PROCLUS

On the Existence of Evils

PROCLUS
On the Existence of Evils

Translated by
Jan Opsomer & Carlos Steel

B L O O M S B U R Y
LONDON • NEW DELHI • NEW YORK • SYDNEY

Bloomsbury Academic
An imprint of Bloomsbury Publishing Plc

50 Bedford Square
London
WC1B 3DP
UK

1385 Broadway
New York
NY 10018
USA

www.bloomsbury.com

First published in 2003 by Gerald Duckworth & Co. Ltd.
Paperback edition first published 2014

British Library Cataloguing-in-Publication Data
A catalogue record for this book is available from the British Library.

ISBN: HB: 978-0-7156-3198-0
PB: 978-1-4725-5739-1
ePDF: 978-1-4725-0103-5

Acknowledgments
The present translations have been made possible by generous and imaginative funding from the
following sources: the National Endowment for the Humanities, Division of Research Programs,
an independent federal agency of the USA; the Leverhulme Trust; the British Academy;
the Jowett Copyright Trustees; the Royal Society (UK); Centro Internazionale A. Beltrame di Storia dello
Spazio e del Tempo (Padua); Mario Mignucci; Liverpool University; the Leventis Foundation;
the Arts and Humanities Research Board of the British Academy; the Esmée Fairbairn
Charitable Trust; the Henry Brown Trust; Mr and Mrs N. Egon; the Netherlands Organisation
for Scientific Research (NWO/GW). The editor wishes to thank Kevin Corrigan and Anne Sheppard
for their comments and Eleni Vambouli and Han Baltussen for preparing the volume for press.

Typeset by Ray Davies
Printed and bound by CPI Group (UK) Ltd, Croydon, CR0 4YY

Contents

Preface

This volume is the result of an intense collaboration during the last three years at the Institute of Philosophy in Leuven. Though we are now academically separated by the Atlantic, we share with some nostalgia pleasant memories of our animated discussions on Neoplatonic philosophy with Gerd Van Riel, Bert van den Berg and Guy Guldentops, and other friends at the De Wulf-Mansion Centre for Ancient and Medieval Philosophy. The translation has profited from the advice and corrections of many people: David Butorac, Maria Desmond, John Steffen and Douglas Hadley in Leuven. A provisional version of the translation was used in a seminar at the Institute of Classical Studies in London and in a seminar at the Philosophy Department of Harvard University: we profited from the comments of Anne Sheppard, Bob Sharples, Richard Sorabji, Harold Tarrant, and the referees for this series. In the preparation of the manuscript for the publisher, we are greatly indebted to the collaborators of the Ancient Commentators Project in London, and in particular to Han Baltussen.

We are very happy that Richard Sorabji has welcomed this Neoplatonic treatise into his monumental series 'The Ancient Commentators on Aristotle'. Even if Proclus would not have appreciated being considered a commentator on Aristotle, he would surely have been pleased that, thanks to this great international project, his treatise *On the Existence of Evils* will find many more readers than ever before (if we exclude readers of the plagiarist Dionysius the pseudo-Areopagite).

Looking back at a wonderful collaboration over the years, which has brought us in contact with many scholars, we have come to understand that Proclus was right when he argued that from 'evil' (in this case the long and arduous philological preliminaries) divine providence can create beautiful things.

2002   J.O. & C.S.

Abbreviations and Conventions

DMS = *De malorum subsistentia, On the existence of evils*
ET = *Elementatio theologica, Elements of theology*
OD = *De omnifaria doctrina* (Michael Psellus)
SVF = *Stoicorum Veterum Fragmenta* (ed. von Arnim)
TP = *Theologia Platonica, Platonic theology*

The chapter and line number references are to Boese's edition of the *Tria opuscula*.

Brackets are used in the translation as follows:

[...] expanding or clarifying the meaning
<...> addenda (implies an emendation of the text)

Introduction

1. The fate of a text

1.1. The treatise in the work of Proclus

Among the works of the Neoplatonic philosopher Proclus (412-485), there are three short treatises that are devoted to the problems of providence, free will and evil.[1] As their modern editor, Helmut Boese, observes, those three '*opuscula*'[2] stand apart somehow in the voluminous oeuvre of the Platonic *Diadochos*, between the great commentaries on Plato and the theological works. Whereas in commenting Proclus has to stick close to the texts of Plato, in his *Elements of Theology* and his *Platonic Theology* he aims at the composition of a grandiose synthesis, which sets other constraints on his philosophising. But here, in the *Tria opuscula* or *monobiblia* as he called them, he seems to enjoy a greater freedom to develop a philosophical problem in itself and to analyse the different arguments that have been offered in the tradition. His style of writing is intermediate as well: not the grand rhetoric of the *Platonic Theology*, not the almost mathematical austerity of the *Elements of Theology*, not the scholastic exposition of the Commentaries. When discussing such fundamental questions as the nature of evil or the problem of free will, Proclus seems to address a larger philosophical audience than the privileged group of students in his school.[3] The problems raised are, indeed, of great philosophical interest and have continued to stir up the debate ever since the Hellenistic schools brought it to the fore: is there providence in the world? And how can it be reconciled with the experience of evil? Is free agency possible in a deterministic universe? What is the nature of evil?

Proclus probably composed the three treatises in the same order as they have been transmitted in the manuscripts. Though dealing with related problems, they each have their own character. The first treatise is, as its title indicates, a discussion of *Ten problems about providence*. That there is providence in this world is undeniable. It is shown by Plato's arguments in the *Laws* and the *Timaeus*, and by the *Chaldaean Oracles*. But what exactly providence is, whether it extends to all levels of reality or only to the celestial spheres, how it exercises its activity in this physical world without losing its transcendence, how it can know contingent events, why it distributes its goods unequally, and how it can be reconciled with evil: those and many other problems Proclus wants to examine in this treatise. Of course, they have already been thoroughly discussed in the philosophical tradition and in the Neoplatonic school in particular. But 'although those problems have been discussed and examined a thousand times, my soul still wants to talk and hear about them, and return to herself, and wishes as it were to discuss with herself and not only receive arguments about them from the outside'.[4]

The second treatise, *On providence and fate and on that which belongs to us, to the engineer Theodorus*, has an entirely different character. In this philosophical letter, Proclus attempts to refute some erroneous views on providence and freedom in reply to his friend Theodorus.[5] This Theodorus, a mechanical engineer with a great interest in philosophy, had sent Proclus a letter wherein he exposed his ideas on providence, fate and on human responsibility (*to eph' hêmin*). In his view, the whole universe is a deterministic system like a mechanical clockwork: freedom is nothing but a word, a beneficial illusion for human life. Theodorus also advocated a hedonistic lifestyle combined with a sceptical attitude concerning the possibilities of human knowledge. Before answering his arguments, Proclus first discusses three basic questions which dominate the whole debate on providence and freedom: (1) the distinction between divine providence and fate (the latter being subordinated to the former); (2) the distinction between the irrational soul, which is connected to the body, and the rational, which transcends the body; (3) the distinction of the various modes of knowledge, ranging from sense perception to suprarational intuition. Theodorus does not share the Neoplatonist philosophical assumptions, though he must have frequented the school, as he is said to remember what 'Proclus' master' (Syrianus) used to say (66,6-8), and is supposed to understand an indirect reference to Theodorus of Asine, who is mentioned as 'your homonym' (53,13).

Notwithstanding the radical divergence of their philosophical positions, Proclus' refutation of Theodorus is friendly and even has a personal character. One has the impression that both men must have been rather close friends. Proclus makes some *ad hominem* arguments with mild irony, for instance when he criticises, in ch. 41, the engineer for not appreciating the importance of mathematics. How could somebody like Theodorus, a lover of philosophy and intellectual speculations, a man of encyclopaedic culture and an expert in geometry and mathematics, defend such a materialistic view on knowledge and the nature of the soul, claiming that there is only a gradual difference between sensible and scientific knowledge? In ch. 45, Proclus criticises the hedonistic philosophy of his friend who argued that 'the good is what is pleasant for each individual and that this is different according to the place where one lives'. – 'I would be ashamed,' Proclus says, 'if, to a man who is my friend, I did not write clearly what I think, namely that such a view is unworthy of my choice of life and of my age.'[6]

If a young man had indeed formulated such a hedonistic view, Proclus would not have been surprised, for the young usually adhere to the opinions of the many. But an old man who gives authority to the intellect should think differently. The fact that Proclus considers this view as unworthy of his old age is adequate proof that this work – and probably the two other treatises as well – was written towards the end of his career. In ch. 22, the reader comes across a highly personal comment: Proclus alludes to a dramatic event in his life, whereby his house and its furniture were destroyed by fire. But, as he confesses, this disaster damaged external goods only and could not take away the wisdom and calmness of his soul. As L. Westerink has argued, Proclus is probably alluding to some religious persecution. Maybe the destruction of the temple of Asclepius, which was adjacent to the school, caused serious damage to his private residence. Or the event could have been related to the persecution that drove Proclus into exile in Asia.[7] This may be another indication for putting the composition of the treatises on providence and evil in the later period of Proclus' life.

The third treatise, *De malorum subsistentia* (*On the existence of evils* = *DMS*), features yet another approach. It is neither a discussion of 'problems', nor a refutation of erroneous views. Proclus here develops in a systematic manner the Platonic doctrine on evil, as he understands it. He knows of course that since Plotinus the question of the nature of evil has often been discussed in the Platonic school. It is his ambition, however, now that he has some 'time off', to write down a critical review of the opinions of his predecessors and, above all, to expound the doctrine of the divine Plato, to whom we should turn for enlightenment in all our speculations on this matter.

This was not Proclus' first attempt to articulate his views on evil. In the preface of the treatise, he explicitly refers to the discussions of evil in his commentaries (1,17-18). We indeed find substantial discussions of evil in his Commentaries on the *Timaeus* (1,372,25-381,21, a summary of his views on evil, occasioned by a discussion of *Tim.* 30A2-3), on the *Republic* (1,37,37,2-39,1, a summary of his doctrine of evil; 1,96,5-100,20; 2,89,6-91,18, on the vices of the soul) and on the *Parmenides* (829,23-831,24, on the alleged Forms of evils). Moreover, we know from a marginal note[8] that Proclus also discussed the problem of evil in his *Commentary on the Theaetetus*, now lost. In this dialogue can be found the famous passage on the necessity of evil as the contrary of the good (176A; cf. below: 2.1, T1) which has been the starting point for all Neoplatonic speculations on evil. Proclus most probably also devoted a commentary to Plotinus' celebrated treatise

on evil, 'On what are and whence come evils' (*Ennead* 1,8[51]). As we
will see, Proclus is very critical of the views of Plotinus and in
particular rejects his identification of evil with matter.[9] Many chapters in the treatise actually contain refutations of the views that
Plotinus expressed in *Ennead* 1,8. Reading the *De malorum subsistentia*, we may get some idea of what Proclus may have written in his
no longer extant commentary on *Ennead* 1,8. The fact that Proclus in
his preface refers to his 'commentaries' is again an argument for
dating the composition of the *Tria opuscula* in his later career. This
will have been after the commentaries on the *Theaetetus*, *Timaeus*
and *Republic* and after the commentary on the *Enneads*, but probably
before the *Commentary on the Parmenides*.[10] This last commentary
precedes the composition of the *Platonic theology*, Proclus' last work.
In the first book of the *Theology*, Proclus devotes a whole chapter
(1.18) to the problem of evil.[11] This chapter may be considered as the
final expression of his views on a problem with which he has been
struggling from his earliest works on.

1.2. The tradition of the text

The treatises on providence and evil must have enjoyed some success
outside the school. They were known to John Philoponus who quotes
some sections from the *De decem dubitationibus* in his refutation of
Proclus in *De aeternitate mundi* (written *c.* 529). In the middle of the
sixth century, John of Lydia quoted a long passage from the last
chapter of *De malorum subsistentia* (61,5-18) in his *De mensibus*
(4,35, pp. 93,15-94,3 Wünsch). But the unimaginable and unforesee-
able success of the *Tria opuscula* was mainly due to the Christian
author who hid his real identity and instead presented himself as
Dionysius the Areopagite. This author was probably active around
500. In his celebrated work, *On the divine names*, ps.-Dionysius
makes extensive use of Proclus' treatise, *On the existence of evils*. The
long digression on evil in 4,18-34 can be considered as an adaptation
and a summary (often a very mediocre one) of Proclus' arguments in
DMS.[12] Whereas in his other works, Dionysius cleverly attempts to
hide his debt to the pagan Proclus, in this section his dependence is
evident to the point of becoming embarrassing (it even made some
scholars suppose the whole digression on evil to be a later interpolation). Dionysius follows Proclus step by step, here and there adding a
critical remark so as to modify his views in a Christian way. One
major divergence from Proclus is to be found in his treatment of
demons.[13] Dionysius upholds the view that the demons were created
good (Proclus would have accepted this), but that they fell away from
their creator through their own sin. Evil then starts in the universe
with the fall of the angels, who by falling become demons. For Proclus,
it is impossible that demons or other 'superior kinds' would ever lose

their initial perfection. Only the particular souls descending in the bodies can 'fall'.[14] Another important divergence consists in Dionysius' denial that there is evil in irrational animals and in bodies.[15] Although in both these cases he uses the same examples as Proclus, he has twisted the argument so that it leads to the opposite conclusion. By doing so, Dionysius has aligned himself with the Christian orthodoxy, according to which evil can originate only in beings that can make free choices. Apart from these doctrinal differences, Dionysius follows Proclus so closely that his work can even be used for the reconstruction of parts of the lost Greek text of *DMS*.

Whatever Dionysius' intention may have been, the plagiarising summary and adaptation of Proclus' doctrine in *On the divine names* gave Proclus' little treatise a publicity and worldwide readership he could never have dreamed of at the time of writing, the author being but a marginalised pagan philosopher in Athens. Thanks to Dionysius, Proclus' argument of evil as a *parupostasis* of the good became known and was studied not only in Byzantium, but also in the Latin West both through the translations of Hilduin, John Scot Eriugena, and Saracenus, and through the numerous commentators. Until the nineteenth century, Proclus' Neoplatonic doctrine of evil as a kind of privation or a shortcoming would continue to dominate the philosophical debates on evil.

However, the esoteric work of Dionysius did not immediately meet with a favourable readership. When it first began to circulate, some readers doubted its authenticity and orthodoxy. A first and successful attempt to defend the apostolic authenticity of Dionysius' work came from John of Scythopolis, who sometime between 537 and 543 composed a series of scholia to explain the often difficult arguments of Dionysius.[16] In the scholion dealing with the argument on evil, John made use of Plotinus' *Ennead* 1,8 without, however, mentioning his source. Actually, he uses Plotinus – of all authors! – to support Dionysius against the 'Greeks' who uphold a dualistic position because they claim that evil is to be identified with matter. As we will show later in this introduction, Proclus attacked Plotinus on this very point – for being too much of a dualist – and, as we have already pointed out, Dionysius merely copied the arguments of Proclus. It is mind-boggling to see how John used Plotinus (the objections that Plotinus first formulates against his own thesis in order to refute them later) to argue against views entertained by the same Plotinus, and defend theses upheld by Dionysius (and Proclus). It is even more remarkable that he did not use Proclus himself to elucidate the points that Dionysius wanted to make. But of course, he could hardly have done so without revealing the secret pagan source of the apostolic Dionysius. It was safer for John to use Plotinus.

Or should we suppose that John of Scythopolis was not acquainted with these works of Proclus and that his silence about Dionysius' dependence upon Proclus was sincere? It may seem unlikely that an author in the early sixth century knowing Plotinus' treatise on evil should not have known Proclus' more recent treatment of the problem. Never, however, does the scholiast show any knowledge of Proclus, and his silence could therefore be sincere.

In this respect, it is remarkable that the name of Proclus appears in a passage at the end of John's *Prologue to the Dionysian corpus*. The passage in question, however, is an interpolation. The author of the interpolation defends Dionysius against the accusation of plagiarism: it is the other way around – Proclus plagiarised Dionysius! He states:

> One must know that some of the non-Christian philosophers, especially Proclus, have often employed certain concepts (*lexeis*) of the blessed Dionysius. [...] It is possible to conjecture from this that the ancient philosophers in Athens usurped his works (as he recounts in the present book) and then hid them, so that they themselves might seem to be the progenitors of his divine oracles. According to the dispensation of God the present work is now made known for the refutation of their vanity and recklessness.[17]

There are good arguments for attributing this scholion to the converted philosopher John Philoponus. Philoponus was familiar with the Dionysian Corpus and was convinced of its authenticity: three times he quotes Dionysius in his theological work, *De opificio mundi*. Philoponus knew Proclus, too, since he wrote a refutation of the latter's views on the eternity of the world and even quotes from the treatise, *On providence*. The many parallels between Dionysius' and Proclus' discussions of evil may have struck him. He explains these similarities, however, by postulating a dependence of Proclus on Dionysius. This will remain the standard view in the Byzantine tradition, and it was transmitted to the Western world when the *Tria opuscula* were rediscovered thanks to Moerbeke's translation. The authority of Dionysius almost eclipsed the fame of Proclus (who was now considered as the one who plagiarised).

However, scholars continued to read and quote from his works, but without mentioning his name. Thus in the eleventh century Michael Psellus inserted large extracts from the *Tria opuscula* into his compilation, *De omnifaria doctrina*.[18] But the most extensive use of Proclus came from an unexpected source. At the end of the eleventh century, a Byzantine prince by the name of Isaak Sebastokrator composed three treatises on providence and evil.[19] Already in the formulation of the titles, there is such a similarity with the *Tria opuscula* that one may expect the prince to have exploited Proclus in the composition of his own works.[20] This suspicion was indeed confirmed by the examination of his treatises. Isaak has used Proclus' text as the substrate for his 'own' developments. Of course, he could not mention his pagan source: Proclus had a very bad reputation in Byzantium, and to be associated with him was almost proof of heresy. Isaak was himself charged with the trial against Psellus' disciple, John Italos, who was accused of propagating the heterodox views of Porphyry, Iamblichus and Proclus. The author did his utmost to hide the Proclean origin of the views he exposed. He carefully left out all references to pagan theology which might disturb his Byzantine contemporaries, substituting, e.g., the singular 'god' for the plural 'gods'. Moreover, he cleverly blended Proclus' text on evil with Dionysius' version and with excerpts taken from an early admirer of Dionysius, Maximus Confessor.[21] The result is a surprisingly homogeneous Neoplatonic Christian speculation on evil, providence and free will. Although we may not value much the originality of the author, we are grateful that through his compilation we can reconstruct almost two-thirds of the lost Greek original of Proclus.[22]

That Greek original was still circulating in the Byzantine world in the thirteenth to fourteenth centuries, as is evident from the insertion of eight fragments in a florilegium that was copied in Byzantium in 1311.[23] But the most important witness of its existence is William of Moerbeke who happened to discover a manuscript of Proclus' treatises when he resided in Corinth as archbishop and made a complete translation in February 1280. After his death, the Greek text was irrevocably lost.

1.3. Moerbeke's translation

As can be learned from the colophon, William of Moerbeke completed his translation of the *Tria opuscula* in Corinth in February 1280. When he arrived in Corinth, the Flemish Dominican could look back on a long career during which he had combined his duties as an official at the papal administration with his translation work on Aristotle, Archimedes and the Greek Commentators.[24] His appointment as Latin archbishop of Corinth offered him a 'sabbatical', a wonderful opportunity for discoveries of unknown Greek philosophical texts and for more translations. After the *Tria opuscula*, he embarked on his last project, the translation of Proclus' commentary on the *Parmenides*, which he finished just before he died.[25]

The translation of the *Tria opuscula* has been preserved in thirteen manuscripts dating from the early fourteenth to the seventeenth century. They can be classified in two groups. On the one hand there are manuscripts that derive from a Parisian exemplar: *Arsenal 473* (A), which once belonged to the Augustinian convent at Pont Neuf. On the other hand, there are manuscripts deriving from a model in Italy. The most important manuscript in this second group is *Vaticanus latinus 4568* (V). Although rather young (*c.* 1500), it had been copied from an old exemplar, which was very close to – if not identical with – Moerbeke's original copy. The most noteworthy feature of the Vatican manuscript is the presence of numerous Greek words in the margin of the translation. The Greek terms correspond to Latin terms in the translation and are obviously meant as an aid in those cases where the equivalencies are not self-evident.[26] Who is responsible for these annotations which are precious traces of the lost Greek original? Not the copyist of *Vaticanus* himself, since he appears to have some difficulty replicating the Greek characters he read in his model. Neither do the marginal notes stem from a reader who consulted the Greek original that was still available to him.[27] They show instead the practice of the translator himself. We know indeed that Moerbeke, when translating, often left an empty space when he could not immediately find a good equivalent for some Greek term (for example in a poetical expression) or when the text was corrupted. In the margin, he jotted down the missing Greek, hoping to return to the passage later. Such a practice can be witnessed in the autograph manuscript of his translation of Archimedes and in one manuscript of the Commentary on the *Parmenides, Ambrosianus A 167 sup.* This last manuscript, copied in Ferrara in 1508, contains in the margin numerous Greek terms and even some quotations from poetry that had been passed over by the translator.[28] In this case again, the scribe is not himself responsible for the Greek notes: he copied what he read in his model. As in the case of *Vaticanus* (copied at about the same time), we must postulate that the model of *Ambrosianus* contained in the margin the annotations of the translator himself. This lost manuscript, which probably contained the *Tria opuscula* as well as the commentary on the *Parmenides*, may have been Moerbeke's personal copy.

In addition to the *Vaticanus*, there are two other manuscripts of Italian origin: *Macerata, Bibl. Communale 5.3.D.30* (S), which once belonged to Colucio Salutati, chancellor of the republic of Florence, and *Oxford Bodleian Digby 236* (O). Both manuscripts date from the middle of the fourteenth century and have many errors in common, which proves their dependence on a common model. In comparison with A and V, the role of the manuscripts OS for the constitution of the text is only marginal. However, when they confirm V or A, they usually represent the authentic text. On this point, we have considered it necessary to correct in some passages the excellent edition of Helmut Boese, who tends to underestimate the importance of this branch of the tradition.[29] D. Isaac, in his edition for the Collection G. Budé, even eliminated O and S from the apparatus.

As the subscriptions inform us, Moerbeke made his translation of the three treatises in just a few weeks. This would not have been possible if he had not applied a translation method that he had elaborated and perfected in his long experience as translator. His primary aim was to provide the Latin scholars with a translation that corresponds exactly – word for word – to the Greek original. He did not have the ambition to produce literary Latin.[30] On the contrary: he manipulated the Latin, stretching the language to the extreme so as to produce a perfect 'calque' of the original while using Latin words, conjugations and declinations. Even the smallest particles are translated. Over the years, this method was ever more standardised and became an almost mechanical technique. His last translations are the most literal ones. Thus Moerbeke attempted to respect, as far as grammar allows, the order of words of the Greek original. To give a simple example of an easy phrase, this is the opening sentence of ch. 58: 'Dubitabit autem utique aliquis qualiter et unde mala providentia ente.'

One of the major problems a Latin translator is confronted with is the absence of the article in Latin. In Greek texts, and particularly in philosophical texts, the article plays an essential role. It is used, among other things, to substantivise adjectives (e.g. *to agathon, to kalon*) and participles (e.g. *to on*) or even whole phrases. To cope with that difficulty, Moerbeke expanded the use of the demonstrative or relative pronoun, writing *ipsum bonum, ipsum pulchrum* or *quod secundum naturam*. But this was not possible in all cases. In his last translations, he introduced the article *le* of medieval French as a standard translation of the Greek article (even sometimes using the genitive form *del*), as in *le unum, le non bonum, le volatile, le mixtum, le non eodem modo, le agonum, le otiosum, le speciei factivum, le preter naturam, le secundum intellectum, le immensuratum, le ornantium unumquodque, le bene, le credibile, le sursum, le et usque ad hoc omnia bona et esse et fieri propter eam que in ipso malitiam* (58,15-16: a whole sentence is substantivised). The article in Greek also makes it possible to determine a substantive by a series of complements inserted between the article and the substantive. When the article is not rendered in the translation, the complements float around. In such cases, the introduction of *le* was little help. Moerbeke then tried to connect the complements with their substantive by construing relative phrases of the type *is qui*. There are innumerable examples of this construction in the Latin version of the *Tria opuscula*. As an example, we take a closer look at *DMS 50*:

6   *eum qui in esse progressum*

22-5   *eorum que ex principio in finem progredientium* [...] *eorum que neque ex principio secundum naturam apparent neque in determinatum aliud consummantium* (the translator has not been consistent: he should have written either *apparentium* ... *consummantium* or *apparent* ... *consummant* instead of mixing the personal with the participle construction)

26   *principalem acceperunt eius quod est facere ipsa dictam*
      causam (note the awkward word order)
27   *eius quod preter naturam*
28   *eorum que preter rationem fiunt*

Does it need to be pointed out that all of this results in a Latin that is nothing short of barbarous?

2. Proclus and the Neoplatonic doctrine of evil

2.1 Platonic pre-texts

As Proclus states in the introduction to his treatise on evil, every study of any philosophical problem whatsoever should always start from Plato, 'for if we fall short of this theory, we will give the impression that we have achieved nothing'. Moreover, 'we shall understand more easily the words of our predecessors and shall always be closer to an understanding of the problems once we have discovered the thought of Plato and, as it were, kindled a light for our subsequent inquiries'. Yet, 'to get a grasp of Plato's doctrine on evil' may not be an easy undertaking, the main reason being of course that we do not posses a fully developed theory of evil from the Master. We do have some various remarks interspersed throughout the dialogues and we could speculate on what kind of theory of evil Plato would have produced in the light of his general approach to philosophical questions.[31] Yet a systematic doctrine of evil such as we find it in the later Neoplatonists is absent from the works of Plato.

Nonetheless the discussion in the Neoplatonic schools took the texts of Plato as their starting point and as their ultimate authority. The doctrine of evil as it is (re-)constructed by them is *supposed* to be Plato's. Both Proclus and Plotinus' treatments of the problem of evil abound with citations from the dialogues. Of these pre-texts, we have selected some that are most crucial for Proclus and for Platonists in general.

At *Theaet.* 176A5-8, Socrates makes a casual remark, that, although fairly detached from the main flow of the argument, has become the *locus classicus* for Neoplatonic discussions of evil:

T1   It is impossible, Theodorus, that evil things will cease to exist
        (*out'apolesthai ta kaka dunaton*), for it is necessary (*anankê*)
        that the good always has its (sub)contrary (*hupenantion ti tôi*
        agathôi aei einai); nor have they any place in the divine world,
        but by necessity (*ex anankês*) they revolve about our mortal
        nature and this place.

From this passage (extensively used by Plotinus as well) Proclus has garnered the following pieces of doctrine: (1) there will always be evils in this world; (2) there is a kind of necessity or inevitability[32] about their existence; (3) there are no evils in the divine world; (4) evils enjoy a relation of subcontrariety – not just of contrariety – with the good (cf. below: 2.4.5). This passage is immediately followed by the famous advice to 'flee this place' and assimilate oneself to the god (*homoiôsis theôi*) as much as possible (176A8-B3).

A little bit further on Socrates speaks of a kind of paradigm of evil, referring to the different patterns of life that people choose (176E3-5):

T1'   There are two paradigms set up in reality, my friend. One is divine and supremely happy (*tou men theiou eudaimonesta-tou*); the other is ungodly and is the paradigm of the greatest misery (*tou de atheou athliôtatou*).

This passage was used in the Neoplatonic debates on whether there are Forms (Ideas) of evils.

The next key passage comes from the second book of the *Republic* (379B-C). Since a god is good, and what is good can only do good things and no bad things, he is not the cause of (*aition*, 'responsible for') all things, but merely of the good ones. For the evils he is not responsible (*tôn de kakôn anaition*).

T2   Therefore, since a god is good, he is not – as most people claim – the cause of everything that happens to human beings, but of only a few things, for good things are fewer than bad ones in our lives. He alone is responsible (*aition*) for the good things, but we must look for some other causes for evils (*alla atta aitia*), not a god. (*Resp.* 379C2-7)

Besides the principle that the god is not responsible for evils, Proclus gathers from this text that one should not look for one single cause of evils, but rather for a multiplicity of indeterminate causes, i.e. causes that do not cause evil for evil's sake, but rather by accident.

The idea that god is not responsible for evils is confirmed in the myth of Er (*Republic* X). The message announced to the (ephemeral) souls involves that they are responsible for their own choices:

T2'   The responsibility lies with the one who makes the choice; the god has none (*aitia helomenou, theos anaitios*, 617E4-5).

Proclus sets great store by the idea that the souls are themselves responsible for any evil they commit, and condemns the attempts to put the blame on matter. He wants to save the moral responsibility of the souls: 'Where would be their self-motion and ability to choose' (33,23) if we attribute the cause of their descent to the activity of matter? The souls make their own choices, and when they have chosen badly, they deserve their punishment (33,21-22).[33]

In the *Timaeus*, it is emphasised that the demiurge did not want evil to exist in the universe, but instead that everything be similar to himself, *insofar as this was possible.*

T3   He was good, and one who is good can never become jealous of anything. And so, being free of jealousy, he wanted everything to become as much like himself as was possible (*panta hoti malista eboulêthê genesthai paraplêsia heautôi*). (*Tim.* 29E1-3)

God wanted (*boulêtheis*) that all things should be good and nothing bad (*agatha men panta, phlauron de mêden*), insofar as this was attainable (*kata dunamin*). (*Tim.* 30A2-3)

The god who creates this world wants to make it similar to his own good nature. Flaws are not part of the divine plan, and the gods can therefore not be held responsible for them. Indeed, even for the demiurge it may not be possible completely to preclude shortcomings, as Timaeus intimates.

Taking these canonical texts as their incontestable starting points, combining them with some other valuable indications gleaned from the works of Plato, and applying their own argumentative acumen and philosophical insights, various Platonists have developed their views on evil.[34] The most extensive and also the most carefully argued treatments of the problem are Plotinus' and Proclus'. Since Proclus undeniably takes issue with the views expressed by his famous predecessor, we will first discuss the solution proposed by Plotinus, and Proclus' criticism of this doctrine, before turning to the latter's own views on the problem.

Perhaps it needs to be pointed out first that it is Proclus' view, not Plotinus',[35] that was to become authoritative within the School and is most representative of the Neoplatonic doctrine of evil.[36] On the other hand, Proclus was certainly not the originator of the views we find in *DMS*, nor of the objections to Plotinus. That honour should probably go to Iamblichus.[37]

2.2. *Plotinus Ennead 1,8[51]*

A central text in the Neoplatonic discussions of evil is *Ennead* 1,8[51], which Plotinus wrote shortly before he died. Since Porphyry, it has been known as 'On what are and whence come evils'. It is a challenging text, in which Plotinus makes a strong and clear point: matter[38] is the origin of all evil; it is evil as such.[39]

Evils of the body (e.g. disease) and that of the soul (vices) are secondary, so Plotinus argues. Prior to these secondary evils, there must be a primary evil, which is the cause of the derived evils, and 'that in which they participate'. How can we know what this primary and absolute evil is? Since evil is 'that which is contrary to the good', and all being is good, evil will be contrary to being (i.e. the Platonic Forms) and to the good that is beyond being, i.e. the primary Good or the One. Evil as such, Plotinus claims, consists in the complete absence of goodness and form; it will be a kind of non-being. Of course, it could never be the kind of non-being that is *beyond* being (the One). Hence it must be a non-being which is lower than being. Nor is it absolute non-being, for then it would not exist at all – but evil is a reality. Neither is it the non-being of motion and rest, which, together with being, belong to the so-called Greatest Forms[40] of the *Sophist*. Evil is then that kind of non-being that does exist, but is completely opposite to the Forms. Therefore it must be identical with matter. For this is what matter is: absolute indeterminateness, absolute disorder, absolute darkness, complete absence of goodness.

Plotinus indeed identifies the substrate with privation, thus violating an Aristotelian thesis. Aristotle had defined the substrate as that which persists through a process of change, whereas privation is that which disappears as a result of the change. But according to Plotinus, the privation does not disappear, but persists. The substrate – matter – is identical with privation, complete absence of form and light, that is, and therefore with evil. This is also why Plotinus claims that matter can never truly receive form. The soul tries to invest matter with form, but fruitlessly: the privation remains.[41]

Matter is unlimited in comparison to limit, formless in comparison to formative principles, in perpetual need, always undefined, nowhere stable, subject to every kind of influence, insatiate, complete poverty. These characteristics are not incidental, but in a way make up the nature of matter-evil, insofar as each part of evil will have all of its characteristics and other things will have any of these characteristics through participation. For these reasons, evil may be considered a nature of its own, the substance of evil, says Plotinus, if indeed there can be such a thing as a substance of evil, the first evil, a *per se* evil (1,8[51],3). This then becomes the source for evil in other beings: they can become evil only if they are in contact with matter, although not everything that is in contact with matter is always evil.

Plotinus' account of the evil of the soul is rather sophisticated, as Denis O'Brien has splendidly demonstrated: matter in itself is not a sufficient cause of evil in the soul. There must also be a certain weakness of the soul itself. Yet this weakness is in its turn caused by matter. Matter and weakness are both part causes of evil in the soul, and together they form a sufficient cause of vice.

However, matter is not like the One, an absolute, self-subsisting principle. Matter is generated by something else, more specifically by a particular soul, which is itself an image of the higher soul and is said to be 'sensation' and 'the nature which is found in plants'.[42] By descending and generating an image of itself, this lower manifestation of soul produces the non-being which is matter. Yet the production of matter is not due to some form of evil that would have pre-existed in the soul. This constitutes a crucial difference with Gnostic doctrine on the origin of matter.[43] Although there is no evil at all in the soul's production of matter, once matter is there (which is to be understood in an ontological rather than a chronological sense), it is the principle of all evils. The soul becomes evil only when it descends a second time and is affected by the presence of matter. It would not have come to be in matter if matter were not already there. So, 'matter is evil first and the first evil' (1,8[14,50-1]). It is important to notice that Plotinus is arguing for the subtle position that matter has no independent existence – it is not ungenerated – but is nonetheless the ultimate principle of evil.

If evil is entirely due to one source, matter, and the Good cannot be held responsible for its existence, Plotinus seems to get away with a paradoxical combination of dualistic and monistic ideas. He wants to be a monist, yet cannot help sounding as a dualist[44] in calling matter evil itself (*autokakon*) and the principle (*arkhê*) of evil.

By this analysis of matter-evil, Plotinus is able to do justice to the key passage in Plato's *Republic*, according to which the god is the cause of everything, yet is responsible for good things only, not for bad things (cf. *Resp.* 2, 379B15-16 = **T2′**). Indeed, according to Plotinus, matter is produced by the superior principles. Therefore its existence does not contradict the axiom that everything is produced by the One (the Good). Yet, as the lowest product in the hierarchy of beings, it is also the principle, in the sense of the beginning[45] and the cause of all evils. For as the lowest, it constitutes the degree of least possible perfection, in other words, of greatest imperfection.[46] With matter, the procession has reached a stage where something is produced that is of itself incapable of returning to its principle. It cannot even truly receive the forms that soul tries to impose on it.

It is important to remark that the gradual loss of perfection is itself not caused by any other principle. Matter is just the end of the process. It is that which has nothing good in it, and therefore, claims Plotinus, it is evil.[47] Now, if matter is the first evil and that which causes all other evil, the second part of the famous sentence from the *Republic* can be maintained, too: the good is not responsible for evil. For Plotinus, this is the essential element of his theodicy.

Plotinus also offers an extensive exegesis (chs 6-7) of *Theaetetus* 176A, another of the key passages (cf. above, **T1**). Plotinus discusses the inevitability of the existence of evils, due to the necessity of a contrary[48] of the good. He explains that by 'this place' (the region haunted by evils), Socrates does not mean the earth, but the universe.

The sought-after 'escape', then, cannot mean that one should fly to the stars, but rather that one should try to become virtuous and rational while living on this earth. The words 'mortal nature' (about which the evils 'revolve') stand for the vices of the soul, which one should avoid. Therefore 'to be among the gods' means to become intellective to the extent that this is attainable for humans. The necessity of evils in particular draws Plotinus' attention. It is not the case that whenever one half of a pair of contraries exists, the other too exists by necessity. So there must be a special reason why for the good this is the case. Any vice is obviously contrary to some virtue. But human vice is not contrary to *the* good, but rather to some good, namely to the good by which we master matter. Absolute evil is not contrary to some good, but to being (i.e. substance, *ousia*) as such or that what is beyond substance (6,27-8). This, however, raises a serious problem, since Aristotle[49] had explicitly denied the possibility of a contrary of substance. Faced with this difficulty, Plotinus argues that while it is true of particular substances that they have no contrary, this has never been proven for substance as such. So, against Aristotle he maintains that there is a contrary of the being of the forms, and this is the non-being that is called matter and that is to be equated with evil as such.[50]

The necessity of evils can also be understood in a different way: if the good is not the only thing that exists, there must be an end to the procession going out from it. And this level, after which nothing can come into being, is evil.

2.3. Proclus' criticism of Plotinus

Plotinus' discussion of evil unquestionably provides a foil for Proclus' *De malorum subsistentia*. In the first lines of the treatise, Proclus already refers to his predecessors in general, who discussed the problem of evil in a substantial way. The kind of questions that Proclus mentions are exactly those of Plotinus: does evil exist or not? What is the mode of its existence? Is evil always an accident of something else, or does it also exist on its own? Where does evil come to be? Where does it originate? Does its existence not contradict that of Providence? Although Proclus speaks of predecessors in the plural and nowhere in the treatise mentions any of them by name, there can be no doubt that he primarily has Plotinus in mind. Of course, Proclus examines the views of other thinkers, too, gently criticising or correcting them. For instance, he discusses the view of those who think that evil does not exist at all.[51] Or he discusses the theory that makes a maleficent soul the cause of all evil, a view he elsewhere ascribes to Plutarch and Atticus.[52] Yet on the whole, it is Plotinus who is considered the main predecessor and also opponent, especially in the chapters on matter (*DMS* 30-7). When Proclus at the beginning of this section presents the view of those who think that matter is evil, he is almost quoting from *Ennead* 1, 8 [51], 3, where Plotinus develops the view that there is an evil that is primary and absolute, and in which other things participate when they become derivative evils.

The very first words of *DMS* are clearly reminiscent[53] of the title that Porphyry posthumously assigned to *Ennead* 1,8 – *On what are and whence come evils* – and of the opening phrases of Plotinus' treatise. Throughout the entire text, Proclus keeps alluding to his famous predecessor, mostly in order to distance himself from Plotinus' views and interpretations. Basing his account mainly on the same Platonic texts, Proclus will nonetheless arrive at conclusions that differ considerably from those of Plotinus. One example may suffice: from the myth of the souls in the *Phaedrus*, Proclus infers that according to Plato the souls are corrupted *before* they descend and come in contact with matter. Hence, matter cannot be the cause of the evil of which the souls give evidence.[54]

However, Proclus' objections to Plotinus are only partly exegetical. Most arguments are based on his understanding of the 'Platonic' metaphysical system.[55] It is Proclus' general interpretation of Plato that makes him reject Plotinus' doctrine of evil. For Proclus, it is excluded that matter would be the principle of evil because there can be no single principle that causes all evil. Whereas all that is good is ultimately produced by one cause, with evils it is the opposite: there can only be a multitude of causes (cf. ch. 47). Moreover, if there were a single cause for evil, it would have to be evil to a higher degree than the evils caused, or rather, it would have to be the greatest possible evil, absolute evil, evil itself. But this would amount to a dualism of principles, which any decent Platonist should keep clear of, and which Plotinus definitely wanted to avoid. However, any theory that makes matter a principle of evil ends up being a dualism of some sort, irrespective of whether matter is considered an absolutely independent principle or as being itself generated by something else.

In ch. 31, Proclus presents the advocates of the thesis that matter is the ultimate cause of all evil with a dilemma:[56] either matter is an ultimate principle, itself not generated by any other principle, or it derives its existence from another principle. The first horn of the dilemma amounts to a coarse, Numenian-styled dualism that was certainly not shared by Plotinus.[57] Proclus dismisses this thesis in a few lines: there cannot be two independent first principles that eternally oppose one another; if there were two 'firsts', another, higher principle would be needed to give existence and oneness to both of them. Elsewhere (36,7-12) he adds the objection that if there were an eternal principle, on equal footing with the Good, the Good would never enjoy tranquillity: it would always have to fight its opposite.

The second horn of the dilemma corresponds to the Plotinian position: what if matter, being the source of all evils, is itself generated? Then, says Proclus, the good will inevitably be the cause of evils. But then it will itself be evil, as the cause is in a greater degree what its product is. Also, another absurdity follows: since Neoplatonic causation is not a one-way process, but reversion is an essential aspect of it, the evils produced by matter will be good, for they will assimilate themselves to their ultimate cause. A double conclusion would follow: 'the good, as the cause of evil, would be evil, and evil, as being produced from the good, would be good' (31,20-1). Plotinus had wanted to hold simultaneously that matter is intrinsically evil and the principle of evil, on the one hand, and that it is the result of the emanation, on the other. By claiming that an inferior soul produces matter innocently, he tried to escape the consequence that the superior principles, and ultimately the One, are responsible for evil. Proclus objects that this goes against the Platonist metaphysical axiom that the cause is like the effect in an eminent way. That which produces evil must therefore be even more evil than the effect. Plotinus' ingenious construction clashes with the laws of causation, which hold that the effect is implied in the cause and that the product reverts to its cause. It is indeed questionable whether this position is tenable if one accepts the standard late Neoplatonic metaphysical laws. Even if it is granted that the descent of the soul and the resulting generation of matter is not yet evil itself, from where could evil get its evil nature if not from its principle?[58]

Proclus not only refutes the view that matter can be the *principle* of evil, he also denies that it could be the principle *of evil*, as matter is not even itself evil. The reason is not only that matter is *necessary* for the universe (chs 32, 34, 36-7), but more importantly that matter is produced by the Good, and it is impossible that the Good produces something evil (ch. 35). That matter is produced by the One can, according to Proclus, be inferred from the *Philebus*.[59] Proclus more particularly refers to a casual remark made by Socrates (23C9-10) 'we agreed earlier that the god (*ton theon*) had revealed a division of what is into the unlimited and the limit'. The Neoplatonists commonly interpreted 'to reveal' (*deixai*) as meaning 'to produce'. Moreover Proclus holds the view, which he develops more fully elsewhere,[60] that matter is simply the lowest manifestation of unlimitedness. Hence it is produced by the Good, and hence it is not evil.[61]

One could object that, as the lowest stage in the procession, matter is not good. But granting this[62] is not yet to admit that matter is evil. Matter cannot be evil, for it has been produced by the good and for the sake of the good. In a loose way of talking, matter can be called both good (as contributing to the whole) and bad (as deficient with respect to the higher levels), but *sensu stricto* it is neither. Its nature is intermediary, in that matter is *necessary* (*DMS* 36; 37,1-6). Matter indeed contributes to the generation of the world, and in this sense may even be called good. For matter desires the good, as it is eager to receive form (Plotinus had claimed that matter is not even capable of truly receiving the forms impressed on it).

Plotinus argued that evil is contrary to all the forms and hence to the Good. In order to do so, he had to claim that matter-evil is contrary to the forms as such, thus violating the Aristotelian principle that there is no contrary of substance. Plotinus claimed that this may hold for particular substances, but not for substance *as such*. If the rule does not apply to substance in general, there may be a contrary of the supreme, unqualified Good after all. Proclus wants to distinguish between these two: if one wants to maintain that the absolute evil exists, one should make the case that it is contrary to the good, not just to being. Moreover, whereas a contrary of *a* form exists, it is impossible for something to be entirely contrary to *all* the forms – to the good of the forms – or to the Good. If evil is that which is contrary to the good that exists in other things, and not to the good on its own, evil, like its contraries, can only exist *in* other things, and not on its own. Hence evil cannot be matter, for matter exists on its own: 'matter is a substrate, and not in a substrate' as Proclus had said earlier, when he paraphrased the view of his opponents. They indeed concluded that if matter is evil, it can only be 'essential evil' (*kat' ousian kakon*) and not evil as an accident (*DMS* 30,2-8). Therefore, if Proclus can prove that evil does not exist on its own, he has refuted the identification of matter and evil.

Proclus' most potent argument is based on the Aristotelian definition of contrariety: contraries belong to the same genus. So if the first good had a contrary, both would belong to the same genus. But there can be no genus prior to the Good, since the Good is the very first principle. This is clearly directed against Plotinus. The latter had taken *Theaet.* 176A to imply that evils must necessarily exist, since there has to be something contrary to the good (1,8[51],6,16-17). Next Plotinus contested the absolute validity of the Aristotelian premise that there is no contrary of substance (1,8[51],6,36-48): while admitting that there are no contraries of particular substances, Plotinus claimed that substance as such does have a contrary, i.e. non-substance, matter-evil. The contrary of substance is non-substance and the contrary of the nature of the Good is the nature and principle of evil: 'for they both are principles, the one of good things, and the other of evils. And all the things which are included in one nature are contrary to those in the other; so that also the wholes are contrary and even more so than the other things [i.e. particular goods or evils].'[63] For ordinary contraries still have something in common, as they belong in the same genus or species. They are, as it were, not *absolute* contraries. Then how could one not call contraries things that are furthest removed from each other and that have absolutely nothing in common? All the characteristics, or rather pseudo-characteristics, of evil are completely contrary to what is contained in the divine nature, for even its being is false. In order to uphold the claim that matter-evil as non-substance is the contrary of substance, which is good, Plotinus had to truncate Aristotle's definition[64] of contraries as 'things which stand furthest apart in the same genus' to 'things which stand furthest apart'. An extreme contrariety would imply, so he claimed, that the contraries have nothing at all in common, not even a genus (1,8[51],6,54-9).

This construction is completely rejected by Proclus: he reaffirms the Aristotelian axiom that contraries are always in the same genus. In ch. 45, he also strongly renounces the idea that a substance could have a contrary: 'And in general all evil is outside the substance and is not substance. For nothing is contrary to substance, but good is contrary to evil' (*DMS* 45,15-17).

Proclus firmly re-establishes Peripatetic orthodoxy. This is also the case when he rejects the Plotinian equation of matter with privation. Aristotle, in his discussion of change (*Phys.* 1.9, 192a13-25), had explained that privation is the contrary of form and in its own nature is nothing. It differs from the substrate, which desires form and only accidentally is not, and most importantly, persists through the change. Privation, as being the complete absence of form, is to be considered 'an evil agent' (*kakopoios*). Privation is the contrary of what is divine, good, and desirable, whereas matter desires these very same things and yearns for it. Plotinus, on the contrary, posited that matter is complete privation, total absence of form, and hence evil.[65] The conflation between matter and privation allowed Plotinus to claim that privation, which Aristotle said is an evil agent, does not disappear as a result of any process of change. This is also why Plotinus said that matter can never truly receive form:[66] matter remains in a state of absolute privation.

Proclus deals with privation in a separate chapter (*DMS* 38) after his discussion of matter. In doing so, he implicitly upholds the Aristotelian distinction between privation and matter.[67] On the other hand, he does not concede (to Aristotle) that privation is evil. Privation of a form could never be (the primary) evil, but is merely a privation of being, for the good transcends being. If evil is to be a privation, it should not just be a privation of a form, but a privation of the good. As we will see later, Proclus insists on making this distinction. At any rate, mere 'Aristotelian' privation cannot be *kakopoios*.

Matter is then not contrary to the good of the forms and *a fortiori* not to the supreme Good. In fact, nothing is contrary to the Good. Absolute evil would be, if it existed. But evil does not exist on its own; matter does.

2.4. Proclus' own views

2.4.1. Does evil exist or not? With this 'ontological question' Proclus opens the discussion.[68] He examines two opposite views that are current among his predecessors.

Some have tried to eliminate evil from the universe and have reduced the apparent evils in it to an inferior good. Although this position has had a long tradition – especially the Stoic[69] habit to explain away all physical evils in a desperate attempt to develop a consistent theodicy comes to mind – it is evident that Proclus is here engaged in a discussion within the Neoplatonic school. Proclus explains that evil cannot be a lesser good, because when a lesser good gets stronger, it comes closer to its principle, whereas evil that increases is less and less good. Therefore evil has to be regarded as being somehow contrary[70] to the good: in the case of evils there is an *opposition* to the good, and not just a lessening of it. The other contending party insists on the reality of vice, as it can be witnessed in psychology and politics. The existence of evil cannot be denied, so they claim. In typical fashion, Proclus will aim at a middle position between these two extremes.

His own answer to the ontological question is complex: absolute evil does not exist. It would be even below absolute non-being, and the latter does not exist at all – for logically absolute non-being is to be considered the contrary of being, whereas absolute evil is the logical contrary of the good that is beyond being. So neither absolute non-being, nor absolute evil exist. But relative evils do exist, i.e. evils that are contrary to a particular good. Hence it is better to speak about evils in the plural, since every evil is opposed to a different good. Evils are real, but there is nothing that is absolutely and intrinsically evil, let alone an evil principle.

Evils can only exist in natures that are partial, while universal beings remain free of corruption.[71] For if the latter admitted of corruption, their evil would take on a universal aspect as being opposed to some universal good – but that is impossible. Universal beings participate unchangingly and perfectly in the higher orders, always and immutably preserving the goodness that flows from the latter. The transcendent Forms produce the lower orders 'by overflowing', without losing anything of their intrinsic character. They produce because of their goodness, for it is better to produce than not to produce. However, due to the abundance of their power, they do not only bring forth the beings that eternally participate in them, but also beings whose participation is only intermittent and that cannot preserve uncontaminated and unchanged the power that comes from their source (ch. 7). To sum up, Proclus distinguishes three levels: the transcendent Forms, the eternal participants, and finally the intermittent participants, the only ones to be susceptible to corruption.[72] Intermittent participants are always partial beings.

A possible objection needs to be dealt with: one could suppose that the procession could have stopped at the level of the eternal participants. Then there would have been no evil. Proclus replies that the superior orders, including the eternal participants (and even the intermittent participants), *have to* produce, because of their goodness. Therefore the very production of lower beings in itself does not imply evil in any way. To doubt this would be to blame the very principle of procession (the hierarchy of being). Also it is inconceivable that the eternal participants would be the last of beings, for then they would be unproductive. But this would be at variance with their goodness. As Plato says in the *Timaeus* (41B), the universe would not be complete if it did not also include the lower beings. A perfect universe requires gradations of perfection.[73]

This explains the necessity of evils, implied by *Theaet.* 176A (**T1**). Because of the existence of the partial and intermittent participants, occurrences of various evils will be inevitable. This, however, is different from saying that these evils are *caused* by the higher principles. The latter bring forth beings that are to some extent deprived of the good. However, privation of the good is not the same as privation of a form. Whereas the latter is mere absence, privation of the good is only possible when the good is not completely absent. What is more, the good gives strength to its own contrary. It is only by mixing with the good that the contrary of the good has the power to fight the good (ch. 7).

Evils occur only in particular beings and are relative. This means that they come about in relation to a particular good. They are relative in another sense, too: evil is not absolute because it could not exist by itself. Everything that is evil needs the power of the good and cannot exist on its own. It is at all times mixed with the good.

2.4.2. Before Proclus even tackles the question where evils exist, he has already eliminated several possibilities: it cannot exist on its own and cannot be a universal being (this already rules out prime matter as a candidate), but neither can it be a particular being that enjoys an unchanging participation in the higher realms. Therefore evil can only occur in particular beings that sometimes fail to participate in the good, and only insofar as they fail to do so (beings that always and completely lack a participation in the good could not even exist). These intermittent participants are beings that have their existence in time and are able to change the form of their being.

Proclus devotes a large part of his treatise to the question of where evils 'make their entry into being'. One by one, he examines the stages of the ontological hierarchy, starting from the gods and moving downwards. Evil is not to be found in the gods, nor in the three 'superior kinds' – angels, demons, and heroes – nor in the divine souls, nor in universal bodies, not even in matter or in privation. The only beings susceptible to evil are the lower particular souls (both ordinary human souls and the so-called images of souls, that is irrational souls) and particular material bodies. Particular souls are capable of both 'ascending' and 'descending', in other words, of 'not acting in accordance with their own nature', and therefore of 'choosing what is worse'. However, this should not be called their power, but rather their weakness and lack of power. Images of souls, i.e. irrational souls such as they are found in animals, are equally vulnerable, because they may change to a state that is either better or worse than their own nature. Particular bodies, too, or more precisely their nature (nature being the governing principle of body), can become perverted. This happens either when the rational principles they receive from universal nature are too weak and become subdued by the contraries that surround them, or when the internal order of their nature is dissolved (because individual bodies are particular beings, several equally partial reason-principles coexist in them and may conflict). Contrary to the particular souls, that can be affected in their powers and activities only, particular bodies can be corrupted even in their essence. At the beginning of ch. 55, Proclus recapitulates his survey of the ontological *loci* of evil: 'We have said earlier already that one kind of evil is in the souls, another in bodies, and that evil in souls is twofold, one residing in the irrational type of life, the other in reason. Let us repeat once again: there are three things in which evil exists, namely, the particular soul, the image of the soul, and the body of individual beings' (55,1-4). Here Proclus explains that in the three cases evil consists in a falling short of the principle that is proximately better: intellect in the case of the soul, reason in that of the irrational souls, and nature in the case of body.

In all these types, evil is never due to a deficiency of the superior principles that bring forth and regulate the existence of these partial beings: evil is always due to the weakness of the recipients. It is because these beings are partial and therefore weak that they are incapable of fully receiving the goodness that flows down towards them. Never is there anything wrong with the causing principles themselves. The recipients alone should be blamed.

Basically then there are two levels at which evils occur: that of particular (human and animal) souls, and that of particular material bodies. It is important to notice that Proclus never attempts to connect those two levels causally: neither is matter responsible for the vices of the souls, nor do the souls produce the evil that inheres in material bodies. The souls are not susceptible to evil *because of* their contact with the body or with matter, as Plotinus and many other Platonists seem to suggest. No, it is of their own weakness that souls descend to the body and the material world. And it is wrong, claims Proclus, to explain the soul's weakness through the contact with matter, as Plotinus did. The soul itself is responsible for descending

and ascending, and makes its own choices.[74] Also the corporeal world
with its inherent corruptibility and decay is not explained as the
result of a fall of the souls or of original sins, as in some Gnostic or
Christian Platonists.[75]

2.4.3. This brings us to the question of the causes of evil.[76] From ch.
40 onwards, Proclus looks at the problem of evil from the perspective
of causation: 'We should look at the causes for evil and ask ourselves
whether there is one and the same cause for all evils or not. For some
say there is, but others deny this' (40,2-3). Three major types of
explanation have been offered in the philosophical tradition. First,
there are those who maintain that there is a source or fount from
which all evils spring, just like there is a source of all good things.
Second, some philosophers (like Amelius, the disciple of Plotinus) look
for a paradigm of evil on the level below the One, that of the intelligible: just like there is a Form of the just, there would be a Form of the
unjust. A third group of philosophers posits a maleficent soul as the
principle of evil.[77] These then are the three main options, for 'if one
should posit a unique cause of evils, then it is cogent to think that this
cause is either divine, or intellectual, or psychical' (40,18-19). Indeed,
for a Neoplatonist only Gods, Intellects and Souls can be ranked as
proper causes. Proclus argues that none of these can be the cause of
evil. There can be no supreme principle of evil, coeval with and
opposing the good, for to think this would imply adopting a contradic-
tory and self-refuting kind of metaphysical dualism. Neither can
there be some intelligible paradigm of evil, for how could there be
imperfection among the Forms? Equally unacceptable is the hypothesis that a maleficent soul is the ultimate principle of evils, for every
soul is by nature good, deriving its essence, as it does, from the higher
ontological levels, which are all good.

Since Proclus had already ruled out the view that matter or privation would be the principle of evil, all possibilities seem to be
exhausted: 'if these are not the causes of evils, what then will we
ourselves claim to be the cause of their coming to be?' (47,1-2). But
perhaps one should give up looking for one single cause of evil. Since
it has already been established that it is better to speak of evils in the
plural, one should also forsake looking for unity among their causes:[78]
'By no means should we posit one cause that is a unique, *per se* cause
of evils. For if there is one cause of good things, there are many causes
of evils, and not one single cause' (47,2-4). Proclus rejects the reduction of plurality to unity in the case of evil.[79] Unlike the many good
things, whose goodness can be traced back to a supreme good, evils
constitute an indeterminable multitude and therefore cannot be attributed to a single principle and cause. In this aspect, evils cannot
resemble their opposite, for good things are characterised by unity
and concord, evil things by discord and dissimilarity. Evil only exists

as a shortcoming, as parasitic upon some kind of being or activity. It is mixed with some form of good, that is. Therefore one will look in vain if one tries to find a single cause that is the *per se* cause of all forms of evil. Proclus gently points out that this can be learned from Plato himself, who in the *Republic* (379C6-7 = **T2′**) has said that 'we must look for some other factors – and not God – as the causes of evil' (*alla atta dei zêtein ta aitia*). Commenting upon this passage, Proclus explains that Plato is here using the plural *aitia* and that he has qualified it by adding the indeterminate pronoun *atta*.[80]

All attempts to reduce evil to one cause or to some source ultimately amount to hypostasising evil. However, evil is not a principal *hupostasis* existing on its own and for its own sake, but a *par-hupostasis*, that is, it can only exist as a side-effect of things existing and happening in the true hypostases. What the later Neoplatonists[81] mean when they use the term *parupostasis* can only be understood properly in the context of a causal analysis. This is perfectly obvious if one keeps in mind that the noun *hupostasis* itself has always preserved something of the verbal meaning of *huphistêmi / huphistamai*, 'to bring forth', 'to produce'.

The notion of a *parupostasis* is tied to the recognition that a proper causal analysis of evils *qua* evils – of failures, misses, shortcomings – is impossible. In chs 48-9 Proclus looks at the four Aristotelian modes of causality, only to conclude that they fail to explain evil. First, evil is not the result of an efficient cause, for every cause on its own account (*per se*) only produces what is good, that is, the intended effect which can be characterised as the good appropriate to the cause (for each cause produces what is similar to it, fire heat, snow cold). Therefore, the shortcomings in the effect are not due to the activity and the powers of the cause as such, but to its lack of power and weakness and deficiency. It is clear that the verb 'to produce' here has an almost normative sense: it is not just to produce an effect, but to produce something that is desirable because it is appropriate to the agent. Its counterpart is destruction: evil is whatever destroys, harms, hurts, etc. To call particular souls efficient causes of evil is therefore only partly justified. Properly speaking, they are not 'real' efficient causes, since they do not produce evil out of power, but out of weakness.

It would be equally impossible to envisage a true paradigmatic cause of evil. For the Forms bestow determination and perfection on all beings, and are certainly not a cause of imperfection. Socrates' talk at *Theaetetus* 176E (**T1′**) of 'a godless paradigm of the deepest unhappiness' only seemingly points to a Form of evil. It cannot be denied that some souls imitate vice, passion and foulness they see, instead of assimilating themselves to the ideal paradigms of perfection. However, Proclus argues that these base models could only be called paradigms in a metaphorical sense, and fall short of the paradigmatic nature of the Forms.

Proclus does not even mention the possibility of a material cause for evils, because, as he has explained earlier, matter as such is not evil and can therefore never be a cause of evil.

So the only possibility left would be that there is some final cause for evil. However, this too is inconceivable. Someone might object that there is a sense in which there is a final cause for evil. For is not the Good the final cause for everything that exists? Since (relative) evils do exist, one could argue that the Good is their final cause. Proclus replies to this objection by saying that it is better to avoid talking about the good as the cause of evil. The good is not the motivating cause for a failure *qua* failure. For no one can maintain that it is for the sake of the good that we fail or transgress. The Good may be the final cause of all things, including evils, *qua* existing, but not of evils *qua* evils.

Hence, none of the modes of causality gives us a cause of evil, at least if we take 'cause' in its proper sense as a principal factor (*proêgoumenê*) from which follows by necessity a certain effect in accordance with the nature of the cause:

> And perhaps it will be better to make neither the efficient cause, nor the natural paradigm, nor the *per se* final cause the principal cause of evils. For the form of evils, their nature, is a kind of defect, an indeterminateness and a privation; their *hupostasis*, is, as it is usually said, more like a kind of *parupostasis*. (*DMS* 49,7-11)

The crucial notion of *parupostasis* is explained in ch. 50, the key chapter of the entire treatise. It is remarkable that just when Proclus is introducing his specific treatment of *parupostasis*, he again suggests that evils may well be uncaused in a way:

> We must next consider what the mode of evil is and how it comes into existence from the above-mentioned causes and non-causes. Here we must bring in the aforementioned *parupostasis*. (50,1-3)

In order to exist in a proper sense (*kuriôs*), an effect must result from a cause which proceeds according to its nature towards a goal that is intended. In such a case, there is an essential or *per se* relation between the cause and its effect. Whenever an effect is produced that was not intended or is not related by nature or *per se* to the agent, it is said to exist besides (*para*) the intended effect, parasitically upon it, as it were.

> For there is no other way of existing for that which neither is produced, in any way whatsoever, from a principal cause, nor has a relation to a definite goal and a final cause, nor has received in its own right an entry into being, since anything whatever that exists properly (*kuriôs*) must come from a cause in accordance with nature – indeed, without a cause it is impossible for anything to come about – and must relate the order of its coming about to some goal. (50,3-9)

Just as a failure *qua* failure is never intended by an agent, evil *qua* evil is never caused by a cause, nor in view of a (final) cause. It only exists parasitically upon an intended action, as it is never produced by an agent acting *per se* and directly intending this very result (when we say that someone intentionally commits an evil deed, this person's action can be explained as aimed at what seemed good to him or her[82]). Evils are not the outcome of goal-directed processes, but happen *per accidens*, as incidental by-products which fall outside the intention of the agents. Therefore, its seems that we must rank evils, failures and shortcomings of all kind among the accidental beings.

> In which class of things should we, then, place evil? Perhaps it belongs to the beings that have their being accidentally and because of something else, and not from a principle of their own? (50,9-11)

Therefore, Proclus continues, it is better to call its mode of existence a *parupostasis*, rather than a *hupostasis*, a term that belongs to those beings 'that proceed from causes towards a goal'. *Parupostasis* or 'parasitic existence', on the contrary, is the mode of existence of 'beings that neither appear through causes in accordance with nature nor result in a definite end'. The basis of Proclus' argument is certainly Aristotle's distinction between a causality *per se* and a causality *per accidens*.[83] The accidental is not necessary, but indeterminate (*aoriston*); and of such a thing the causes are unordered (*atakta*) and indefinite (*apeira*).[84] The examples of the man discovering a treasure when digging a grave, or meeting a debtor when going to the agora are fairly well-known. Evil effects then seem to belong to the class of beings *per accidens* without principal antecedent (*proêgoumenai*) causes. In fact, evil is due to the non-attainment by an agent of its appropriate goal.

> Therefore it is appropriate to call such generation a parasitic existence (*parupostasis*), in that it is without end[85] and unintended (*askopon*), uncaused in a way (*anaition pôs*) and indefinite (*aoriston*). (50,29-31)

It is remarkable that Proclus flirts with the idea that evils are somehow uncaused. The notion of an uncaused motion also figures in a text that is part of the *Mantissa* (ps.-Alexander).[86] Referring to Aristotle's analysis of accidental causation, the author of what is known as ch. 24 of the *Mantissa* argues that chance events cannot be explained under the heading of any of the four Aristotelian types of causation. A chance factor is not really a cause: 'So what followed on this cause came about without a cause (*anaitiôs*), for it did not do so on account of a proper cause.'[87] There is somehow non-being in things that are contingent and especially those that come about as a result of chance, and this non-being in a sense stems from the causes (insofar as these causes are not really *their* causes). The notion of an 'uncaused motion' is highly problematic, as Robert Sharples has convincingly argued.[88] To regard an event as 'uncaused' does not imply that it is completely divorced from preceding causes. There would be no discovery of a treasure without the preceding digging. However, the event is uncaused because it cannot be explained as the outcome of a particular process. Here one may refer to Richard Sorabji's interpretation of Arist. *Metaph*. 6.3. He argues that coincidences are indeed uncaused, if we understand 'cause' in terms of the ability to give an explanation.[89] *Qua* coincidences, such events are indeed uncaused. It is not improbable that Proclus had knowledge of Peripatetic analyses such as we find them in the *Mantissa*. A passage in Syrianus' *Metaphysics Commentary*[90] even provides evidence for a link between an Aristotelian analysis of accidental causation and chance and Neoplatonic treatments of the same subject.

That Proclus in his explanation of the occurences of evils seems to accept some sort of 'uncaused events' is astonishing and even perplexing. For elsewhere[91] Proclus fully endorses the famous axiom formulated by Plato at the beginning of the cosmology of the *Timaeus*: 'Whatever is produced must be produced by a cause; for it is impossible for something to be produced without a cause' (*Tim*. 28A4-6). Why then does Proclus in his account of evil seem to admit some form of uncaused in the universe? The reason is, of course, that he wants to eliminate at all cost any reduction of evil to the divine first cause. In fact, any explanation of evil in causal terms would integrate evil into the metaphysical structure of the universe and would inevitably lead us to the first cause as the ultimate explanation of evil. Whatever causes evil must itself be produced by principles in the hierarchy of the good, so that the good could ultimately be held responsible after all. But this is of course inadmissible (cf. **T2**). The only possibility to exculpate god (to make him really *anaitios*) is to understand evil itself as an uncaused event that does not have a proper or principal existence (*proêgoumenê hupostasis*), but is rather something that just happens without an antecedent cause (not insofar as it happens or exists, that is, but insofar as it is evil).[92]

Proclus wants to keep the god(s) free from all blame (from all causal responsibility for evils, that is) and at the same time allow for a domain in reality where real contingency is given. This is the world in which we live, populated by particular beings that can only participate intermittently in the higher orders.

> The procession beginning from on high ceases when it has got as far as those things which can both change and make to subsist along with themselves some sort of aberration (*paruphistanein tina paratropên*[93]). (*in Alc.* 117,22-5, p. 97 Segonds)

The consequence of this is that failure, perversion and disorder become a real and inescapable possibility. Evil is possible because not all levels of reality can accept the gifts of the superior orders in the same way.[94]

> For if there is something that, at times, has the capacity of participating in the good but, at other times, is deprived of this participation, then there will necessarily be a privation of participation of the good. (7,25-7)

2.4.4. The uncausedness of evils *qua* evils is also the bottom line of the *theodicy* that Proclus presents in the final chapters of the *DMS* (chs 58-61): only insofar as they are good are evils produced by the god(s). *Qua* evils, they remain 'uncaused somehow'. This also sheds new light on Proclus' view that evils can only exist because they are mixed with the good. Had it been possible that pure and unmixed evils existed, then there would have been a problem for Providence. But now that they turn out to be invariably mixed with some good, it is obvious that Providence and our trust in it need not be endangered: Providence only produces the good in them.[95] 'After all, saying that god is the cause of all things is not the same as saying that he is the only cause of things' (58,16-17; cf. **T2 & T2′**). Evils *qua* evils are not the result of his productive activity. They rather follow from the activities of particular bodies and souls. These are the 'other causes, which, as we have said, are able to be productive not on account of power, but on account of weakness' (61,9-10). But a cause bringing about an effect through weakness, not through power – that is, not intending the actual result –, is not really a true cause of *that* effect.[96] And therefore evils remain in a way uncaused, as Proclus said earlier. At any rate, the gods remain free from all blame. In the same way as they have a unitary knowledge of plurality, and an undivided knowledge of divisibles, their knowledge of evils is good (61,17-24).[97] And since for the gods knowing and producing coincide, they produce evils in a good way; in other words, they cause them *qua* good, not *qua* evil.

This interpretation resolves the conflict between belief in divine

Providence and the experience of evil that has haunted Greek philosophy for ages.[98]

> How can evil belong to being if there is Providence? (*De dec. dub.* 5,26)

> If there is evil, how will it not stand in the way of that which is providential towards the good? On the other hand, if Providence fills the universe, how can there be evil in beings? Some thinkers indeed yield to one of the two lines of reasoning: either they admit that not everything comes from Providence, and [acknowledge there is evil, or they] deny the existence of evil, and maintain that everything comes from Providence and the good. (*DMS* 58,2-6)

Traditionally Platonists attributed the first view to Epicurus, who was known for his rejection of Providence[99] and to Aristotle, who was believed to have limited the activity of Providence to the supralunary realm, whereas the Stoics were generally considered to have played the reality of evil (and that of contingency) down[100] in favour of the omnipresence of divine Providence. The Stoics actually claimed that many of the so-called evils are in fact not evil when seen from a universal perspective. Indeed, there seemed to be no way around either detracting from Providence or minimising evil. But Proclus – no doubt following a specific Neoplatonic tradition: the Iamblichus-Syrianus lineage – has managed to build himself a carefully balanced middle position, so that at the end of his treatise he can proudly say:

> If I am right in stating this, all things will be from Providence and evil has its own place among beings. (61,16-17)

However, Proclus in his all-encompassing theodicy has also incorporated the originally Stoic idea that seeming evils no longer appear evil when seen from a universal perspective. In the case of both particular souls and particular bodies, many if not all of their sufferings and difficulties – even the destruction of bodies – are good when seen 'from above'. The evils of souls and bodies are never unqualifiedly evil: they are at the same time good. What is more, they are not just good from a universal perspective – the destruction of a body, e.g., will give rise to the birth of a another body out of the components of the first – often they are even good for these particular beings themselves. A soul that suffers, for instance, may actually be undergoing a punishment that it deserves, and thereby become better. Indeed, a soul would not benefit from unmerited rewards (chs 58-60).

2.4.5. It remains to be explained in what sense evil is a contrary and a privation.[101] First of all, it is clear that evil has to be understood as a privation, rather than as a positive essence in its own right. However, a privation of form (i.e. 'Aristotelian' privation) is merely an absence, and a complete privation would lead a being to non-existence, which would entail the end of all evils for this being. It is not this kind of privation that Proclus has in mind. Also evil cannot be equated with privation as such or absolute privation, as Plotinus believed. As we have already explained, absolute privation, absence of every positive qualification, that is, does not exist according to Proclus. But at any rate, privation conceived as the absence of form and being could never give us evil. For evils are not just contrary to being, but contrary to the good[102] (or rather contrary to *a* good, as only relative evils exist).

An important distinction must be made between a privation of a form and a privation of a good. Whereas a privation of a form is a mere absence and in no way evil, the so-called privation of the good actively opposes the good and is therefore evil. The difference between an ordinary privation and a privation of a good can be explained by the example of not-seeing versus blindness. The absence of sight in the case of a stone, e.g., is not an evil, for to be deprived of a form or quality is not in itself evil. But the absence of sight where there *should* have been sight – in a human being, e.g. – *is* an evil and is no longer called not-seeing, but blindness. Blindness is an evil when it is a defect of a particular power that has the capacity to see, and 'coexists' with that power.

Privations of forms, says Proclus, are always total privations: nothing of the positive disposition remains and, by consequence, there is nothing left to oppose the corresponding form or disposition. For a pure lack cannot have any force to oppose the disposition of which it is the privation.[103] It is different with privations of the good. A disease is more than an absence of order and functioning. It has the power to attack and undermine a given order in the body.[104] This kind of 'privation' derives its power from the good, and should therefore be called not a contrary, but a subcontrary of the good.[105]

Proclus derives the notion of the subcontrary from *Theaetetus* 176A (**T1**).[106] Subcontrariety, as Proclus defines it in chs 52-4, is a special form of contrariety whereby a particular evil derives its being and power from the good it is opposed to. It is a privation that somehow coexists with the good disposition of which it is the negation and which through this coexistence shares in that disposition's form and power. Evil, as has been explained, is never a complete privation: somehow it always coexists with the good disposition or form or capacity, of which it is the privation. Therefore, evil not only weakens this disposition by its presence, but it also derives its power and even its specific form[107] from it.

The notion of the subcontrary allows Proclus to maintain a form of contrariety between particular, i.e. relative, evils and the good, without attributing any independent being to them. Evil can never exist on its own, in its own right – not insofar as it is evil. It has a kind of existence only insofar as it is *parasitic* on true being and on the good. Because evils always parasitise upon good dispositions, they can usurp the power of those dispositions and use it against the good.[108]

Evil is thus a privation 'deriving its power from the nature <of which it is the privation> through its interwovenness with it, and only thus can it establish itself as something contrary to the good' (7,30-1). That is why it can fight the disposition upon which it is parasitic, something that is not possible for other privations, which 'do not exist at all', as Aristotle says (in other words: the disposition of which they are the privations has disappeared completely).

3. Structural analysis

A. *Overview of chapters*

Introduction (ch. 1)

Does evil exist? (chs 2-10)
First point of view: evil does not exist (chs 2-3)
The opposite point of view: evil exists (chs 4-7)
Proclus' own view (chs 8-10)

Where does evil exist? (chs 11-39)
Is there evil in the gods? (chs 11-13)
Is there evil in the three superior kinds (angels, demons, and
    heroes)? (chs 14-19)
Is there evil in the souls? (chs 20-6)
    Transition (ch 20)
    The immaculate souls (chs 21-2)
    The fallen human souls (chs 23-4)
    The irrational souls (chs 25-6)
Is there evil in nature? (chs 27-9)
Is matter evil? (chs 30-7)
    The view of the opponents (Plotinus) (ch. 30)
    Counter-arguments (chs 31-5)
    Proclus' own view (chs 36-7)
Is privation evil? (ch. 38)
Corollary: are evils of bodies greater than evils of souls? (ch. 39)

The causes of evil (chs 40-9)
One or many causes of evil? (ch. 40)
(1) There is no divine principle of evil (chs 41-2)

(2) There is no intelligible form of evil (chs 43-4)
(3) The maleficent soul is not the source of evil (chs 45-6)
Proclus' own view concerning the causes of evil (chs 47-9)

The mode of existence and the nature of evil (chs 50-4)
The mode of existence of evil (ch. 50)
The nature and properties of evil (ch. 51)
How can what is contrary to the good act against it? (chs 52-4)

Different types of evils (chs 55-7)
Providence and evil (chs 58-61)

B. Summary of chapters

Introduction

Chapter 1
We shall examine in this treatise the nature and the origin of evil, and
also where it occurs, what are its causes, what is its mode of existence
and what is its relation to providence. Those questions have been
often discussed by our predecessors. But it might be good, now that
we have some free time, to give a critical survey of their views,
starting however with Plato. For whoever wants to understand the
nature of evil, can only do so by understanding Plato's teachings.

1. Does evil exist? (chs 2-10)

First point of view: evil does not exist

Chapter 2
If the Good is the cause of everything and the Good only causes good
things, evil cannot exist. Everything participating in being also participates in the One-Good. The Good is beyond being and every being
strives towards the good. But what is contrary to the good, does not
strive for the good. If therefore evil is completely contrary to the Good,
evil is not one of the beings. So what is said in the *Theaetetus* (176A)
is wrong, that evil exists because there must be something contrary
to the good.

Chapter 3
If the Good is beyond being, and absolute non-being is the contrary of
being, and evil that of the good, evil must be beneath absolute
non-being. People indeed prefer non-being (death) over evil (a miserable life). If the demiurge wants everything to be good, how could
there be evil?

The opposite point of view: evil exists

Chapter 4
Vices show the reality of evil. For in society, and, prior to that, in our own souls, we experience vice and vices to oppose virtue and the virtues. Vices are not just lesser goods, but truly contrary to the good.

Chapter 5
As it is shown in the *Republic*, evil is that which corrupts. Now, without corruption there would be no generation, and without generation the world would be incomplete. For in the *Timaeus*, it is said that the mortal kinds are necessary to complete the universe. There are different kinds of corruption: that of bodies, and that of souls.

Chapter 6
The relation of evil to good is not that of an increasing of deficiency, but is a relation of true contrariety. For everything that can be either more or less comes closer to its principle by leaning towards the 'more'. Injustice by increasing does not come closer to the good. Hence injustice is not a lesser good, but a contrary of the good.

In Plato's *Theaetetus* (176A), Socrates affirms the existence and even the necessity of evil, but this also means that it exists because of the good.

Chapter 7
Why is evil necessary? Because there should not only exist beings that participate unchangingly in the Forms, but also intermittent participants. The latter cannot directly participate in the Forms, but only through the intermediary of the eternal participants. The eternal participants could not exist if not also the intermittent participants existed, for otherwise they would themselves be the lowest of beings and they would be infertile. The intermittent participants, then, will have a lesser participation in the good: there will be a privation of the good.

However, compared to other privations, that are mere absences, privation of the good is a special case, as it cannot exist when the good is completely absent. It is, on the contrary, the good which lends power to its own privation, as can be seen in the evils of the soul and in those of the body.

Proclus' own view

Chapter 8
Evil is twofold: pure evil, and evil mixed with the good. Likewise, the good is twofold (the absolute good, and good mixed with non-good), and so is being (being itself, and being mixed with non-being), and also non-being (absolute non-being, and non-being mixed with being).

Chapter 9
Absolute non-being does not exist at all, while relative non-being
does. A *fortiori* does absolute evil not exist, since it is even beyond
absolute non-being just as the good is beyond being. But evil that is
mixed with the good exists. It is contrary to a particular good, but not
to the good in general, as it owes its existence to the good.

Chapter 10
Plato is right when he says, in the *Timaeus*, that according to the will
of the demiurge everything is good and nothing bad. But what is said
in the *Theaetetus* too is correct, namely that evils will always, by
necessity, exist. Insofar things are produced and known by the demiurge, they are good. However, not everything is capable of always
completely remaining in the good. Conclusion: all things are good,
since there is no evil that has no share in order and is unmixed; yet,
also evil exists, namely for the particular things that cannot always
remain in the good unmixedly.

2. Where does evil exist? (chs 11-39)

Is there evil in the gods?

Chapter 11
The gods (i.e. the henads) are the highest and produce all reality. The
gods themselves have their existence through the good, and hence
cannot be evil.

Chapter 12
They lack nothing. If even souls can be free from evils, how could
there be evil in the gods?

Chapter 13
For the gods 'to exist' and 'to be good' are identical. Their goodness is
unchanging.

Is there evil in the three superior kinds (angels, demons, and heroes)?

Chapter 14
It is impossible that *angels* have any evil in them, as they are
continuous with the gods, know the latters' intellect and reveal the
gods to the lower beings.

Chapter 15
Since angels occupy the first rank among the three superior kinds,
they are necessarily good, for whatever has the first rank in any order
is good.

Chapter 16
Is it in *demons* that evil exists for the first time? Some believe that certain demons are evil by nature. Others claim that the demons responsible for the eschatological punishment of the soul are evil 'by choice'.

Chapter 17
Demons are (1) neither evil to themselves, (2) nor evil to others. They are not evil to themselves because (1a) deriving their existence from the gods they could not be unchangingly evil, and (1b) if they are only sometimes evil to themselves, they cannot be demons by nature; true demons are not even now and then evil to themselves. They are not evil to others, (2) for in punishing wrongdoers they only perform a task that serves a good purpose.

Chapter 18
There is no evil in *heroes*, as their nature always remains the same. Their so-called passions are for them in accordance with their nature, and hence not evil.

Chapter 19
In assisting in the punishment of the souls of the deceased, the heroes do nothing but perform the task assigned to them.

Is there evil in the souls?

Chapter 20: Transition
All classes examined before were not susceptible to a change affecting their specific order. But those that come next have the potency of ascending or of moving to generation, which makes the occurrence of evil a possibility.

Chapters 21-2: The immaculate souls
The better souls (such as the souls of Orpheus or Heracles) remain in contact with the divine when they descend to the world of becoming. The larger part of their life is dedicated to contemplation and to providence over the whole together with the gods. If they come down, it is for the benefit of the things here. There is no passion or depravity in their behaviour. Nevertheless even these souls are not immune to 'oblivion', which is common to all souls that descend. In their case, oblivion only means a temporal ceasing or disturbance of their activities, their internal intellectual disposition remaining untouched. Since their nature remains untouched, there is only the mere semblance of evil in them.

It is indeed appropriate that there is an intermediate class between

the (divine) classes that remain completely free from evil, and those
in which evil really exists.

Chapters 23-4: The fallen human souls

Most souls are incapable of imitating their presiding gods in a life of
contemplation and universal providence. They fall from on high, 'toil
and limp' (*Phaedr.* 248B), become weak and suffer all sorts of evil.
These souls form a manifold tribe transmuted continuously by various choices and impulses. In the case of these souls, not only the
activities are hampered, but the internal faculties are curtailed. In
their care for their mortal bodies, they become interwoven with
secondary (irrational) forms of life.

This is for the souls indeed a weakness, to fail to participate in the
divine banquet and to precipitate downwards. However, they retain
the power to get up there again, though this will not be easy. This is
confirmed by the myths of the *Phaedrus* and the *Republic* that reveal
the ultimate fate of the human souls.

The origin of evil for us is the continuous connection with what is
inferior; it is also oblivion and ignorance.

Chapters 25-6: The irrational souls

Is there evil in the irrational souls, that are but images of a soul, parts
of a worse kind of soul, which the Athenian stranger calls 'maleficent'?
These irrational souls (the souls of animals) are inferior to the irrational soul that exists in us, and therefore it would be very unlikely if
they did not run the risk of becoming evil as well. Now, if such an
'image' belonged to the rational soul of an individual (as is the case of
the irrational soul of human persons), its evil would consist in not
conforming itself to reason. But in the case of animals, who only have
an irrational soul, evil arises when they lack the appropriate virtue,
that is, when they fall short of their own nature. When a being does
not act according to its nature, it is either a change to what is better
or to what is worse than its nature. These irrational souls may then
become better or worse on account of their acquired habits.

Is there evil in nature?

Chapter 27

There is no evil in the nature of the universe as a whole, nor in the
nature of eternal beings. For particular beings, however, one thing
will be in accordance and another not in accordance with nature. For
each particular nature, there will be something else contrary to it.
Corporeal things may undergo what is contrary to their specific
nature, because the latter is distinguished from and opposed to other
partial natures. Thus a particular nature may become impotent
because of the power of contraries surrounding it or because of a

defect of its own substantial power (which is possible since it has come down from universal nature).

Chapter 28
For natural beings evil consists in the fact that they do not act according to their nature. Thus ugliness occurs when the rational form does not prevail over its matter and disease when the order of the body is dissolved. These deficiencies, however, are only possible in material individual bodies, not in the universal bodies (such as the elements), nor in the immaterial bodies, as are the celestial bodies, which remain invariably the same and uniform in their activities. A special case are the pneumatic vehicles of the souls: though immaterial, they follow the vicissitudes of their respective soul in its ascent and descent.

Chapter 29
To summarise, individual bodies that exist in matter have evil even in their substance; others are outside matter and have no evil in their substance, but in their activities they may be hindered by what is contrary to them. Universal bodies always and invariably preserve their order (some because there is no disorder in them, some because the disorder is always overcome).

But how, then, should one interpret what Plato says in *Timaeus* 30A of 'that which moves in a irregular and disorderly fashion'? For this is a substrate for both the material and the eternal bodies. Proclus answers that 'disorder' and 'irregularity' have a different sense when applied to the substrate 'up there'.

Is matter evil?

Chapter 30: The view of the opponents (Plotinus)
Summary of the main arguments of *Ennead* 1,8[51],3. If good is twofold – one being absolute and nothing other than good, the other being the good in something else – then evil too will be twofold: the absolute and primary evil, and the evil participating in the former. Primary evil, which is absolute unmeasuredness and imperfection, must be identified with matter which is without any form or determination.

Chapters 31-5: Counter-arguments
Chapter 31
If one admits that in bodies evil occurs when matter prevails and in souls weakness comes about when they assimilate themselves to the material, the conclusion that matter is the source of all evil seems inescapable. This inference, however, is unacceptable. A series of arguments follows in order to refute the equation of evil with matter.

(1) If matter is the principle of evil,

(1a) either there are two ultimate principles, which is unacceptable, as there cannot be two firsts,

(1b) or matter stems from the good [which happens to be Plotinus' view], but then the good will be the cause of evil, and hence the good will be evil (as its cause is to a higher degree what the product is) and evil will be good (as products always assimilate themselves to their cause).

Chapter 32

(2) Matter is necessary for the universe.

(3) Matter is called unmeasured not as being the mere absence of measure [since matter is not identical with privation], nor as something that actively opposes measure [since matter according to Plotinus is inert], but as the need for measure – matter desires measure and therefore cannot be evil.

Chapter 33

(4) Evil existed in the souls prior to their descent to matter: in the *Phaedrus*, it is clear that the souls make the wrong choices prior to their descent; and in the *Republic*, it is said that they are weakened before they drink from the cup of oblivion.

Chapter 34

(5) In the *Timaeus*, matter is called the mother and wet-nurse of generation; it contributes to the fabrication of the world, and is therefore good.

(6) The disorderly 'previous condition of the world' should not be equated with precosmic matter as such; it refers to matter in which partial – and hence conflicting – forms are present.

(7) In the *Philebus*, it is said that matter is produced by the One and according to the *Republic*, god does not cause evil things.

(8) The 'irregular motion' of the *Timaeus* is not matter, nor due to matter.

Chapter 35

Matter is generated by god: exegesis of *Philebus* 23C. As the lowest manifestation of unlimitedness, matter is produced by the Good, and hence it is not evil.

Chapters 36-7: Proclus' own view

Matter is neither good, nor evil, but necessary.

Evil does not exist in itself, but only in other things, for it is contrary to the good in other things, not to the first good. Indeed, nothing can be contrary to the first good, as (1) contraries are mutually destructive and (2) contraries must belong to the same genus.

Is privation evil?

Chapter 38

If matter is not evil and must be distinguished from privation, perhaps privation is an 'evil agent', as it is contrary to the form and a cause of destruction? But this view is not correct. Since the Good is not identical with, but beyond being, evil cannot consist just in the privation of being. The presence of a privation does not yet entail that there is evil. Complete privation even amounts to the disappearance of evil, since it destroys the subject of the evil. What does not yet exist, or no longer exists, is not evil. Two meanings of 'disorder and unmeasuredness' must be distinguished: this expression may refer to pure absence of order and measure or to something contrary to these. If the evil is contrary to the good, it cannot be a mere privation, since a privation is without form and power.

Corollary: are evils of bodies greater than evils of souls?

Chapter 39

As evil exists both in souls and in bodies, we must examine the ranking of evil. Is the evil in the souls greater or lesser than the evil in bodies?

Evil may either destroy the substance itself of a thing, or handicap its powers, or merely obstruct its activities. As the soul can never be corrupted in its substance, but only in its powers and activities (and the divine souls only in their activities), it seems that the evil that touches the soul is less radical than the evil that extends to the substances of bodies. But from another perspective that psychic evil appears to be worse in that it is contrary to a greater good (moral virtue) than is corporeal evil. Also, corporeal evil when it intensifies leads to non-existence, whereas evil of the soul leads to an evil existence. This again proves that matter is not the primary evil.

3. The causes of evil (chs 40-9)

Chapter 40: One or many causes of evil?

Is there one and the same cause for all evils or are there many?

If one posits a unique cause, it must either be a divine or an intellective or a psychical principle. (1) Some indeed maintain that there is an ultimate principle of evil opposed to the Good [the position of the Manicheans]. (2) Others [like Amelius] admit forms of evil in the intelligible realm. (3) Others again [like Atticus or Plutarch] posit a maleficent soul. The last two groups invoke Plato in support of their views.

Chapters 41-2: There is no divine principle of evil (1)
It is easy to refute the view that there is a 'fount of evils'. For as has
been argued (in chs 11-13), all the gods and all the founts only cause
what is good. If evil exists, it cannot have a divine origin, but, as Plato
said, 'there must be other causes for it'.

However, in exercising their universal providence, the gods also let
some forms of evil exist by 'measuring their unlimitedness and adorn-
ing their darkness'. In this sense, one may call the divine cause 'the
fount of evils', not as the principle of the generation of evils, but as
providing them with limit and integrating them in the whole order.
The gods are not cause of evil *qua* evil, but cause of the order in evils.

Therefore, not only the barbarian theologians, but also the most
eminent of the Greeks admit that the gods have knowledge of both
good and evil. If there were absolute evil, unmixed with the good, it
could not be known by the gods. For the gods create all beings they
know, as their knowledge is creative. The gods know and produce evil
qua good.

Chapters 43-4: There is no intelligible Form of Evil (2)
How could one explain the incessant existence of evils without there
being a paradigm? If evil is perpetual, it must proceed from an
immutable cause, which points to the nature of the Forms. This
argument, however, is wrong. There can be no intelligible paradigm
of evils, since all Forms are perfect and good. If the evils were images
of an intelligible Form, they would try to assimilate themselves to
what is perfect and blessed.

Further, the demiurge did not want evil to exist in the universe and
wished 'to generate all things similar to himself'. The demiurge
creates through the Forms which exist in him in an intellectual
manner. If there existed Forms of evil, he would necessarily produce
evils corresponding to these Forms.

But is the perpetuity of evil not a sufficient argument for the
hypothesis of a Form of evil? We must distinguish between what is
'eternal' and what is perpetual and merely recurs.

Chapters 45-6: The maleficent soul is not the source of evil (3)
Some consider the soul that is called 'maleficent' (*Laws* 10) as the
cause of all evils. We must ask them whether this soul is evil by its
very essence or is good by nature, though acting in different ways
(better or worse). If the latter is the case, not only the irrational soul
must be called maleficent, but also the 'better' soul from which it
derives its good, since that soul too can change from better to worse
states. If, however, it is evil in nature, from where does it derive its
evil being? It must come from the demiurge and the encosmic gods,
which are all good. But nothing that comes from the good is evil. If the
Athenian Stranger calls this soul 'maleficent' because of the evil in its

activities and potencies, we must say that even this soul is not always in the same state, but may act in different ways. Besides, it may even be made good-like when it adapts its activities to the better soul. It is no wonder that it can thus improve itself, as it has the capacity to revert upon itself, which is lacking in all bodies and in the irrational souls.

It would, however, be absurd and sacrilegious to consider this soul [which is the source of the irrational life] as the cause of evils. It is neither the cause of evil for the bodies, nor for the better soul. For the latter, evil comes from the soul itself when the mortal life-form is connected with it in its descent. But even before the descent, there was already weakness in the soul. For souls do not flee from contemplation when they are both capable and agreeable to remain in the intelligible. Therefore, evil was already present in the soul, and is not the consequence of the secondary (irrational) lives the soul attracts in its descent.

Chapters 47-9: Proclus' own view concerning the causes of evil
It is wrong to search for one single cause of evils. Whereas one should posit one single cause for all good things, the multitude of evils can only be explained by many particular indeterminate causes, some for souls, some for bodies, which cannot be reduced to one principle. Socrates, too, appears to suggest this when he says (*Resp.* 379BC) that the divinity cannot be held responsible for evil and that 'we must look for some other (*alla atta*) factors as causes of evil'.

Moreover, those multiple causes of evil are not principal or essential (*per se*) causes. Although some particular souls and corporeal forms could be called *efficient* causes of evil, they are not really 'reasons or powers' but rather lack of power and weakness. Although one could speak of a *paradigm* of evil, as does Socrates in the *Theaetetus* (176E), this is not an immobile intelligible form, but rather things external and inferior, which the soul wrongly takes as a model. And certainly there are no *final* causes of evil. For souls do everything for the sake of the good, even when they act badly. However, those bad acts are not done for the sake of the good, but result from a failure to reach the good. That is why evil is said to be involuntary.

4. The mode of existence and the nature of evil (chs 50-4)

Chapter 50: The mode of existence of evil
Since evil is not produced from a principal cause nor related to a final cause, it has not received existence in its own right. It belongs to the class of accidental beings that exist because of something else and have no principle of their own. For we do everything for the sake of (what we consider to be) good. If, then, the contrary effect occurs, it is

appropriate to attribute to it only a parasitic existence (*parupostasis*), because it is 'unintended and uncaused', 'supervenient and adventitious'. The failure to attain the appropriate goal is due to the weakness of the agent that stems from the contrariety between its diverse powers.

Chapter 51: The nature and properties of evil
How can we know the nature of evil which is formless? We can know it indirectly by considering what the good is at the different levels of reality and denying its attributes. The properties of evils are explained as privations of the forms of goodness that characterise the different ontological levels of Proclus' theological metaphysics.

Chapters 52-4: How can what is contrary to the good act against it?

Chapter 52
Evil is not complete privation, but as parasitising upon the good, it uses the very power of the latter to combat it. For it coexists with the disposition of which it is privation and thus not only weakens this disposition, but also derives power and form from it. Privations of forms, being complete privations, are mere absences of dispositions and as such not evil, whereas privations of the good actively oppose the corresponding dispositions and are contrary to them.

On its own account, evil is neither active, nor powerful. But it receives power from its contrary, the good. The stronger the power of the good that inheres in evil, the greater will be the evil actions. When the good is weakened, evil will be greater as a privation, but as far as its action is concerned, it will be weaker. The greater the evil, the less effective it becomes.

Chapter 53
In the admixture with evil, the good becomes weaker, whereas evil profits from the presence of the good. Thus, in bodies, a disease can develop thanks to the natural order which strengthens it, and in souls vice will use the power of reason on behalf of its desires.

Chapter 54
In that it is ineffective, impotent and involuntary, evil is deprived of the triad of the good: will, power and activity.

Socrates in the *Theaetetus* (176A) rightly calls evil a 'subcontrary' (*hupenantion*) of the good. It does indeed not have a relation of complete contrariety, since this would put it on the same level with the good. Neither is evil a pure privation, because a privation has no power to produce anything. It is a privation that coexists with its contrary disposition and through sharing in its power and activity establishes itself as an active contrary. Therefore, it is called a sub-contrary, and it is clear that *parupostasis* is really meant.

5. Different types of evils (chs 55-7)

Chapter 55
There are three types of things in which evil exist: particular rational souls, irrational souls and individual bodies (not in the universal bodies). For the rational soul, evil consists in being contrary to intellect, for the irrational soul in being contrary to reason, for the body in being contrary to nature. The most general division of evil is that between evil in souls and evil in bodies. From the *Sophist* (228E-230E), it can be gathered that among the evils of the soul again two types should be distinguished: 'foulness' (e.g. ignorance), which is a privation of intellect, and 'disease', which amounts to discord in the soul.

Chapter 56
So there are three basic types of evil, and each of these kinds will in turn be twofold. For the disease of the soul can be a privation of knowledge or of skill, and its disease may affect either the theoretical activity (when it is disturbed by sense-images) or the practical life (when impulses are not according to reason). As for the body, it can be evil either because it is foul and ugly (deprived of form, that is) or because it is diseased (because of the dissolution of order and proportion).

Chapter 57
Since all evil is unmeasuredness, i.e. privation of measure, the three basic types correspond to the three principles of measure governing the beings in which evil can exist: nature is a measure for the bodies, reason for the irrational life, intellect for the rational souls.

6. Providence and evil (chs 58-61)

Chapter 58
Concerning evil and providence, we are confronted with a dilemma. If providence governs the universe, it looks like we have to deny the existence of evil. If evil exists, it seems that not everything comes from providence. But a perspective may be found wherein evil is integrated with the providential order. For, as has been said already, there is no absolute evil unmixed with the good. Because of its participation in the good, evil can be included in the works of Providence, not as an evil, but insofar as it is good.

To say that god is cause of all things is not equal to saying that he is the only cause of all things. For intellect, soul and nature, too, are causes for the things posterior to each of them. That is why some forms of evil may come to existence from these causes without affecting the universal providence of the gods.

How, then, is there an admixture of good in the evils stemming from the *soul*? The evils of the soul are twofold: some are internal to the soul, as, for instance, wrong choices that affect the soul alone; others are exterior, e.g. actions in which the soul manifests its anger and desire. All those evils may have good effects.

Chapter 59

Thus evil actions may happen for the rightful punishment of others. This action is good both for the person undergoing it and for the agent, if s/he performs it not for his/her own motives (revenge), but in accordance with the universal order. Through the performance of evil actions, people also make the evil that is concealed in their soul visible, which may contribute to their healing, as is shown in the case of remorse. Just as doctors open ulcers and so make evident the inward cause of the disease, so Providence hands souls over to shameful actions and passions in order that they be freed from their pain and start a better life.

Even internal passions may have a providential effect. For if the soul chooses the inferior, it will be dragged down towards baseness: it always gets what is deserved. Thus even a bad choice has something good, but it brings the soul to a form of life that is in accordance with its choice.

Chapter 60

How can evil in *bodies* be good? Two kinds of evil inhere in bodies: foulness and disease. Foulness is a state contrary to nature, though not a disease, as when monsters are born from normal animals. Although in a particular case this is against nature, it nevertheless happens in accordance with universal nature. For even in a monster, natural forms and reasons are present, though in unusual mixtures.

Corruption and destruction stemming from diseases are in accordance with nature in a twofold manner. From the perspective of universal nature, the corruption of one being is a necessity for the generation of another. But for the particular being, disease seems to be against its nature, because it destroys the existence that it has in accordance with its form. However, even for this particular being, corruption is a natural process, if this being is not considered as a separate whole, but as a part contributing to the whole universe.

Chapter 61

To conclude, all things that come to be, even if they are evil from a partial or inferior perspective, are good insofar as they derive ultimately from the good. For it is not possible that evil exists without being connected with its contrary, the good. All things are because of the good and yet the good is not the cause of evils. For never does evil *qua* evil derive from there; it stems from other causes which produce on account of weakness. As it is said by Plato in his second *Letter* (313E), 'all things (including things that are not good) are around the King of everything and exist because of him'. But god is not the cause of all things, but only 'of all good things'. For he is cause of evil things only insofar as they are beings and good.

The gods know and produce (activities that in their case coincide) evils *qua* good.

4. The principles of the translation

Our translation is primarily based on the Latin translation made by William of Moerbeke, yet aims at rendering as much as possible the meaning of the lost Greek original of Proclus. This means that where Moerbeke has made obvious mistakes of interpretation or translation, or where he was following a clearly inferior textual tradition, we try to restore the likely original meaning. This can often be done in a fairly reliable way through a comparison of the Latin with the Greek paraphrase of Isaak Sebastokrator. However, for those chapters where there are no Greek parallels, we are obliged to make a 'mental' retroversion of the Latin into Greek before translating it into English. This is a difficult, though not impossible procedure, because Moerbeke, as we have explained, made an extremely literal word for word translation, respecting as much as possible the phrasing of the original text. Moreover, we can use indices of the editions of Moerbeke's other translations, where the Greek text has been preserved, to recover the Greek terms behind unusual Latin expressions. With the help of the *Thesaurus linguae graecae*, we could find parallel texts in other works of Proclus. As a matter of fact, Moerbeke's very mechanical method of translating word for word was a blessing, as it enabled us to reconstruct the lost Greek with a fairly high degree of plausibility. There are, however, many passages where the Latin translation remains unintelligible. Moerbeke may have made mistakes, translating a Greek genitive by a Latin genitive (where the ablative was required) or wrongly connecting or splitting words; he may not have known the meaning of certain terms, not understood the construction of a phrase or an argument, or – and those are the worst cases – skipped some words or a whole line misreading a homoioteleuton, as he was working too fast. Some of those errors can be easily detected in the chapters where a comparison with the Greek text is possible thanks to Isaak Sebastokrator.

Other obscurities in the text may be explained by accidents in the manuscript transmission of the Latin translation. Finally, the Greek manuscript that Moerbeke used for his translation had already many errors and omissions. Whatever the reasons may be, when there are no Greek parallels of the Latin, we often had to resort to conjectures, lest we be left with a nonsensical text. Fortunately, we have at our disposition the excellent edition of the *Tria opuscula* by Helmut Boese, which has not been superseded by the more recent edition in the Collection Budé. Boese not only offers a sound text of Moerbeke's Latin translation, based upon a thorough examination of the manuscript tradition. He also adds, where possible, on the right-hand side, a Greek parallel text, as it can be reconstructed from Isaak Sebastokrator's paraphrase and from parallels in other Greek sources. The Greek text given by Boese should not be considered as an edition of Sebastokrator: it is a rather hybrid reconstruction, intended solely as a means towards a better understanding of the Latin. For a full edition of the Byzantine treatises, we made use of D. Isaac's Budé edition of the *Tria opuscula*.

In principle, in our translation we follow the Latin text as given in Boese's edition. We take into account, however, the Greek parallels as well as the editor's numerous remarks in the *apparatus* to the Latin and Greek versions, where he gives valuable suggestions concerning various mistakes made by Moerbeke and helps us to retrieve the original meaning or to supply lacunae in the text. In many cases, however, we had to introduce new conjectures. Whenever we deviate from Boese's edition, we offer a justification of our text and translation in the Philological Appendix at the end of this volume. This Appendix contains, besides emendations and interpretations of Boese and some other scholars and editors of the past (Thomas Taylor, Victor Cousin, Daniel Isaac, and in particular L.G. Westerink), several suggestions of our own making. It also explains some of the cases where, despite there being little doubt that the Latin text is sound, the meaning of the original Greek is almost lost under the barbarous Latin phrases. A few striking examples will do more to give an idea of the state of the text than a long exposé.

* At 21,15-16, Proclus quotes from book ten of the *Republic* (621A6-7): 'it is necessary for every soul to *make (facere)* a certain quantity of the cup of oblivion'. It should of course be 'to *drink* a certain quantity'. Moerbeke's Greek text most probably read *poiein*, which is a corruption for *piein* (pronounced the same way in later Greek).

* At 23,6 the words *quidem entibus* make no sense, but should be translated as if the text read *manentibus*, since Moerbeke presumably mistook *menousais* for *men ousais*.

We would not like to give the reader the impression that we have changed the text at random, nor *ad libitum*, just in order to make it philosophically meaningful. In general, we have adopted an attitude that was as conservative as possible, sticking to the text of Moerbeke, yet correcting it where we could explain how a certain confusion in the translation or transmission of the text had occurred. For obscure passages, we always tried to find parallel texts in the other works of Proclus: here we were fortunate to use the *Thesaurus linguae graecae* in search of parallels. Finding a successful emendation was often a time devouring activity. Alas, however great the ingenuity of the successive editors and translators, the text remains full of *cruces*. In those impossible cases, we had to translate *ad sensum*.

Proclus often quotes and paraphrases Plato. When translating these passages we allowed ourselves to be inspired by existing translations. In particular we made a thankful use of the translations gathered in Hamilton & Cairns (1973 [=1963]) and Cooper & Hutchinson (1997), and for Aristotle we consulted Barnes (1984). Finally, we sometimes looked at Taylor's translation (1980 [=1833]) of the *DMS* in search of a fitting English expression

Since we aim at translating the original Greek text of Proclus, insofar as we can reconstruct it, and not a medieval version of it, we did not consider it very useful to make Latin-English and English-Latin Glossaries. Making Greek-English Glossaries would have been conjectural. Therefore we decided in agreement with the general editor to drop the Glossaries altogether. We have, however, compiled a Subject Index, which includes technical philosophical terms (such as *hupostasis, parupostasis, hupenantion*).

Notes

1. On the life and work of Proclus, see the introduction of H.D. Saffrey and L.G. Westerink to their monumental edition of the *Platonic Theology* (1968, pp. IX-LX). The best survey of Proclus' works remains Beutler (1957), col. 190,18-208,34.

2. Thus they are mostly quoted since Helmut Boese's edition (1960).

3. cf. *DMS* 11,34-5.

4. *De dec. dub.* 1,13-16.

5. On Theodorus, see Ziegler (1934).

6. *De prov.* 45,4-6.

7. See Marinus, *Vita Procli* 15. On the interpretation of *De prov.* ch. 22, see Westerink (1962), pp. 162-3.

8. More precisely a scholion to *in Remp.* 1,37,23 (2,371,10-18 Kroll). According to the scholiast, who is obviously well-informed, Proclus discussed the problem of evil in his *monobiblion*, 'On the Existence of Evils', in his treatise on the speech of Diotima in the *Symposium*, in his *Commentary on the Theaetetus* and in his a commentary on the third (?) *Ennead*, 'Whence come evils?'. The last three texts are lost. P. Henry (1961 [=1938]), 8 n., suggests reading 'first Ennead' instead of 'third Ennead', yet R. Beutler considers this emendation unnecessary, pointing out that the reference could be to *Enn.* 3,2-3 [47-8], *On Providence*. See Beutler (1957), 198,4-52. Because of the title, 'Whence come evils?', we are inclined to believe that the scholiast had *Enn.* 1,8[51] in mind. Proclus' comments on the *Enneads* (not necessarily

a full-blown commentary on all of them) are further mentioned in a few other places. Some excerpts are preserved in Psellus: see Westerink (1959). It is at any rate very likely that this commentary covered *Enn.* 1,8. It is not difficult to understand how *Theaetetus* 176A (cf. below: 2.1) and *Enn.* 1,8 offered a splendid opportunity to discuss the problem of evil. This is less evident for Diotima's speech. However, Proclus may have attempted to explain the remark of Diotima that Eros is neither good nor evil (201E-202B). At 205E, Diotima formulates the well known principle that the good is 'what belongs to oneself' (*oikeion*), evil 'what belongs to another' (*to allotrion*).

9. cf. below: 2.3.

10. According to Marinus (*Vita Procli* 13, 1. 330 Masullo), the *Timaeus Commentary* is one of the first works of Proclus. This was not however his first discussion on evil, since Proclus refers in 1,381,14-15 to earlier treatments of the question: this may have been in the commentaries on the *Theaetetus* or the *Republic* which in the Neoplatonic curriculum preceded the *Timaeus*. In the *De prov.* (50,11-12), there is an implicit reference to the commentary on the *Republic* for a more extensive discussion of the authenticity of the *Epinomis*: See *in Remp.* 2,133,27-134,7. The short discussion in *in Parm.* on the question whether there are ideas of evil (829,26) seems to refer to chs 43-4 of *DMS*. Of course, in principle it cannot be excluded that Proclus inserted some of these cross-references into his texts only later.

11. See the excellent 'notes complémentaires' (pp. 151-4, referring to pp. 82-8) in the edition by Saffrey and Westerink (1968).

12. The comparison of the digression on evil with *DMS* has been the decisive argument that proves ps.-Dionysius' dependence on Proclus. See the renowned studies of Stiglmayr (1895) and Koch (1895), and also Steel (1997).

13. cf. Rordorf (1983), p. 242 (and pp. 242-4 for Isaak Sebastokrator's treatment of the same problem).

14. The question of the fall of the angels offers Dionysius the opportunity to insert the long digression on evil: see *De div. nom.* IV, 18, p. 162,6-14 Suchla. Dionysius raises the question how the demons could become 'evil both for themselves and for the others'. This phrase is taken from Proclus' discussion of the demons in ch. 17. But Proclus argues there that demons are neither evil for themselves, nor for others. In his adaptation of ch. 17, however, Dionysius tries to lessen the differences between him and Proclus by insisting that even after their fall the demons keep the angelic nature they received from the creator.

15. *De div. nom.* 4,25, p. 173,1-9; 4,27, pp. 173,17-174,3 Suchla. In the last paragraph Dionysius denies that there is 'evil in bodies'. The cases of illness or deformity are not considered as 'evil' but as 'less good' (yet in 174,2 he seems to admit that there is evil in bodies, too). Proclus, on the contrary, would never have accepted that 'evil' is a 'lesser good' (see ch. 6).

16. On the scholia of John of Scythopolis, see the excellent study by P. Rorem and J.C. Lamoreaux (1998). We summarise some of their results.

17. See *scholia De div. nom.* PG 4, 21D. We made use of the (partial) translation by Rorem and Lamoreaux (1998), pp. 106-7.

18. Edited by Westerink (1948).

19. Three Byzantine princes of the name Isaak Komnena Sebastokrator are known to us: the elder brother of Alexis I, his third son, brother of Johannes II (1118-43), and the third son of Johannes II (1143-80). The third of these can be safely ruled out. D. Isaac (1977), pp. 25-7, considers the second as author of the treatises. We propose (with Boese) to identify the author with the first Isaak, the elder brother of Alexis I, who played a role in the process against Italos as well (1082). See also Carlos Steel (1982b), pp. 365-73; De Libera (1995), pp. 35-6.

20. It was L.G. Westerink who first suspected this and informed Boese.

21. See Steel (1982b).

22. Boese did not aim at reproducing Isaak Sebastokrator's text, only using it where it could help for the reconstruction of Proclus' Greek. The complete text of the three treatises of Sebastokrator has been published by J. Dornseiff, J. Rizzo and M. Erler in *Beiträge zur klassischen Philologie*, Meisenheim am Glan (1966, 1971, 1979). Those editions are now replaced by the new edition of D. Isaac, which appeared as appendices to his editions of the *Tria Opuscula* in the Collection Budé (Paris, 1977, 1979 and 1982).

23. See Steel (1982a), to be complemented by Ihm (2001).

24. On the life and work of William of Moerbeke, see Brams and Vanhamel (1989).

25. Moerbeke (who was appointed archbishop in 1278) did not stay in Corinth until his death in 1286. He returned to Italy for a mission as papal legate in Perugia (1283-84) and probably remained in Italy during the last years of his life.

26. The list of those Greek glosses may be found in the Appendix of Boese's edition, pp. 267-71.

27. Here we disagree with Boese, who attributes the marginal notes to a reader of the texts: '*marginalia* [...], *quae, etiamsi argumenta, quibus ea a Guilelmo profecta esse probari possit, non deficiant, potius tamen a lectore quodam, posteriore quidem, Graecum autem Procli textum etiam tunc inspiciente, addita esse veri simile est*' (p. XVII). Boese considers this explanation as the more plausible and promises a more extensive essay on this question (see p. XVII, n.1), which, however, never appeared.

28. On this manuscript and the Greek notes it contains, see Steel, introduction to his edition of the Latin translation of Proclus' commentary on the *Parmenides* (1982), pp. 3*-5*, 49*-53*.

29. We follow OSV against Boese in the following cases: 4,6; 26; 28; 6,20; 9,8; 14,7; 21,21; 27; 27,5; 28,13-14; 36,1; 38,11; 39,34-5; 45,8; 46,1; 5; 14; 19; 50,43; 58,7; 61,4. The most important corrections are discussed in our Philological Appendix.

30. On Moerbeke's method of translation, see Steel, introduction to his edition of Proclus' commentary on the *Parmenides* (1982), pp. 43*-54*.

31. For reconstructions of Plato's views on evil, see Cherniss (1954); Guthrie (1978), pp. 92-100; Hager (1987), pp. 13-33. Schröder (1916), pp. 10-33 and Greene (1944), pp. 277-316; 420-2 are still useful.

32. Compare Alexander Aphr. ap. Simpl. *in De cael.* 359,20-6.

33. cf. *DMS* 20,7-8; 24,32-40; *in Tim.* 3,313,18-21.

34. For a survey of the Hellenistic and Middle Platonic discussions of evil, see Opsomer & Steel (1999), pp. 229-44.

35. Simplicius even speaks of the *heterodox* who claim that matter is the evil <principle>: *in Phys.* 9,256,25.

36. Simplicius regularly expresses ideas similar to those found in *DMS*; cf. *in Ench.* xxxv; *in Phys.* 9, 248,21-250,5; 251,20-7; 256,25-31; 361,1-9 (see also 346,22-3; 357,34). For late Neoplatonic discussions of evil, see also Schröder (1916), pp. 202-5.

37. cf. Simpl. *in Cat.* 418,4-6, and below.

38. On matter and evil in the Platonic tradition, see Hager (1962).

39. For meticulous analyses of Plotinus' view, see esp. O'Brien (1971; 1999); O'Meara (1997; 1999), pp. 13-30; Sharples (1994).

40. These participate in Difference with respect to Being, i.e. they are different from being, i.e. they are not being.

41. cf. Rist (1969), 157; O'Brien (1999), pp. 63-6; Opsomer (2001b), pp. 9-10.

42. *Enn.* V, 2 [11], 1,18-21.

43. O'Brien (1993), pp. 31, 35.

44. cf. Alt (1993), pp. 55-81.

45. cf. Rist (1969), 159.

46. cf. *Enn.* 1,8[51],7,16-23.

47. To this view Proclus objects that what is not good is not therefore evil.

48. Instead of the more usual *enantion*, Plato has the variant *hupenantion*. Whereas for Plato there is no noticeable difference in meaning, Proclus, contrary to Plotinus, sets great store by this detail.

49. *Cat.* 5, 3b24-32; *Phys.* 1,6, 189a32-3.

50. For a more extensive analysis, see Opsomer (2001b), pp. 27-9.

51. cf. Opsomer & Steel (1999).

52. cf. *in Tim.* 1,382,2-11; *DMS* 40,5-7.

53. See our notes ad loc.

54. *DMS* 33,1-12. For further examples, we refer the reader to the notes to the translation.

55. For a more extensive discussion of Proclus' criticism of Plotinus, we refer the reader to Opsomer (2001b).

56. cf. O'Meara (1997), pp. 42-6; Schäfer (1999); Opsomer (2001b), pp. 17-20.

57. In his treatise on matter, Plotinus himself rejects this coarse dualism. Cf. 2,4[12],2,9-10. Gnosticism, especially its Iranian variant, Manicheism, was known for this kind of dualism. Pépin (1964), pp. 54, 56, makes the observation that to many Christian authors the Platonic doctrine of the uncreatedness of matter comes down to making it a second god. We would like to point out, however, that although the uncreatedness of matter seems to be implied by the *Timaeus*, most Neoplatonists – and certainly Plotinus and Proclus – did not regard matter as ungenerated (which is to be understood in an ontological, not in a chronological sense). Eusebius, *Praep. ev.* 7,18,12; Basilius, *Hom. in Hex.* 2,2; Ambrosius, *Exam.* 1,7,25; Tatianus, *Or. ad Graec.* 5,3; Tertull., *Adv. Marc.* 1,15; Titus Bostrenus, *Contra Manich.* 1.5, p. 3,38; 1.4, p. 3,24 de Lagarde; Serapion of Thmuis, *Adv. Manich.* 12,1-8; 26,5-14 Fitschen.

58. cf. O'Brien (1971), p. 146; Narbonne (1994), pp. 129-31; O'Meara (1997; 1999, p. 109; 111); Schaefer (1999; 2000); Opsomer (2001b), sect. VIII. See Greene (1944), p. 382. Hager (1962), 96-7, on the contrary, reproaches Proclus his scholastic-mindedness that blinded him to Plotinus' 'sublime insight'. See also Schröder (1916), p. 195, who qualifies Proclus' criticism of Plotinus and his incorporation of the entire preceding tradition as 'scholastische[r] Pendanterie und Begriffsspaltung mit Hilfe rein formaler Gesetze'.

59. cf. Van Riel (2001).

60. e.g. *TP* 3.8; *in Tim.* 1,385,9-17.

61. cf. *DMS* 34, with our notes.

62. Proclus seems to grant provisionally or dialectically the idea that, as the lowest product, matter is not good. Plotinus claims that at this point of the emanation, nothing of goodness is left. Matter is completely incapable of returning to its principle. Plotinus believed of course that matter is produced by some lower principle. Proclus, however, maintains that matter is caused directly by the Good, according to the axiom, commonly accepted from Iamblichus onwards, that higher causes are to a higher degree causative of a given product than its immediate cause, and that their influence extends further down the ontological scale. Therefore matter is not just not-evil, but even good in a sense, and it reverts towards its principle, that is, it desires the good and is able to receive the forms (*DMS* 36,23-8).

63. 1,8,6,32-6 (transl. A.H. Armstrong). Simplicius (*in Cat.* 5, 108,21-110,25 Kalbfleisch) criticises this view of Plotinus using partly the same argument. These arguments may ultimately go back to Iamblichus: cf. Chiaradonna (1998), p. 602; Opsomer (2001b), pp. 31-5.

64. *Cat.* 6, 6a17-18.

65. cf. O'Brien (1999), pp. 55, 64-6.

66. cf. O'Brien (1999), sect. XIV-XV.

67. See also *DMS* 32,14-16: 'Nor is it a removal of measure and limit, for it is not identical with privation, because privation does not exist when measure and limit are present, whereas matter keeps existing and bearing their impression'. Cf. Simpl. *in Phys.* 9,246,17-248,20.

68. See Steel (1999), pp. 84-92.

69. They do, however, expressly affirm the reality of moral evil. Cf. below.

70. 'subcontrary', to be more precise: cf. below: 2.4.5. If absolute evil existed, it would be the true contrary of the good and a nature of its own in the full sense. But Proclus argues that only relative evils exist without there being an evil principle in which the relative evils participate in order to be evil. In Plotinian terms, Proclus' position comes down to the claim that only 'secondary' evils exist without there being a primary evil. Yet Proclus does want to preserve the idea of an opposition to the good. However, this opposition can no longer be explained as a relation of complete contrariety.

71. cf. *TP* 3,94,15-21.

72. See, e.g., *ET* 63; *TP* 1,83,21-84,9. Cf. Segonds (1985), I, p. 97 n. 5-6 (*notes complémentaires* pp. 189-90).

73. cf. *De dec. dub.* V, 28,4-11; *DMS* 5,10-16. See Plot. 3,2 [47], 2,8-10.

74. cf. *DMS* 20,7-8; 24,32-40; 33,21-3, and T2′.

75. One may think of Origen or Augustine, for whom all evil is either a sin or a consequence of sin.

76. For a more extensive analysis, see Opsomer & Steel (1999), pp. 244-60.

77. Proclus probably has Plutarch of Chaeronea and Atticus in mind. See, however, Opsomer (2001a), pp. 191-3.

78. See also Iambl. *De myst.* 4,7; Orig. *Contra Cels.* IV 64 Vol. I, p. 334,33 Kö., p. 552 Delarue.

79. Contrast Plotinus 1,8[51],3,21-4. See O'Meara (1997), pp. 38-9.

80. *DMS* 47,11-17; *in Tim.* 1,375,20-376,1; *in Remp.* 1,38,3-9.

81. The term was used before Proclus: cf. Syrianus 107,8-9; 185,20-2; Julian, *Eis tên mêtera tôn theôn* 11,21; Greg. Nyss. *in Eccl.* 5,356,9-15; *De opif. hom.* 164,6-8; *Contra Eun.* 3,7,58,2-6 (cf. Basil *Hom.* 1,7,21; 6,3,60); 3,9,5,1-3. According to Simplicius (*in Cat.* 418,4-6), Iamblichus had developed a number of arguments to show that evil exists *en parupostasei* and is the result of some failure. As a philosophical term, it makes its first appearance – as far as we know – in Porphyry (*Sent.* 42,14; and also 19,9; 43,23; 44,29; 31; 35; 45; 47), but Iamblichus appears to have been the first to apply it to the existence of evil. It is not impossible that the term had already been used by the Stoics to designate the relation of the incorporeal *lekton* to the corporeality of language. At any rate, Neoplatonic philosophers use this terminology when discussing this Stoic doctrine: cf. Iambl. ap. Simpl. *in Cat.* 361,10-11; 28; 397,10-11; Syr. *in Metaph.* 105,25-30; Lloyd 1987, p. 146. It may very well have been this context that has given rise to the term being used as referring to a reality that has no existence as a substance or as a quality of a substance, but is nevertheless not nothing. Cf. Sext. Emp. *AM* 8,11-12 (*SVF* II 166); Iambl. ap. Simpl. *in Cat.* 8,361,6-11 (*SVF* II 507); Simpl. *in Cat.* 8,397,10-12; Syrianus *in Metaph.* 105,19-31. See Opsomer & Steel (1999), p. 249; Opsomer (2001b), p. 35 n. 118.

82. The only agents that are capable of evil are partial beings. Their lack of understanding follows from their partial nature (their limited perspective). Universal beings contain in themselves the reasons that are sufficient to make their activity perfect.

83. cf. *Metaph.* 6,2-3 (also 5,30; 11,8; *Phys.* 2,4-6).

84. *Metaph.* 1065a24-6.

85. *imperfectam*, which probably is a translation of *atelê*.

86. For a more extensive treatment of this text, see Opsomer & Steel (1999), pp. 251-5.

87. *Mant.* 171,14, trans. Sharples.

88. Sharples (1975), pp. 44-6.

89. Sorabji (1980), pp. 3-5.

90. *in Metaph.* 194,9-13.

91. See *in Tim.* 1,262,1-29; *in Parm.* 835,6-838,3.

92. Other similar problems are examined in Chiaradonna (1998), pp. 601-3; Opsomer (2000b), esp. pp. 129-30; (2001b), p. 26 n. 87.

93. For this term, see Segonds (1985), I, p. 97 n. 4 (*notes complémentaires* p. 189).

94. cf. *TP* 1,86,14-16.

95. cf. *DMS* 58,7-16.

96. The evil effects are actually side-effects. The weakness of partial causes can be understood in many ways: these causes fail to adopt a universal perspective; (hence) may take an apparent good for the real good; they fail to foresee the interaction with other partial (or also universal) causes; they may themselves comprise conflicting reason principles, etc.

97. Compare Amm. *in De int.* 136,1-137,11.

98. See already Plato *Leg.* 885B; 901DE. Proclus regards this problem as essential for the entire 'Platonic theology': cf. *TP* 1.15, p. 76,10. For a more elaborate overview of the history of this problem, see Opsomer & Steel (1999), pp. 229-43.

99. For his famous argument against providence, see Lactantius *Ira* 13,20-1 = Usener, *Epicurea* fr. 374. See also Sext. Emp. *PH* 3,9-12.

100. This is not completely fair to the Stoics, who did emphasise the reality of vice. However, it remains open to debate whether by practically denying evil on a cosmic scale the Stoics can still claim a place for evil at the level of human action. Is not Plutarch (e.g. *De Stoic. rep.* 1048D; 1049D, and esp. 1050A-D) right to point out that this amounts to an inconsistency? For the Stoic view of evil, see Long (1968).

101. For a more extensive discussion of this problem, we refer the reader to Steel (1999).

102. cf. *DMS* 38,7-11.

103. As Simplicius remarks, the privations that Aristotle discusses in the *Physics* are merely 'absences' (*apousiai*) of forms, not a lacking or missing (*apotukhia*) of a form: cf. *in Phys.* 417,27-418,1; *in De cael.* 430,8; *in Ench.* xxxv, 74,6-24.

104. This is also the case for blindness, which hinders a normal functioning of the body.

105. *DMS* 7,39-42; 38,13-25; 52,5-10.

106. cf. *DMS* 54,12-22; 6,29-7,2.

107. On the specific differences of evils see chs 55-7, and on its characteristics, derived from the forms of goodness to which it is opposed, see ch. 51.

108. See Plato *Resp.* 352C (referred to at *DMS* 52,10-15); 344C; 348E.

Proclus
On the Existence of Evils

Translation

On the Existence of Evils

[Introduction]

1. What is the nature of evil, and where does it originate?[1] These questions have already been examined by some of our predecessors, who have pursued the theory of evil neither incidentally nor for the sake of other things, but have considered evil in itself, [examining] whether it exists or does not exist, and if it exists, how it exists and from where it has come into being and existence.

It is, however, not a bad thing that we too, especially because we have the time for it, summarise the observations rightly made by each of them. We will start, however, with the speculations of the divine Plato on the essence of evil things. For we shall understand more easily the words of those predecessors and we shall always be closer to an understanding of the problems once we have discovered the thought of Plato and, as it were, kindled a light[2] for our subsequent inquiries.

First, we must examine whether evil exists or not; and if it does, whether or not it exists in intelligible things; and if it exists in the sensible realm, whether it exists through a principal cause[3] or not; and if not, whether we should attribute any substantial being to it or whether we should posit its being as completely insubstantial; and if the latter is the case, how it can exist, if its principle is a different one,[4] and from where it begins and up to which point it proceeds; and further, if there is providence, how evil can exist and where it originates.[5] In short, we have to consider all the questions we usually raise in our commentaries.[6]

Above all and before all, we must get a grasp of Plato's doctrine on evil, for if we fall short of this theory, we will give the impression that we have achieved nothing.

[Does evil exist?]

[First point of view: evil does not exist]

2. The natural starting point for examining these questions should be whether evil belongs to beings or not.[7] Indeed, how is it possible that something exists which utterly lacks a share in the principle of beings? For just as darkness cannot participate in light nor vice in virtue, so is it impossible that evil should participate in the good.

5 Suppose light were the first cause;[8] then there would be no darkness in the secondary beings – unless it had its origin in chance and came from somewhere other than the principle. Likewise, since the good is the cause of everything, evil can have no place among beings. [For there are two alternatives.] Either evil, too, comes from the good – but then the question arises: how can that which has produced the nature

10 of evil still be the cause of all good and fine things? Or evil does not come from the good – but then the good will not be the good of all things nor the principle of all beings, since the evil established in beings escapes the procession from the good.

In general, if anything, in whatever way it exists, derives its existence from being, and if that which participates in being must necessarily participate in the One as well – for it is at the same time being and one, and before it is being it is one – and if it neither was

15 nor will be permitted to secondary beings to do what they do without the beings above them – for Intellect must act with Life, Life with Being, and everything with the One – then evil again is subject to one of the following alternatives: either it will absolutely not participate in being, or it is somehow generated from being and must participate at the same time in the cause beyond being. And a direct consequence

20 of this argument is the following: either there is no principle, or evil does not exist and has not been generated. For that which has no share in being is not being, and that which [proceeds] from the first cause is not evil. In both cases, however, it is mandatory to say that evil is nowhere.

If, then, the good is, as we say, beyond being and is the source of

25 beings – since everything, in whatever way it exists and is generated, strives for the good according to its nature[9] – how then could evil be any one thing among beings, if it is actually excluded from such a desire? Thus, it is far from true to say that evil exists because 'there must be something that is completely contrary'[10] to the good'.[11] For how could that which is completely contrary [to something] desire the

30 nature that is contrary to it? Now, it is impossible that there is any being which does not strive for the good, since all beings have been generated and exist because of that desire and are preserved through it. Hence, if evil is contrary to the good, evil does not belong to beings.

3. Why should we say more? For if the One and what we call the nature of the good is beyond being, then evil is beyond non-being itself – I mean absolute non-being, for the good is better than absolute being.[12] Thus, one of these two implications follows. <Non-being is either absolutely-not-being or what is beyond being. But it is impossible that evil is beyond superessential non-being, which is the good.> If, <on the other hand> non-being is absolutely-not-being, then evil

5 even more is not; for evil is even more wraith-like, as the saying goes,[13] than that which absolutely does not exist, since evil is further removed from the good than non-being. This is what is shown by those

who give priority to non-being over being evil.[14] However, that which is further removed from the good is more insubstantial than that which is closer; thus, that which is absolutely not has more being than the so-called evil; therefore evil is much more deprived of being than that which is absolutely not. 10

Besides, if – according to Plato's account[15] – the father of this world not only gives existence to the nature of good things, but also wants evil not to exist anywhere, then how could evil possibly exist, which the demiurge does not want to exist? For it is inconceivable that what he wants is different from what he produces; on the contrary, in divine substances willing and making always coincide.[16] Hence, evil is not 15 only not wanted by him, but it is even without existence, not [only] in the sense that he does not produce it – for it is not right even to think this – but in the sense that he even causes it not to exist; for his will was not that evil would not be produced by him, but rather that it would not exist at all. What then could still produce its being when that which brings it to non-being is the father who gives existence to 20 all things? For what would be contrary to him, and from where could it come? Evil agency, indeed, does not spring from him – for this is not right for him – and it would be absurd [to think] that it could originate elsewhere; for everything in the world stems from the father, some things directly from him, as has been said, other things through the proper activity of other beings.[17]

[The opposite point of view: evil exists]
4. The argument that banishes evil from being could go like this,[18] and along these lines it may sound probable. The argument that gives voice to the opposite viewpoint, however, will require that we first look at the reality of things and declare, with that reality in mind, whether or not evil exists; so we must look at licentiousness itself and 5 injustice and all the other things that we usually call vices of the soul and ask ourselves whether we will accept calling each of them good or evil. For if we admit that each of these [vices] is good, we must necessarily affirm one of the two following: either virtue is not contrary to vice – that is, virtue on the whole is not contrary to vice on 10 the whole, and particular virtues are not contrary to the corresponding vices – or that which opposes the good is not in every respect evil. But what could be more implausible than each one of these positions, or what could be less in accordance with the nature of things?

For the vices oppose the virtues; how they oppose one another becomes clear if one takes a look at human life, in which the unjust are opposed to the righteous, and the licentious to the temperate, and 15 also if one looks at what one might call the discord within souls themselves[19] – for instance, when people lacking continence[20] are drawn by reason in one direction, but forced by passion in the other direction; and in the fight between the two the better is overcome by

the worse, but sometimes the worse by the better. For what else is happening in these people than that their souls' temperance is in discord with their licentious manners? What is happening in those
20   who are fighting with anger? Is it not something similar? And what about the other cases of evil in which we perceive our souls to be in discord? Indeed, in general the manifest oppositions between good and evil men exist long before in a hidden way within the souls themselves. And the stupidity and disease[21] of the soul are then extreme when the better part in us and the good rational principles
25   that exist in it are overcome by worldly, vile passions. But to adduce many more examples would be foolish, would it not?

Now, if vices are contrary to virtues, as we have said, and evil is in every respect contrary to good – for the nature of the good itself is not so constituted as to be in discord with itself, but being an offspring of
30   one cause and one henad, it maintains a relation of likeness, unity, and friendship with itself, and the greater goods preserve the lesser goods, and the lesser goods are beautifully ordered by the more perfect – then it is absolutely necessary that the vices be not merely vices (*kakiai*) 'by way of speaking',[22] but each of them must also really be evil and not just something less good.[23] For the lesser good is not
35   contrary to the greater good, just as the less hot is not contrary to the more hot nor the less cold to the more cold.[24] Now if it is agreed that the vices of the soul belong to the nature of evil, it will have been demonstrated that evil pertains to beings.

5. And this is not the only reason. Evil is also that which corrupts everything. Indeed, that this is evil has been shown by Socrates in the *Republic*, where he makes the correct observation that the good of each thing is that which preserves this thing, and that therefore all things have an appetite for the good. For all things have their being
5   from the good and are preserved by the good, just as, conversely, non-being and corruption occur on account of the nature of evil.[25] Thus, it is necessary either <that evil exists or> that nothing is corruptive of anything. But in the latter case, 'generation will collapse and come to a halt';[26] for if there is nothing corruptive, there can be no corruption; and if there is no corruption, there can be no generation either, since generation always comes about through the corruption
10   of something else. And if there is no generation, the whole world will be 'incomplete', 'as it will not contain in itself the mortal classes of animals; and they must exist if the world is to be sufficiently perfect', says Timaeus.[27] Hence, if the world is to be a 'blessed god',[28] then it must perfectly preserve a 'similarity' with the 'completely perfect
15   animal';[29] if this is true, even 'the mortal classes' must complete the universe; and if this is true, there must be generation and corruption; and if this is true, there must be both principles corruptive of beings and generative principles, and different principles for different classes of beings. For not all things have their generation or corrup-

tion from the same principles. If, then, in the classes that have been
allotted generation there are congenital corruptive principles which   20
destroy the powers of those beings, then evil must also exist. For this
is what evil has been said to be, namely, that which is corruptive of
each of the things that are generated in which it exists primarily and
per se.[30] Indeed, some things are able to corrupt the soul, others the
body, and what is corrupted is in each case something different.
Neither is the mode of corruption the same, but in the first case it is
a corruption of substance, in the other of life; and in the first case   25
substance is led towards non-being and corruption, while in the other
case life flees from being and, in short, to something else that is not.[31]
Thus, it will be the same argument that keeps the whole world perfect
and posits evil among beings. And so, evil will not only exist because
of the good, but evil will also be good because of its very being. This,
then, may seem extremely paradoxical, but it will become more clear   30
later.

6. If, however, we should not only be content with the above
arguments, but pursue the inquiry also in another way, let us then
develop the following argument as well. Every good that admits a
difference of more and less is more perfect and is situated closer to its
source when leaning to the more. When, however, it is weakened   5
according to the less and has become less perfect because of its
deficiency, it is removed downwards from its own monad.[32] This is also
the case for the equal: that which is 'most equal' is most cognate and
as it were continuous with its monad; the 'more equal' occupies the
second rank after this level; the 'less equal' takes the last rank. And
the same reasoning holds for the hot and the cold, the beautiful and   10
the ugly, the great and the small.

So, do we not speak also of more and less injustice (*adikia*) and
licentiousness (*akolasia*)? Or do we call all people licentious and
unjust to the same degree? We shall definitely deny that. Moreover,
as regards injustice that can be more or less, [must we not accept that]
the less it is injustice, the less distant it is from the nature of the good,   15
whereas with injustice of the greater degree, the more it possesses the
passion of injustice, the more it is deprived of the good? Yes, we must
certainly concede this. But, as regards all the good that may be more
or less, we have said that by increase it comes closer to the first good,
and that the perfectly good is the same as the supreme good. But
augmentation of injustice is, as we have said, in every way a defi-   20
ciency of the good; hence, it no longer makes sense to call injustice
good, neither a greater nor a lesser good; no, it should be called
unqualifiedly evil. For when a lesser good increases, it becomes good
to a greater degree. Indeed, what is less hot and what is less cold
becomes [by increase] more what each of them is, while injustice by
increase does not become a greater good. How, then, could that which
stands contrary to the good not belong to evil things?[33]   25

That is what this argument will confidently state about the existence of evil. And one could also adduce a text of Plato for further
corroboration of the above argument, namely, the text in which he
seems to include the nature of evil things among beings, not only

30   asserting but also demonstrating it. For, in the *Theaetetus*,[34] Socrates
vigorously defended the thesis that 'evils will not cease to exist', and
that their existence is not superfluous nor as it were incidental; for
their existence is something necessary and good. Evil is 'necessary',
he says, and thus evil is good. If, however, evil is good, evil certainly
exists, according to his argument, and it belongs to beings not only
because it has been so produced that it 'will not cease to exist' and thus

35   belongs to beings, but also because it has its origin, its entry into
being, on account of the good.[35]

    7. What then shall we say is the reason for the necessity of evil? Is
it its opposition to the good, as Socrates suggests to us?[36] As we have
said in other works,[37] all the forms, and also that which exists beyond
the forms, cannot produce [immediately] after themselves a being
that participates in them in a [merely] contingent way, nor do they

5   limit their activity[38] to those beings that can enjoy them immutably
and always in the same way. But because of the abundance of their
power and the excellence of their goodness they do not only produce
the orders that are continuous with them, participate in them and,
without being mingled with privation, preserve in uniformity every-

10   thing that comes from them. No, they also produce the most remote
realisations (*hupostaseis*) of their activities, where that which comes
from the causes can no longer remain uncontaminated and unchange-
able. For there must exist not only those beings that sometimes
participate in the forms and sometimes are cut off from the illumination and power that comes from them. For these intermittent
participants would not be able to participate in the forms[39] that are

15   completely separate from all things and transcend all properties that
exist in others and are themselves participated only. Nor must exist
only those beings that are uninterruptedly dominated by the impressions of the forms, unless the inferior things, too, were generated
which enjoy only an intermittent participation. For [otherwise] all
good things would be the lowest [in the hierarchy] of beings, and the
eternal beings would exist at the level of matter; they would be sterile

20   and weak and have all other [attributes] we usually predicate of
things subject to generation and corruption.[40] For it would be those
superior beings instead of these below that have these characteristics,
as if the lower beings were non-existent.[41] If then these [lower] things
too are necessary because of the all-powerful and all-good activity of
the first causes, then the good will not be present in all things in the

25   same way, and the generation of evil will not be expelled from beings.
For if there is something that, at times, has the capacity of participat-

ing in the good but, at other times, is deprived of this participation, then there will necessarily be a privation of participation of the good.[42]

It is impossible, however, for a privation to exist in its own right, nor can privation ever be totally detached from the nature of which it is privation.[43] In a way, privation derives its power from this nature through its being interwoven with it, and only thus can it establish itself as something contrary to the good. Other privations[44] are mere absences of dispositions, deriving no being from the nature to which they belong. But the good, because of the excellence of its power, gives power even to the very privation of itself. Just as, in the whole of reality, the good created the first power,[45] so, in each being, the good that is somehow present in it generates its power in it. This way, as we have said, the privation of the good that is interwoven with it gives strength to its own shadowy character[46] through the power of the good. It becomes opposed to the good, yet, by mixing with the good, has the strength to fight against what is close to it. But this privation [of the good] is not in the same situation as other privations. For these others do exist even in the complete absence of the [corresponding] disposition, whereas this privation does not exist when the good is completely absent. Indeed,[47] there is no form of life so bad that the power of reason is completely extinguished. Some reason remains inside, expressing itself feebly; though surrounded by all kinds of passions, understanding never leaves the upper [part of the] soul. And in those things that are utterly deprived of the opposite [healthy] state, not even the shadow of a body remains; nor does the disease persist, for where there is no order at all, it is also impossible that the body is preserved. Disease is a lack of order, but not of all order. This is shown by the cycles of nature, which measure with numbers whatever is disorderly.[48] More on this elsewhere.[49]

[Proclus' own view]

8. If, as we have said, one should not only adduce the above arguments but also unfold the doctrine on the existence of evils from Plato's teaching, what has already been said is sufficient even for those who are capable only of moderate comprehension. However, as in a court of justice, we should not only listen to the contending parties, but also pass some judgement of our own. Let this then be, if you like, our verdict. To begin with, evil is twofold: on the one hand, pure evil on its own, unmixed with the good; and on the other hand, evil that is not pure nor unmixed with the nature of the good. For the good too [is twofold]: on the one hand, that which is primarily good and as it were the good itself, and nothing else but good – it is neither intellect nor intelligence nor real being; on the other hand, the good that is mixed with other things. And the latter sometimes is not mixed with privation, whereas elsewhere it does have such a mixture. For that which intermittently participates in the primarily good is mani-

festly entwined with the non-good. Indeed, the same holds for being
15   itself and the nature of being: in the higher realm being is really being
and merely being, but in the last beings, being is somehow mixed with
non-being. For take that which in one respect is, but in another is not,
that which at times is, but is not for countless times, that which is this
but is not all other things: how could one say that it is, rather than
that it is not, when it is completely filled with non-being?

20   And non-being itself, too [, is twofold]:[50] on the one hand, that which
absolutely does not exist – it is beyond the lowest nature, whose being
is accidental – as it is unable to exist either in itself or even accidentally, for that which does not exist at all does not in some respect exist,
in another not. On the other hand, [there is] non-being that is
together with being, whether you call it privation of being or 'other-
ness'.[51] The former [i.e. absolute non-being] is in all respects
25   non-being, whereas the latter [i.e. relative non-being] is in the higher
realm 'not less than being', as the Eleatic Stranger asserts,[52] but when
it is present among the things that sometimes are and sometimes are
not, it is weaker than being, but nonetheless even then it is somehow
dominated by being.

9. Hence, if someone were to ask whether non-being is or is not, our
answer would be that what absolutely does not exist and has no share
whatever in being has absolutely no being; however, we would concede to the questioner that what somehow is not, should be counted
among beings.

The same reasoning, then, holds for evil, since this is twofold too:
5   on the one hand, that which is exclusively evil; on the other hand, that
which is not [exclusively evil], but is mixed with the good. We will
rank the former beyond that which absolutely does not exist, inas-
much as the good is beyond being, and the latter among beings, for,
because of the mediation[53] of the good, it can no longer remain
deprived of being and because of its being it cannot remain deprived
10   of the good. Indeed, it is both being and good. And that which is in all
respects evil, being a falling off and as it were a departure from the
first good, is of course also deprived of being: for how could it have an
entrance into beings if it could not participate in the good? But that
which is not in all respects evil, is on the one hand 'contrary'[54] to some
good, though not to the good in general; on the other hand, it is
15   ordered and made good because of the pre-eminence of the wholes
that are good. And it is evil for those things which it opposes, but
depends on other things [i.e. the wholes] as something good.[55] For it
is not right that evil oppose the wholes, but all things ought to follow
in accordance with justice[56] or not exist at all.

10. Therefore, Plato in the *Timaeus* is right in saying that in
accordance with the will of the demiurge, 'all things are good and
nothing is bad'.[57] In his discussions with the geometer, however, he
contends that 'evil things cannot possibly cease to exist'[58] and that 'by

necessity'[59] they have come to exist among beings. For all things are made good by the will of the Father and, with respect to his productive activity, none of the things that are or come to be are evil. However, when he distinguishes degrees in nature he does not escape the consequence that there is evil for particular things, evil which destroys the good [in them].[60]

It is the same with darkness:[61] darkness that is completely unmixed with its contrary and [utterly] deprived of light has no being; but darkness that is produced in light and limited by it from all sides, belongs to beings. And for the sun nothing is dark, for even to darkness it imparts a weak clarity; for the air, however, darkness is a privation of the light that exists in it. Thus, all things are good to the father of all, and there is evil in those things that are not capable of remaining established in complete accordance with the good; for this reason evil is 'necessary', as we have said earlier.

In what sense evil exists and in what sense it does not is clear from our argument. For both those who assert that all things are good, and those who deny this, are right in one respect and wrong in another. Indeed, it is true that all beings are, but non-being, too, is interwoven with being. Therefore all things are good, since there is no evil that is unadorned and unmixed. And also evil exists, namely, for the things for which indeed there is evil: it exists for the things that do not have a nature that is disposed to remain in the good in an unmixed way.

[Where does evil exist?]

[Is there evil in the gods?]

11. After these questions we should examine in which [class] of beings, and how, and whence evil has come to exist. For, as we have seen, to being also belongs the nature of evil. So we should start from the beginning and explore, to the best of our abilities, where there is evil.

The gods, their reigns, numbers, and orders have the first portion of being, or rather they possess all beings and the intellective essence. Riding mounted on this essence,[62] they produce all things, preside over all things, proceed to all things, are present in all things without being mixed with them, and adorn all things in a transcendent manner; neither is their intelligence hindered by their providential activities, nor is their parental authority weakened by the purity of their intelligence: for their intellective activity is identical with their being, and they have providence because of their goodness and because of their fertile power.[63] This power does not want to remain in itself, but as it were brings forth that which the gods are allowed to engender, that is to say, all beings, all the classes that are superior to the souls, the souls themselves, and whatever may be on a lower level of being than the latter.

In fact, the gods themselves are beyond all beings, and they are the measures of being, since all being is contained in them as is number in the monads.[64] Beings, then, proceed from the gods, some beings remaining in the gods, other beings falling away from the unity of the gods into a secondary or yet lower nature, according to the principle of degradation. These beings are established in the order of the

20   participating entities, since they depend on the goodness of the real gods. The gods, however, exist in accordance with the good itself and the measure of all things; they are nothing else but the henads of beings, their measure and goodness, their summits, if you like, and as it were the 'flowers and supersubstantial lights',[65] and everything

25   like that; they allow participation on the level of true being and the first substance, and they produce by themselves all good and fine things, the intermediate things, and whatever kind of beings there are. Suppose someone asked us about the light which the king of all that is visible,[66] the god who has a rank analogous to the good,[67] spreads over the whole world: is this light in itself susceptible of

30   darkness or not? There would be many ways in which we could lead the questioner through circuitous arguments to reject such ideas, now celebrating the simplicity of its nature, then its continuity with its generating principle, then again something else. In the same manner we must speak about the gods. Perhaps we should not raise questions while remaining in the divine abodes; however, since we speak to

35   simpler minds as well, we must use many examples from both poetry and conversations[68] that may imbue the souls of a young audience. We should explain then in which way what is called evil does not exist in the gods.

12. We have to remember that the gods adorn all things, that they are lacking in nothing, that they live in complete blessedness, and that life for them means 'to live in abundance'.[69] For we have these ideas about the gods in our thoughts that are not deflected [by lower things] and this is from where we take them. And why speak about the gods? As a matter of fact, even 'souls of good fortune'[70] that acquire

5   intellect 'grow wings'[71] and, having assimilated themselves to gods, remain in the good. In them no evil is present nor will it ever come about. Total mirth,[72] an unharmed life, and a choir of virtues,[73] these things lead such a soul to a superior place, 'to a banquet, a feast',[74] far away from the evils of this world, not for the purpose of vanquishing

10   these evils, but so as to introduce in them, with the help of the gods, an order according to justice; these souls remain themselves in the gods. But when they are filled with the contemplation of the higher world, they become sated with their food, which is for them the beginning of excess, worldly pleasures and overboldness, but not yet pure evil.[75] If, then, even in the case of souls that are divine there is no evil, how could there be evil in the gods themselves? There is no

15   warmth in snow, as they say, nor cold in fire.[76] Hence there is no evil

in the gods either, nor is there anything of a divine nature in evil things.

13. All this must be said for the benefit of those who need it. But one should also keep in mind that for the gods 'to be gods' means 'to exist in accordance with the good'. For just as [particular] souls come from the universal soul and particular intellects from the entirely perfect intellect, likewise the very first series of goods, for which being and existence is nothing other than to be one and good, will come from the first good, or rather – if one may say so – from goodness itself, that is, from the henad of everything that is good. Similarly, for the particular intellects to be and to exist is nothing other than to think, and for the souls it is nothing other than to live.[77] For if all things that proceed from their principle accomplish their procession through likeness and in continuity,[78] then those things that proceed from the first unity are the first henads; and from the one good proceeds the multitude of goods. Now what could still be 'evil' or 'the nature of evil' for those beings that have their existence in accordance with the good? For the good itself does not allow evil. For the good is measure and light, whereas evil is darkness and absence of measure; the former is the cause of all foundation and all power, the latter is without foundation[79] and weak;[80] the former is that which sustains everything,[81] the latter that which corrupts each thing in which it is present, each according to its own rank; for, as we have explained, not everything has the same mode of corruption.[82]

Should we say, then, that it is not true that the gods are good, or should we say that they are good but change? This is what happens in particular souls, which always exhibit different types of life.[83] But in so saying we would be affirming something unholy with respect to the very existence of the gods. For that which is congenial with the non-good, is not good – and what is like this is not a god. Neither is that which changes similar to the One, which is better than any activity. For that which, through similarity, is in accordance with the One and eternal stems from what is before eternity,[84] and that which is located in immobile activity derives its existence from that which is beyond the level of primary activity.[85] Hence evil is not in the gods, neither absolutely nor in time. For both eternity and time are wholly posterior to the gods. These are substances and about substance; the gods are prior to substance and being.[86] Beings proceed from the gods, who are not beings themselves. And a god is whatever is good, whereas [substance and being] is what derives from this, namely true being.

[Is there evil in the three 'superior kinds', angels, demons, and heroes?]

14. Next, after the gods, let us direct our attention, if you like, to the order of angels, and consider whether this order, too, is to be regarded as completely good, or whether this is where evil [appears] for the first time. But how could we still call the angels messengers of the gods, if evil were present in them in whatever way? For everything that is evil is far distant from the gods and strange to them and like darkness in comparison to the light which is there. And evil is not only in ignorance about itself – it does not know that it is such[87] – but it is also ignorant about everything else and particularly about everything that is good. For it will probably flee and lose itself, incapable as it is of knowing either itself or the nature of the good. But the class that is the interpreter of the gods stands in continuity with the gods, knows the intellect of the gods, and reveals the divine will. Moreover, it is itself a divine light, [proceeding] from the light that resides in the sanctuary, that is, it is the light that [goes] outside, that appears, and is nothing other than the good proceeding and shining forth first from the beings which remain inside the One.

Indeed, it is necessary to make the procession of all things a continuous one. One thing is by nature consequent to the other because of its similarity.[88] Continuous with the source of all good, then, are the manifold good things, that is the number of henads, which remain hidden in the ineffability of the source. In continuity with them is the first number of beings emerging [from them], standing as it were in the portals[89] of the gods and revealing their silence.[90] But how can there be evil in those things for which 'to be' precisely means to reveal the good? For where there is evil, good is absent and is not revealed; it is hidden, rather, by the presence of the contrary nature.

That which reveals the One, however, has the character of unity. And in general, the revealer of something is in a secondary degree what the revealed was before its activity extended towards other things. Hence the angelic tribe eminently resembles the gods on which it depends,[91] so that, by its revelatory similarity, it may convey their property to the lower beings.

15. If you want to show not only in this way but also from another perspective the beneficent character of the order of angels, look, then, at all the kinds of beings and all their series; [you will see that] what occupies the first and principal rank in each order possesses also the truly good that cannot become evil, and rightly so. For, in each order, that which is first must bear the image of the prime cause,[92] since everywhere first natures are analogous to this first cause, and they are all preserved by participation in it. Whether you divide all beings into intelligibles and sensibles, or likewise the sensible again into heaven and generation, or likewise the intellective into soul and intellect, everywhere that which is the very first and most divine is not susceptible to evil. Therefore, not only in the aforementioned divisions but also in the threefold empire of the superior classes,[93] the first level must be immaculate, intellective, unmixed with evil, and

somehow correspond to the good. Indeed, the procession of the first
class is accomplished because of goodness, just as the race of demons 15
is constituted in accordance with the power and fertility of the gods;
this explains why they have received the middle position among the
three classes. For power pertains to the middle, just as intellect and
the circular reversion to the principle pertain to the third class.[94] Now,
what corresponds to reversion belongs to the heroes. But it is goodness that is active in angels, determining their existence by its own 20
unity. Hence it would be impossible to explain how this goodness
could still allow evil to enter surreptitiously into the nature of angels.
Thus only that which has a good nature shall obtain the rank of
angels, and evil shall not – definitely not. For the angels are the
interpreters of the gods, they are situated at the summits of the
superior classes, and their being is characterised by the good. 25

16. But is it in demons, then, that evil exists for the first time? For
the demons are next in line to the choir of angels. Well, there are
people who claim that demons even have passions. Some argue that
demons have passions by nature even, and depict in tragic style their
deaths and consecutive generations.[95] Others claim that demons have 5
passions only as a result of choice, and say that some demons are base
and evil – namely those demons who defile the souls, lead them to
matter and the subterranean place, and draw them away from their
journey to heaven.[96] Those who say this even believe that Plato was
the patron of this doctrine, as he posited two paradigms in the
universe, one 'divine', luminous, and of good form (*boniformis*), the
other 'ungodly', dark and mischievous.[97] Moreover, they say, some 10
souls are carried in one direction, some in the other; and those who
have moved downwards suffer punishment. Likewise some of the
souls in the underworld rise to the other side of 'the mouth' [of the
cave][98] and escape from that place, while others are drawn by 'fiery
and savage ghosts' towards 'the thorns' and 'Tartarus'.[99] Thus, accord- 15
ing to their argument, it is this whole race of demons, as it has been
described – I mean that deceptive, malicious race that destroys the
souls – which is the first to admit of evil. And they have it that even
the nature of these demons is differentiated by good and evil.[100]

17. One should ask these philosophers at least the following question – for the fathers of these arguments are divine, too:[101] the demons
that you hold to be evil, are they evil in themselves, or are they not
evil in themselves but only for others? For if they were evil in
themselves, a dilemma would arise: either they remain in evil per- 5
petually, or they are susceptible to change. And if they are always evil,
[we will ask:] how can that which receives its existence from the
gods[102] be always evil? For not to be at all is better than always to be
evil. On the other hand, if they change, they do not belong to the
beings that are demons in essence, but to beings that are such by
relation:[103] for the latter may be both better or worse, and [that is] 10

another kind of life.[104] Demons, however, without exception, always fulfil the function of demons, and every single one of them always [remains] in its own rank.

To say they are good in themselves but evil for others in that they lead them to something worse would be just as if one called some schoolmasters and pedagogues mischievous because, having been appointed to chastise wrongdoings, they do not allow those who make 15 mistakes to have a better position than they deserve. Or it would be as if one called evil those who stand in front of temples and stop every defiled person outside the precinct because they will not allow them to participate in the rites taking place inside. For it would not be evil that those who deserve it remain outside, but rather to deserve such a place and such prohibitions. Therefore, if some of the demons that 20 exist in the world lead souls upward while other demons keep souls that are not yet able to ascend in their own habits of life, none of those demons can rightly be called evil, neither those who detach the soul from this realm nor those who detain them here. For there must also exist demons to detain in the earthly realm the defiled person who is 25 unworthy of travelling to heaven. Thus, neither in these demons does reason seem to find evil; for each of them does what it does according to its own nature, always in the same manner. And that is not evil.

18. What, then, about the class of the heroes? Well, in the first place, does not their being, their essence, and their existence consist in a conversion towards the better? And, further, does not each of them, by its very being, always perform its own task, each having been ordered by their father to take providential care of different 5 things? If, then, they always do this in the same way, there is no evil [in them], for all evil is by nature unsteady and unstable;[105] by contrast, that which always is, is exactly the opposite. For '<not> always' means potentiality. And this 'potentially' characterises those things for which there is also evil. But in general, the changing of their type of life in whatever way makes them heroes by relation and 10 no longer heroes in essence.[106] For an angel as well as a demon or a hero who is essentially what it is, will by nature always preserve its own rank. They do not act now this way, now that way, but always according to the nature that each of them has received. Moreover, if in heroes as well anger, impulsiveness, and other so-called evils[107] 15 stemmed from a perversion of their natural condition, there would indeed be evil in them also – a disorder of their power and a deviation in every direction from the perfection that is appropriate to them. For evil is powerless, imperfect, and of a nature too weak to preserve itself.[108] However, if each hero in performing these things preserves itself and its own nature and its part in the whole allotted to it from 20 eternity, how then could it still be contrary to their nature to do these things? Insofar as [something] is in accordance with nature, it is not really evil, if indeed evil is for each thing [something] contrary to its

nature. In the case of lions and leopards one would not consider rage
to be something evil, but one would do so in the case of human beings,
for whom reason is the best. However, acting in accordance with
[mere] reason is not good for other [beings], namely for those whose
being is intellective.[109] For, as we have said many times already, evil 25
must not be that which is in accordance with nature nor that which
is the best in each thing – for what is such is good. No, evil must
belong to that which pursues what is inferior to its nature.

19. Hence also for all heroes that are led by rash imagination,
[passions] such as rage, irascibility, impetuosity, and obstinacy are
not unnatural; for their being does not consist in reason. Then how
could evil for them be due to these passions? Even if those passions
are hindrances for the souls, where do their [so-called] chain[s] come
from and their downward inclination?[110] For it is not the souls that 5
have not yet fallen which the heroes escort to their place. Surely this
would not be possible. Rather, in conformity with the design of the
universe, the heroes inflict a just punishment on the souls that have
descended and actually need to be punished. And the heroes themselves act in accordance with their nature, whereas the universe uses
them as instruments of healing, just as it uses beasts to devour
human beings[111] and as it uses for other purposes inanimate things 10
that act in accordance with their nature. Indeed, a stone, being moved
downward by nature, strikes that which it meets – after all, collisions
are actions of bodies. And by using the nature of the stone to this
effect, [the universe] in a suitable way meets the need of that which
needs to be hit.[112] Thus, for bodies it is not evil to strike, and in general
it is not evil if things act in accordance with their nature. Every thing 15
acts according to its nature when there is no better action available.
What other life, then, might be better for those heroes that are
allegedly evil than the life they actually lead? Nobody can tell. For
this is their order, this form of activity is determined by the organisation of the universe for the sake of guarding the dead. As their guards
they must, within fixed periods, honour with their surveillance the 20
deeds that happened within the limits of the souls' past. The duration
of the period, however, is fixed by the power of the sufferers. When
the purification is finished, the mouth [of the cave] remains quiet[113]
and all other things are removed from the souls that are ascending;
but when the punishment is still unfinished, some souls through 25
ignorance of themselves desire to proceed upwards, whereas others
are led to their appropriate place by the universe. And as guards of
these souls the heroes serve the will of the universe, directing the
souls to different kinds of punishments, restraining some souls for a
long time, others for a short time, and releasing each soul in conformity with the ordinance of the universe and its law.

The gods and the superior kinds have received a fine treatment 30
from us, we may say: there neither is nor ever will be evil in them.

Indeed, one has to keep the following in mind: all things act in accordance with their rank, the rank in which each of them has been placed, and when they 'abide by their accustomed manner',[114] they preserve invariably that boundary which they have received from the demiurgic principle.

[Is there evil in the souls?]
[Transition]

20. Now we must look at those beings that come next after these [superior kinds].[115] Here, if anywhere, evil might appear to those who are looking for it. If this is not the case, then we would have to say that it is nowhere among beings, neither there [i.e. above], nor in 'this place'.[116] All of the aforementioned classes were indeed not susceptible

5   to a change in kind, that is to a change affecting their own order. For each class is always constituted so as to preserve the same order that it has received. But the beings that come next after them[117] have the potency of sometimes ascending and at other times tending to generation and 'the mortal nature'. And among those beings, some are better and more divine, and in their contact with mortal nature they do not

10   renounce kinship with the divine; others, by contrast, 'have their circles in every way broken and disturbed'[118] and are completely filled with 'oblivion',[119] 'affinity' [with inferior things], and evils.

[a. The immaculate souls]

21. Let us therefore first consider the better [souls]. That they are indeed better, and that they do not allow in themselves any passion belonging to human depravity, is clearly indicated by Socrates in the *Republic*, when he complains that poetry represents the children of the gods on a par with humans as lovers of money,[120] and does not

5   hesitate to call them the offspring of divine parents, while depicting them as replete with evils, such as we see occurring in human nature. However, as is said about them,[121] the larger part of their cycle is dedicated to contemplation, a life free from harm, and a secure providence exerted over the whole together with the gods,[122] and when they descend to [the world of] becoming, it is for the benefit of the

10   places down here[123] – some [souls] making their appearance for the sake of noble offspring,[124] some for the sake of purity, some for the sake of virtue, some for the sake of divine intellect. [In their descent] they are perfected in the procession together with the gods,[125] by the inspiration of good demons,[126] and by the consent of the universe. What evil, then, could there be at all for those [souls], unless you wish to call generation itself evil?[127]

15   To be sure, 'it is necessary' for every soul 'to drink a certain quantity of the cup of oblivion', as Socrates says in the *Republic*.[128] This oblivion, however, is different in different souls: in some cases it involves the loss of a certain disposition, while in others it is only the

burying of activity. Thus, if you like, you may call this ceasing of
activity 'oblivion' when the disposition remains inside like a light that
is unable to proceed externally because of the surrounding darkness;
or you may, if you prefer, call it the 'evil' of these souls. These souls,   20
then, are not subject to the disturbance[129] in generation that occurs
within the living body; for this reason we are accustomed to calling
them 'immaculate',[130] since the evils here below cannot enter into
them. Yet these souls, too, are incapable of preserving in this [earthly]
realm that invariable and immutable life of the intellective realm,
and so they permit that which disturbs them and is unstable to   25
remain in the dependent natures [i.e. their bodies]. Silently these
souls stay inside, until their living body has calmed down; at that
point their beauty shines forth, making it appropriate to call them
'children of the gods'.[131]

22. Whether the generations of souls occur in living beings on
earth,[132] or in other parts of the universe,[133] this is the mode of descent
for all of them,[134] and oblivion and evil go this far. Thus we say of a
light that it becomes darkened,[135] when, on account of the extraneous
nature of its surrounding, which is thick and nebulous, it is incapable
of illuminating that which is near. But to be completely darkened is   5
the state of that which is incapable of preserving even itself. The
descent of these divine souls, therefore, is not the loss of their internal
life; it gives them, however, a weakness as regards action.

The souls, however, that are posterior to these [immaculate souls]
and have lost their internal life, come [down] in oblivion of the   10
heavenly sights.[136] In these there is true death, insatiety, shedding of
the wings,[137] and all the other things we are accustomed to assert
about them. For what else should we posit as an intermediary between the beings that are not susceptible to evil[138] and those that are
altogether perverted,[139] if not a slight and, so to speak, apparent evil?
This is what should be asserted of these souls.

[b. The fallen human souls]

23. Immediately next to these souls comes a truly variegated and
manifold tribe, subject to change by various choices and impulses.
Here even the powers inside the soul itself are curtailed. They 'toil'
and 'limp';[140] they are weak and suffer all the evils[141] that souls are   5
said to partake in because they have fallen from on high, where there
is a life of beatitude, free of sorrow for those that stay there. For each
soul, when it remains on high, 'journeys through the sky and governs
the whole world',[142] contemplating essences[143] and, together with the
presiding gods,[144] ascending to the blessed and most perfect 'banquet'[145] of being, and filling those beings that gaze on [this soul] with   10
nectar[146] from there. For the primary good is not contemplation,
intellective life, and knowledge, as someone has said somewhere.[147]
No, it is life in accordance with the divine intellect which consists, on

the one hand,[148] in comprehending the intelligibles through its own intellect, and, on the other, in encompassing the sensibles with the powers of [the circle of] difference[149] and in giving even to these sensibles a portion of the goods from above. For that which is perfectly good possesses plenitude, not by the mere preservation of itself, but because it also desires, by its gift to[150] others and through the ungrudging[151] abundance of its activity, to benefit all things and make them similar to itself.[152]

But when a soul is incapable of imitating, according to both kinds of life, its presiding gods, it is deprived of the contemplation of true being and is attracted by other, secondary powers which revolve about the world. For these souls this is 'the beginning' of their generation and 'of another cycle'.[153] Although it means impotence, privation of speculation, and thus, for them, evil, from the perspective of the whole it is not even for them evil,[154] but a kind of life different from their primary kind of life, inferior on account of its lack of power: for the primary self-sufficient exists where that which is primarily good resides and power is strongest where self-sufficiency exists.[155]

24. Thus, for the soul this is indeed a weakness, namely, to fail to participate in the banquet,[156] and to precipitate downwards; it is its power, on the other hand, to get up there before sinking into the depths.[157] Indeed, all things do not have the same mode of weakness. For neither do all bodies suffer total decay when they are separated from the power that regulates and preserves them.[158]

Now, as Plato says,[159] 'it happens' that a soul becomes associated with 'the mortal, death-bringing kind', 'becomes heavy and replete with oblivion and falls down.' Such a soul will be led by the universe to the appropriate rank, but will vary the form of its life again and again, until, as it is said in the *Timaeus*,[160] it changes course and moves upward: 'shedding the turbulent mob and its own accretions' and leaving them where they are, it is led 'to being itself, and indeed to the most splendid being'.[161] The soul, therefore, descending from there, will arrive at the meadow and contemplate the souls that are there.[162] But it will also arrive below the throne[163] of necessity and contemplate the plain of oblivion,[164] and no longer contemplate the things that it did when it had a primordial nature.[165] Indeed, for the souls that resided above, the 'plain of truth' and the 'upper meadow' were there to be contemplated.[166]

The 'nutriment from up there' is, however, 'a proper pasturage for the noblest part of the soul',[167] says Plato, whereas the nutriment down here is of a doxastic nature,[168] since the river of oblivion[169] is near. And all of this is not yet terrible, provided that one does not take too much. But when the soul is filled with it, it is led by the universe towards what is similar, folly: as he says,[170] and darkness and what is most bereft of light, the pit[171] of the universe, if one may say so, where an insurmountable multitude of evils surrounds mortal nature and grows upon it all around.[172] For the fractures and distortions of their circles,[173] the 'bonds', and whatever else there is that introduces death into souls, the periods of a thousand years,[174] the punishments,[175] and, so to speak, the most tragic of experiences that the law of the universe brings them, all these are found here. And we shall certainly not be able to flee from these experiences nor rest from our labours, if we do not withdraw from external things and separate our proper good, which is the contemplation of real being, from mortal triviality. Therefore we must strip ourselves of the garments with which, in descending, we became invested, and must proceed naked from here to there,[176] completely purifying the eye of our soul by which we contemplate true being,[177] and instead of sense make intellect the principal ruler of our internal lives.

What then is the origin of evil for us? It is the continuous communion and cohabitation with what is inferior to us. It is also oblivion and ignorance, which come about by looking at that which is dark and not intellectual.[178] But the origin of the good is flight and assimilation to the divine.[179] For up there total good exists, the source of all good things, and, for the souls which arrive there, a truly pure and felicitous life.[180] This is what we had to explain about the soul that is capable of both ascending to that place and descending to this place: how evil, weakness, falling, and everything else we have mentioned are present in it.

[c. The irrational souls]

25. What, then, about the other souls, not those that are parts of [real] beings, but certain images,[181] parts of an inferior soul, which the Athenian stranger calls maleficent?[182] Indeed, these too we have to examine asking the question: are they immune to vice or is there actually evil in them? If those souls are inferior to the human soul – I mean, to the image [of soul] that exists in us – evil in them will consist in not acting according to [their] nature. For if our own souls change continuously with respect to good and bad, it is not possible that in those inferior souls the good [state] or the bad [state] would be invariably present. On the other hand, if they were related to another soul that is prior to them, as is the case with our [irrational] souls, it would obviously be necessary that, when this higher soul is faring better or worse, the image follows and at times is carried upwards, while at other times it is drawn [down] to generation and the realm of matter. For when irrationality is dependent on reason, the worse condition consists in dissidence from reason, in not receiving light from there and [not] correcting one's own lack of measure using the measure that derives from there. For this behaviour reveals not the power of these[183] souls, but their weakness and lack of power.[184] And indeed, for each thing <the good consists in> being led towards that

25

30

35

40

5

10

15

which is better and towards participation in the good that it is born to receive.

But <when the irrationality subsists> by itself, evil <does not consist in acting according to its own nature>, but in lacking the appropriate virtue. After all, for some souls, pleasures and pains occur moderately and do not exceed what is necessary, while for others, who follow their own lack of boundary, pleasures and pains are without measure. And as for virtue, it does not exist in the same way in all beings; in one case it is by possessing the virtue of a horse that one has the good corresponding to one's nature, in another case by possessing the virtue of a lion, or that of another animal. And all species reside in the good, though some more, some less. But if an animal becomes a fox instead of a lion, slackening its virile and haughty nature, or if it becomes cowardly instead of bellicose, or if another assumes any other type of life, abandoning the virtue that is naturally fitting to it, they give evidence that in these [beings], too, there is evil.

26. When a being has the capacity of not acting in accordance with its nature, the change is necessarily either to what is better than its nature, or to what is worse. Thus for these [irrational] souls, too, there is an ascent to that which is better, namely when some activity taking the form of reason manifests itself in them – this kind of power being inspired, as it were, by a leading demon allotted to such a soul. Descent to what is worse, on the other hand, occurs when, because of bodily disfunctioning or inappropriate nutriment, the natural activity of the soul is obstructed by a unnatural state, showing the soul to be replete with those things.

In general, everything that progresses through generation is born in an imperfect state and accomplishes its perfection in time. It is perfected by the addition of something.[185] For each thing's end is [its] good.[186] But an imperfection may always be twofold: it may consist either in the halting of activity <or in> the lack of a disposition.[187] That which is deficient only in its activity is better on account of its natural virtue, and in that it has, prior to its activity, a perfect disposition. But that which is naturally disposed to receive perfection from its natural virtues lacks both the perfection of its nature and this disposition.[188] This, then, is [its] evil: the privation of a virtuous disposition. In the case of such a privation, the underlying nature may be perverted, and possibly even becomes the complete opposite of its own virtue. But if some things may become either better or worse on account of their habits, too, should one be surprised, then, to see an evil nature arise out of these very habits? Take the following examples: one may turn natural haughtiness by means of training into modesty; another may be provoked into a harsher savagery, yet another may in various ways be turned away from its natural virtue. Indeed, all beings have their own virtue, but for some habit advances their virtue, whereas for others habit becomes an obstruction to their

natural path. In some cases nature prevails and softens the damage   25
resulting from [bad] habit, whereas in other cases nature remains
passive and becomes, as it were, alienated from itself, drawn along on
the road of habituation.

[Is there evil in nature and bodies?]

27. Next we have to consider nature itself, as well as all those things
which have their complete being and existence imparted to them by
nature. We must examine whether evil is situated in nature or not,
and for what reason. As regards the nature of the universe, then, or
any other nature of an eternal being that there is, we must not say
nor think that it at any time departs from its own disposition; nature   5
rather remains, that is, governs a body according to nature.[189] For
what else is the function of nature than to preserve and sustain that
in which it exists? And this is common to all causes. As to the
particular nature that pertains to individual things, however, [the
situation is different]: when it completely dominates the substrate
matter, it 'conducts all things rightly and wisely';[190] but when it lets
itself be dominated, insofar as it is partial and uses reasons that are   10
partial as well, it does the complete opposite of what it is disposed to
do. For nature as a whole nothing is contrary to nature, since all
reasons derive from it. But for particularised nature, one thing will
be in accordance and another not in accordance with nature. Indeed,
for each [particular] nature something else will be contrary to its
nature. Thus for the nature of man this particular form of a lion
originates contrary to its nature, since neither the rational principle   15
of this form nor that of other species is intrinsic to it, but only the
rational principle of man. To this nature the rational principles of
others are strange, and likewise in the case of all other things whose
rational principles are specifically different. It is characteristic of this
[i.e. a particular] nature that it may be dominated and act contrary to
nature, but not of nature as a whole nor of any eternal nature.[191]
Indeed, matter that is the substrate of non-eternal natures is often
dominated by the bonds proceeding from nature. Then matter adorns   20
and as it were illuminates its own darkness and deformity, and
invests itself with a foreign ornament.[192] And indeed, in the wholes its
ugliness is thus concealed.[193] Hence, though matter stems from the
principle, not everyone gets to know it, not even those who have
elucidated many of the secrets of nature.[194] But it happens that a
particular nature becomes impotent on account of a defect of substan-   25
tial power; for a particular nature is as it were a ray[195] and impression
of universal nature,[196] a rational principle that is detached from it,
that has flowed downwards into body and is incapable of remaining
pure. Alternatively, [a particular nature can become impotent] on
account of the power of the contraries surrounding it on all sides, for
many are the forces that are external and hostile to mortal nature.

Thus, as we have said, when it is affected by this weakness and allows
30   its own ugliness to prevail, it curtails its own activities and by its own
deformity causes the light that proceeds from it to be darkened.
Indeed, when the reason of nature does not prevail, ugliness is
revealed as passion, and when the order is impotent, as lack of order.
And reason is overcome by the inferior when it becomes irrational
itself.

28. If, then, nature in its activity manifests that it is without
hindrance, we will find that all things are according to nature and
that nowhere in them is there evil. But if the goal of a thing and its
natural course are to be distinguished from what is contrary and an
impediment to nature, and if the rational principle [of a thing] is one,
5   but the things that are contrary to it are infinite in number: would we
not say that there, and nowhere else, is the badness of nature? Indeed,
to a being for whom contemplation is good, the privation of contemplation is evil. But to a being for whom the good consists in producing
and acting in accordance with reason, evil consists in the fact that
reason does not prevail and that its productivity, having been overcome by the inferior, does not attain its goal. One should posit a
10   badness of bodies, then, if the form that is imposed on them can be
overcome by what is inferior. For corporeal foulness arises from
rational form being subdued, and disease of the body from order being
dissolved.[197] Beauty, accordingly, indeed [exists] when the form prevails – it is like a flower draping itself over the forms[198] – and what
there is of health [exists], when the natural order is stably preserved.

And all that has been said, thus far, about things in nature, must
15   be understood as referring to material bodies and individual things,
but not to beings that rank as wholes nor to what lies outside
matter.[199] For where could ugliness be outside matter, which we are
accustomed to call ugliness itself and the last nature, as it is without
measure and beauty and does not even possess the weakest form of
splendour?[200] And where would disorder and contrariety to nature be
20   found in those beings that always exist in accordance with nature and
– since nature always prevails – preserve their well-being invariably?
Individual bodies, which in matter undergo all sorts of transmutations, at times indeed possess order and good; but at other times their
natures are dominated by the contraries of these. But the bodies that
are not individual and that, being wholes, must always remain and
25   complete the world,[201] always possess an order that vanquishes disorder. And of the things that are outside matter, some indeed are always
numerically[202] the same and are uniform in their activities and free
from all mortal toiling. But others, while remaining the same in their
very being and nature, in their activities are led to the better and the
30   worse. That is the case with the instruments[203] of the human soul,
which indeed possess an essence that is in accordance with nature,
but have a kind of life that is always different. And at times, indeed,

they remain in their own beauty, adhering to their natural activity and natural place, but at other times they are dispersed into a foreign region and are drawn into a condition contrary to nature, and then they introduce into themselves the baseness of matter. For each instrument[al body] of a soul, being capable of looking in both directions, follows the soul and its impulses, and, being led in all directions, undergoes all sorts of motions and is assimilated to the appetites of the soul.

29. We have spoken about corporeal nature, said that there is evil in it, and explained how it is different in different things. Of the individual bodies those that exist in matter have evil even in their substance, and they are infinite in number; but others are outside matter, and are indeed finite in number; there is no evil in their substance, but in their activities and transmutations of life they are filled with the contrary. But of the beings that rank as wholes, some possess order exclusively, since there is no disorder in them, whereas others possess order because the disorder is always overcome.[204] For each totality has the character of an order that always prevails, and uniformity exists because of order. Hence, when it is said that everything 'that moves in an irregular and disorderly fashion', whatever it may be, is the substrate not only for material but also for eternal bodies,[205] we must say that 'disorder' and 'non-uniformity' apply to them in a different sense. Down here, indeed, disorder is due to matter and to the mixture of form with the formless, but up there disorder does not consist in the deprivation of form, but in the deprivation of life: up there the substrate is reason and form.[206] Hence, in that realm even that which is disorderly, as it were, is order, yet it is an order that is disorderly with respect to the adornment that comes from above. In the realm of generation, however, disorder is situated in matter, because of the irrational, obscure, and indeterminate character of its nature.[207] For the disorderly character is not accidental to matter nor is matter said to be disorderly with respect to something else, for what is disorderly with respect to something else is not yet the last. No, absolute absence of measure, absolute indeterminateness, absolute darkness:[208] that is the disorder of matter.

[Is matter evil?][209]
30. But fortunately, even before we have been led to examine matter itself, the argument has already brought us to consider the question whether matter is evil, or whether even this is not evil. For it is by no means possible that evil belongs to matter as an accident, because, by itself, matter is without quality and formless; matter is a substrate,[210] and not in a substrate; it is simple, and not some thing in another. If matter is entirely evil – and some say it is[211] – it must be evil in essence, as they also say, making matter the primary evil and 'that

which the gods abhor'.[212] For[213] what is evil other than unmeasuredness and indeterminateness and all kinds of privations of the good?
10 Indeed, good is the measure of all things, their boundary, limit and perfection. That is why evil is unmeasuredness, absolute unlimitedness, imperfection and indeterminateness. Now all these things, [they say,] are primarily in matter; they are not other beings besides matter, but matter itself and what it is to be matter. Hence matter is the primary evil, the nature of evil, and the last of all things. If good
15 is twofold – one being the absolute good and nothing other than good, the other being the good in something else, a particular good, that is, and not the primary good – then evil as well will be twofold, the one being as it were absolute evil and the primary evil and nothing else but evil, the other being evil in something else and some evil, i.e. that which is evil because of that [first] evil, by participation in or assimi-
20 lation to it. And just as the good is the first, the absolute evil[214] will be the last of beings. For it is not possible for anything to be better than good nor worse than evil, since we say that all other things are better or worse by virtue of these. But matter is the last of beings: for all other things are disposed to act or to undergo, whereas matter does neither, as it is deprived of both these potencies. Hence the absolute and primary evil is matter.

31. If, as we have said,[215] in bodies the unnatural arises when matter prevails, and in souls evil and weakness[216] come about when they fall into matter, get drunk[217] with the indeterminateness surrounding it and assimilate themselves to it, why should we dismiss this [explanation] and seek for another cause of evils as a principle of
5 and source for their existence?[218]

But if matter is evil – for we should now move to the other point of view – we must choose between two alternatives: either to make the good the cause of evil, or to posit two principles of beings. For, indeed, everything that exists in any way whatever, must either be a principle of complete beings or stem from a principle. Now, if matter stems from
10 a principle, then matter itself receives its procession into being from the good. If, on the other hand, matter is a principle, then we must posit two principles of beings which oppose each other, viz. the primary good and the primary evil.[219] But that is impossible. For there can be no two firsts. From where would these two come at all, if there were no monad? For if each of the two is one, prior to both there must exist a single principle, the One, through which both are one. Nor does
15 evil stem from the good. For just as the cause of good things is good in a greater degree, likewise that which generates evil will be evil to a greater degree.[220] Neither would the good maintain its own nature, if it produced the principle of evil. If, on the other hand, it is a general rule that what is generated likes to assimilate itself to its generating principle, even evil itself will be good, having been made good by
20 participating in its cause. Hence [in this case], the good, as the cause

of evil, would be evil, and evil, as being produced from the good, would be good.

32. If, however, matter is necessary to the universe,[221] and the world, this absolutely great and 'blessed god',[222] would not exist in the absence of matter, how can one still refer the nature of evil to matter? For evil is one thing, but the necessary is something else; the necessary is that without which it is impossible to be, whereas evil is the privation of being itself.[223] If, then, matter offers itself to be used in 5 the fabrication of the whole world, and has been produced primarily for the sake of being 'the receptacle of generation, and as it were as a wet-nurse'[224] and 'mother'[225], how can it still be said to be evil, and even the primary evil? Again, we speak in many senses of 'unmeasured' and 'unlimited' and all those things. For we may call 'unmeasured' (1) that which opposes measure, or (2) its absence and 10 removal, or (3) the substrate of measure and indeed the need for measure and limit. Now matter is not disposed to (1) oppose nor, in general, to effectuate anything, since it is neither capable by nature of undergoing an effect because of the lack of the potency to undergo.[226] Nor is it (2) a removal of measure and limit, for it is not identical with privation, because privation does not exist when measure and limit are present, whereas matter keeps existing and bearing 15 their impression. Hence the unlimitedness and measurelessness of matter must consist in (3) the need[227] for measure and limit.

But how could the need for limit and measure be the contrary of limit and measure? How can that which is in need of the good still be evil? For evil flies from the nature of the good, as in general every contrary flies the contrary disposition. If then, matter desires and 20 conceives generation, and, as Plato says, nourishes it, no evil will come from it, since matter is the mother of the beings that proceed from her, or rather, the beings that are born in her.

33. If, then, the souls suffer weakness and fall, this is not because of matter, since these [deficiencies] existed already before the bodies and matter, and somehow a cause of evil existed in the souls themselves prior to [their descent into] matter.[228] What else could be the explanation for the fact that among the souls that follow Zeus some raise the head of the charioteer into the outer region, whereas <others> are incapable and sink down, and are as it were blunted by that 5 spectacle and turn away their eyes?[229] Indeed, how can 'oblivion' of being and 'mischance' and 'heaviness'[230] occur in those souls? For 'the horse that participates in evil becomes heavy and verges to the earth',[231] without there being matter [involved]. Indeed, only after the soul has fallen to earth does it enter into communion with matter and the darkness here below. Up there, however, and prior to matter and darkness, there is [already] weakness and oblivion and evil; for we 10 would not have departed if not out of weakness, since even at a distance we still cling to the contemplation of being.

Hence, if souls are weakened before [they drink from] the cup[232] [of oblivion], and if they come to be in matter and descend into matter after the flight from up there, [it can] no longer [be held that]

15 weakness and evils in general occur in souls because of matter. For what could something do to other things that is itself incapable of doing anything? And also, how could that which on its own is without qualities[233] have the capacity to do something?

Does matter draw souls to itself or are they drawn by themselves and become separated through their own power, or [rather] their own powerlessness? If souls are drawn by themselves, evil for them will

20 consist in an impulse towards the inferior and the desire for it, and not in matter. Indeed, for each thing evil is the flight from the better, and even more is it the flight towards the worse. And because of their weakness such souls suffer what they ought to suffer when they have chosen badly. If, on the other hand, souls are drawn by matter – that is, if we attribute the cause of their generation to the attraction matter exercises upon souls, as something that draws them – where

25 is their self-motion and ability to choose?[234] Or how can one explain why among the souls that are generated in matter, some gaze at intellect and the good, whereas others gaze at generation and matter, if matter draws all of them alike to itself, troubling them and doing violence to them even when they are in the upper regions? These will be the conclusions of the argument: it will compel us to demonstrate not just that matter is not evil, but even, trying to prove what is contrary to the first thesis,[235] that matter is good.[236]

34. It may seem that Plato himself, too, is drawn, as it were, to both argumentations. For when, in the *Timaeus*, he calls matter the 'mother'[237] and 'wet-nurse'[238] of generation and a 'co-cause'[239] of the fabrication of the world, it is clear to everyone that he takes matter

5 to be good, since he calls the entire world a 'blessed god',[240] and matter a portion of the world. But in the argument of the Eleatic Stranger[241] he refers the cause of 'the disorder of the universe' to its substrate, when he says that 'the world possesses all things good from its composer', but that the contrary of the good originates in the world 'from the previous condition' of the world. In the *Philebus*,[242] however,

10 he produces matter itself and the whole nature of the unlimited from the One, and, in general, places the divine cause before the distinction between limit and the unlimited. Thus he will admit that matter is something divine and good because of its participation in and origin from god, and that is never evil. For he asserts that 'one must look for some other causes of evil and not consider god as its cause',[243] as is said elsewhere.

15 Perhaps then disorder and evil happen not because of matter, but because of 'that which moves in an irregular and disorderly fashion'.[244] For this is 'the corporeal nature' that, as the Eleatic Stranger[245] affirms, is 'the cause of disorder' for the lowest things of the universe;

it cannot be matter, as there is motion in it, whereas matter is by itself immobile. Nor is this first composite a body without qualities (for 'it is visible', as Timaeus says,[246] whereas that which is without qualities 20 is not visible), but rather with some impression of all the forms, a brew of all forms so to speak. That is why this first composite by its movement produces disorder. For the traces[247] of the different forms leading to different local motions show the irregularity of the motion [of the first composite] in its totality. This then is the 'previous condition'.[248] For as this 'previous condition' is incapable of being dominated by the forms, it shows itself as being unadorned and 25 without beauty. And in wholes reason prevails, but in partial things reason, because of its weakness, is vanquished by a nature contrary to itself; there, reason is led to evil and, as it were, made irrational, dominated as it is by the inferior.

35. How, then, the unnatural enters into bodies will be made clear in a while. But that evil does not stem from matter, not even in the case of bodies, is evident from these arguments. For matter is not identical with 'that which moves in an irregular fashion'.[249] Moreover, that it is wrong to posit matter as the primary evil, is, I think, sufficiently demonstrated by Socrates in the *Philebus*, where he 5 argues that unlimitedness is generated from god.[250] Also if one must straightaway identify the unlimited with matter, matter is from god, since we must say that the primary unlimited and all unlimitedness belonging to being and deriving from a unique cause are generated from god, and especially the unlimitedness that together with limit cannot produce the mixture. For god is the cause both of the existence of limit and the unlimited and of their mixture. This [unlimited], 10 therefore, and the nature of body, qua body, must be referred to one cause, namely god, for it is he who produced the mixture. Hence, neither body nor matter is evil, for they are the progeny of god, the one as a mixture, the other as unlimitedness.[251] That the unlimited is to be placed beyond matter, Plato himself elsewhere clearly indicates, using the following words: 'Did not the three kinds give us all things 15 that come to be, and the constituents from which they come to be?'[252] Hence body – and this too is a unity of all [these], since it is mixed, and constituted by limit and reason, on the one hand, and unlimited-ness, on the other– derives from the divine in two ways: as a whole and on account of its parts. For what else is the unlimited in body but matter? And what else is limit in it but form?[253] What else but the whole is that which consists of both of these? If then 'the things 20 themselves that are generated and their constituents',[254] are (1) the mixed, (2) limit, and (3) the unlimited, and if 'that which produces these three kinds' is something else, 'a fourth kind', as he calls it himself,[255] then we will not say that either matter, or form, or the mixed are produced as a mixture from anywhere else than from god. 25 And what could be evil that stems from there? Just as warmth cannot refrigerate, good cannot produce evil.[256] Hence neither matter nor body may be called evil.

36. Perhaps, then, someone may ask us what our opinion is concerning matter, whether we consider it to be good or evil, and in what respect [we may admit] either of these options. Let this, then, be our decision: that matter is neither good nor evil. For if it is good, it will
5   be a goal, instead of the last of things, and it will be 'that for the sake of which'[257] and desirable. For all good is like this, since the primary good is the goal, that for the sake of which everything [exists], and the object of desire for all beings.

If, on the other hand, matter is evil, it will be a god and an alternative principle of beings, dissident from the cause of good things, and there will be 'two sources releasing their flow in opposite directions', one the source of good things, the other of evil things.[258]
10   Even for the gods themselves there will not be an unharmed life, nor a life free from mortal toiling,[259] since something for them will be difficult to bear, foreign and troubling as it were.

If, then, matter is neither good nor evil, what will it be in its own right? We should repeat what has been often said about matter, that it is a necessity. Indeed, the nature of good is one thing, that of evil
15   another, and they are contrary to each other. But there is another, a third nature, that is neither simply good nor evil, but necessary. Indeed, evil leads away from the good and flees from its nature; but the necessary is everything it is for the sake of the good, and it has a relation to the good. And any generation that befalls the necessary, happens because of the good. If then matter exists for the sake of
20   generation, and if no other nature exists for the sake of matter in such a way that we could call it the goal or the good,[260] then we must say that matter is necessary to generation, that it is not evil and that it is produced by divinity as necessary,[261] and that it is necessary for the forms that are incapable of being established in themselves.[262]

For the cause of all good things had to produce not only beings that
25   are good and that are good by themselves, but also the nature that is not absolutely and intrinsically good, but that desires the good and through its desire – and, as it were, by itself – gives other things the possibility of coming into being. Indeed, through its need for good things this nature [i.e. matter] contributes to the creation of the sensibles. For being, too, imparts existence not only to beings, but also to things that desire a participation in Being itself. For those things,
30   being consists in the desire for being.[263] Hence, that which is primarily desirable is one thing; another thing is that which desires this and possesses good through this; yet another thing is everything that is intermediate, which is desirable to some things, but itself desires other things, namely the things that are prior to it and for the sake of which it exists.

37. If we consider matter itself from this perspective, we will see

that it is neither good nor evil, but only necessary; in having been produced for the sake of good it is good, but taken on its own it is not good; and as the lowest of beings it is evil[264] – if indeed what is most remote from the good is evil[265] – but taken on its own it is not evil, but   5
necessary, as we have explained.

And in general, it is not true that evil exists on its own anywhere, for there is no unmixed evil, no primary evil. For if evil were contrary to the good in all respects, then, given the fact that the good that is on its own and primary precedes the good in other things, evil, too, has to be twofold: evil itself, and evil in something else.[266]   10

But if evil is [only] contrary to those goods that have their being in something else, then *a fortiori* evil is in something else and does not exist on its own;[267] neither does the good of which evil is the contrary exist on its own, but it exists only in something else and not separately. Indeed, what would be contrary to the primary good? I do not mean evil, but what else among beings [would be contrary to the primary good]? For all beings exist because of the good and for the   15
sake of the good. But that the contrary exists because of the nature of its contrary, that is impossible; it is rather the case that [because of the latter] the contrary does not exist. For contraries are destroyed by each other. And in general all contraries proceed from a single summit[268] and genus.[269] But what would be the genus of the first good? Indeed, what could be beyond the nature of the good? What among   20
beings could become homogeneous[270] to it? For in that case it would be necessary that there be something else prior to both of them, of which either one of them would be a part. And the good would no longer be the principle of beings. No, the principle of beings would be the principle that is common to both these.[271]

Hence, nothing is contrary to the primary good, and neither to all things that participate in it, but there is only contrariety to things whose participation is not immutable. Of these, however, we have   25
spoken before.

[Is privation evil?]

38. Here we have to dismiss the discussion of matter, and proceed again[272] to the question of privation, since [there are] also some [who] say that this is evil and completely contrary to the good.[273] For matter remains as a substrate when the form is present, whereas privation has no being at all, as it is always an evil agent and contrary to the   5
forms. And matter desires the good, strives for it and partakes in it, whereas privation flees the good, is the cause of destruction and is completely evil.[274]

But [this is not correct]: if the primary good were identical with being, and were at the same time good and being, and were one nature, then indeed privation would have to be primary evil, for privation is as such non-being and contrary to being.[275] But if, on the

10   contrary, the good is different from being, and both are not identical, then evil, too, must be different from privation. And just as the good is not being but beyond being, and being itself is not as such <good> but a descent from the good and its first illumination and as it were its splendour, so it is with privation: as such [it is not evil]. For the presence of privation does not yet entail that there is evil, whereas total privation implies that the evil nature has disappeared. What I

15   mean is this: the body is diseased, when there is disorder, yet not total disorder. For the total privation of order at once destroys the subject and the evil present in it.[276]

And that which is not yet generated is a privation, but not evil. Fire, for instance, and water and other elements are on their own [privations] of that which may be constituted out of them but is not

20   yet; but none of these are as yet evil. In general, disorder and unmeasuredness, as we have said earlier,[277] can be taken in two different ways: either as an absence of these – I mean, of measure and order – or as a nature contrary to these qualities. For the latter opposes order and measure, while the former is merely the deprivation of these and nothing but their negation; or rather, when these [properties] are present they are what they are, but, when absent,

25   they just leave behind privations of themselves.[278] Therefore, if evil is contrary to the good and discordant with it, but privation neither opposes the disposition of which it is the privation, nor is disposed to do anything, as its being is so weak and wraith-like[279] – as they say – how could we still attribute the evil agency to privation, of which all

30   activity is denied? For activity is a form and a power, whereas privation is formless and weak, and not power but rather absence of power.[280]

Hence, from what has been said, it is evident what the beings are in which evil exists, and what those are in which it does not exist.

[Corollary: are evils of bodies greater than evils of souls?]

39. Because, however, evil exists in souls in one way and in bodies in another, what ranking of evils is to be assumed, where does evil start, and how far does the decline extend? Indeed, is the evil in souls greater than that in bodies, or is the evil in bodies the ultimate evil

5   and the evil in souls a weaker evil? With respect to the evil in the soul, one kind extends to the activity alone, but another dominates the soul altogether, introducing various 'fractures' to some of its powers and paralysing others, as Plato[281] says.[282]

If, indeed, mere obstruction of activity is one thing, and the kind [of obstruction] that extends to the very power another, and yet

10   another the kind that destroys the substance, and if the first kind is a passion of divine souls that are in contact with the realm of generation, the second the evil of souls who bring with them a weaker brightness of intellect, the third already the evil of bodies them-

selves,[283] then the first will be only an apparent evil, the third will be a true evil that curtails being and the nature in which it is present, and the second will be intermediate between these, being evil to the powers but unable to affect substance. 15

In general, that which can damage greater things is a greater evil. Substance is above power and power is above activity. And that which destroys substance at the same time destroys power and activity; that which destroys power [also destroys] activity. Hence the destruction of these [i.e. power and activity] cannot entail that of substance, nor can power be abolished as a consequence of the cessation of activity. 20

Or perhaps, evil that extends to activity is privation and not contrariety, whereas <that which is destructive of either power or substance> is the contrary of <either power or> substance.[284] But the contrary of a greater good is a greater evil. Therefore, the evil in souls is a greater evil than that in bodies. This is not the case for all souls, but only for those whose power can be affected. For those souls whose 25 activity alone can be affected, the evil is lesser and is only the absence of complete perfection and [a certain] decline. One kind of evil [sc. that of souls] is indeed contrary to virtue, the other [sc. that of bodies] to the goods of the body; the first is contrary to what is according to intellect, the second to what is according to nature.[285] To the extent therefore that intellect is better than nature and that what is according to intellect is better than what is according to nature, to that extent what is a deviation from intellect will be a greater evil than 30 what is a deviation from nature. Is it a surprise then, that the latter [sc. the evil of body, which goes against nature] destroys substance, the former [sc. the evil of soul, which goes against intellect] only power? Indeed, when one particular evil destroys the substance and another the power of the same thing, then that which destroys the substance is evil in a greater degree. But when destruction affects different [aspects] of different things, then there is no absurdity in 35 admitting that what destroys the power, being more remote from the nature of the good, exceeds in evil. For instance, the power of one thing may be better than the substance [of another], as in the case of the powers of the soul which are said to generate and preserve the substance of the body. Hence, it is this evil of the soul that Socrates in the *Republic* calls 'an altogether terrible evil', adding that it would not have been such had it been 'lethal'. For then it would swiftly 40 reduce the souls affected by it to non-existence.[286] However, it is better to be non-existent than to have an evil existence, as the first case is a privation of being, and the second a privation of the good. This also shows that corporeal evil is not more troublesome than malice is in souls. For corporeal evil when it intensifies leads to non-existence, whereas evil of the soul leads to an evil existence.[287]

If what we say is correct, we have just given an additional argu- 45 ment for [our claim] that matter is not the primary evil: indeed, body,

which is nearer to matter than souls are, is replete with a lesser evil. But one [would expect] that what is more remote from the good is worse, and that what participates more in evil a greater evil. But in
50   souls the evil is greater and in bodies less, because the order of the souls is different from that of the bodies. Indeed, among the souls those that dwell on high are completely pure, others admit <badness in their activity, and for these evil consists in the privation of> activity, and in yet others the reception of evil extends as far as their powers. And among bodies some always remain in order, whereas there are others whose activity and power vary at different times, and
55   yet others whose substance may receive evil. This much about the order [of evils].

[The causes of evil]

40. Next we would like to examine evil itself: what it is and what its nature is. But first we should look at the causes of evil and ask ourselves whether there is one and the same cause for all evils or not. For some say there is, but others deny this.
5   Some indeed say that there is a fount of evils, and from this fount is produced every evil of whatever kind;[288] others posit a maleficent soul as the principle of the nature of evil and say that the evils are generated from there.[289] Others again take a middle position[290] and leave forms of evils in the intellective nature, from which, they claim, evils have their procession just like all other things.
10   Philosophers come to those conclusions from different suppositions; some of them even make Plato the father of their doctrines.[291] Those, indeed, who place the ideas of all things in the intellective realm adduce what is said by Socrates in the *Theaetetus* as corroboration of their doctrine, namely, that there are two kinds of 'paradigms, the one divine and the other godless'.[292] Others cite the
15   Athenian stranger, who introduces two kinds of soul, 'the one beneficent, the other the opposite of beneficent', and asserts that the universe is governed by the first of these alone, but the mortal realm by both.[293] In general, if one must posit a unique cause of evils, then it is cogent to think that this cause is either divine or intellective or
20   psychical. For gods, intellects and souls have received the rank of causes.[294] Of the other things, some are their instruments, others are their simulacra and images produced in something else.
       41. In answer to those who contend that there is a fount of evils, what has been said before is sufficient. For all the gods and all the founts are causes of good. They neither are nor ever will be causes of any evil. As we have said before,[295] and as Socrates in the *Phaedrus* asserts, if 'everything divine is good, beautiful and wise',[296] either it
5   [i.e. this alleged fount of evil] will act contrary to its nature when contriving the generation of evil things, or everything that takes its

existence from there will have the character of the good and will be the offspring of the goodness that remains in itself.[297] But, as they say, it does not pertain to fire to refrigerate, nor to good to produce evil from itself.[298] Hence, one of two things must follow: either evil must not be said to be evil, if it is of divine origin, or evil exists and has no divine origin. But we have shown[299] above that it exists. Therefore, 'there must be other causes of evil, not god' – as Plato himself somewhere teaches,[300] establishing that for all good things the procession is from one cause, and referring the generation of evil things to other causes, not to the divine cause. For everything that takes its existence from there is good. Hence the whole is good. And the light of goodness, which is as it were the light of the heart,[301] is in the gods, whereas all other light and brightness is from this light, and also all power and every single part of its power.

But blessed and truly happy are those who say that evil things, too, are adorned by the gods, and that the unlimitedness of evil things is measured and their darkness bounded by them, insofar as evils, too, receive a portion of the good and are allotted the power to exist. These people have called this cause by which evils, too, are adorned and ordered the fount of evils, not in that it were the mother that gives birth to them – for it is inconceivable that the first causes of beings would be the principle[s] of the generation of evils – but as providing them with limit and end, and as illuminating their darkness by its own light. Indeed, for evils, too, the unlimited is due to partial causes, and limit to universal causes. Therefore, for particular things evil is real evil, but for wholes it is not evil.[302] For the unlimited exists in them [i.e. in the particular things] not according to power (so that their unlimitedness would enable them to participate in the nature of the good), but because of a lack of power, whereas they are corroborated, in a sense, by the good through the participation of limit.

42. The people who are of such an opinion believe that not even the generation of evils is without order and make god also the cause of the order of evils. It seems to me, however, that not only the barbarians[303] but also the most eminent of the Greeks[304] acknowledge in the gods knowledge[305] of all things, both good and evil, but they let the good things come directly from the gods, evil things only insofar as they, too, have received a portion of good and a power to be and a limit. Evil is not unmixed evil, as we have said repeatedly, but it is evil in one respect and good in another. And insofar as it is good, it is from the gods; but insofar as it is evil, it is from another, impotent, cause.[306] For all evil comes about through impotence and lack, just as the good gets its existence from and in power, for the power is of and in the good.[307] Indeed, if evil were exclusively evil without an admixture, it would be unknown to the gods, who are good and have the power to make all things good that derive their being from them, that is all things of which they have knowledge, since their cognitions are active powers, and creative of all beings of which they are said to be cognitions. Given, however, that evil is simultaneously evil and, in another respect, good, and not partly good, partly evil, and that everything which it is is good and rather good [than evil], because it is such for the whole[308] – [given all this,] neither the knowledge that is in the gods nor the generation that stems from them is to be

20   abolished. No, the gods know and produce evil *qua* good.[309] Hence, in the same way as they know it, they have it, and with them the causes of evils are the powers that impart good to the nature of those evils, just as one might say of the forms that they are intellective powers formative of formless nature.[310]

43. It is a good thing, however, that our discussion has led us to speak of forms and the order of forms. Could evils and the generation of evils pertain perhaps to them, as well?[311] If not, from where do evils, too, obtain the property of being incessant? For everything that exists perpetually, proceeds from some immobile and definite cause.[312] If, therefore, evil perpetually 'revolves about our mortal region',[313] what

5   is this perpetuity and from where does it come? For we cannot say that it proceeds from any other cause than that which always exists in the same manner, that is, from an immutable nature. But this is precisely the nature of the forms, and that which always exists, is good. And what, indeed, will come about in intellect that is not good? If then a being residing in intellect is good, whatever comes about in accordance with the forms is good – for that which is assimilated to

10   the good is good, whereas evil, insofar as it is evil, is not disposed to be assimilated to good. We call the person who assimilates himself to the intellective forms perfect and happy. But it is the complete opposite for the evil person: him we call miserable and unhappy. For the evil person, insofar as he is evil, does not assimilate himself to the intellect.[314] This being the case, it is clear that there will be no

15   paradigms of evils in intellect. For every image is an image of a paradigm. If, however, Plato calls the forms the most divine of beings – for the Eleatic Stranger says that a 'perpetual sameness of existence pertains only to the most divine of all things'[315] – and if, as we have said,[316] the paradigm of evil is 'godless and dark',[317] how could we maintain that such a nature is present in the forms, and derive evil

20   from there? Moreover,[318] if the demiurge of the universe with whom all the forms and the series of forms are to be found, did not want evil to exist in the universe, and 'wished to generate all things similar to himself',[319] and did not wish to generate evil, how then would he still contain a paradigm of evils, he who makes 'all things good and does not allow anything to be bad'?[320] For it is not the case that he creates

25   and generates using some forms only, while being sterile and ineffectual with respect to others. No, by his very being he produces all things, and he acts in an undivided manner.[321] And a form of evil [i.e. if it existed in the demiurge] would generate evil, so that the demi-

urge would not exclusively do what he wanted, and his will would not be in accordance with his nature. It would be as if fire that warms but also dries wanted to do the one but not the other. Hence, one of two things is necessary: either the divine intellect wishes evil things to exist and to be generated, if the demiurge according to his own essence is the father of evils, too; or, not willing them, he will neither generate nor produce them nor possess their forms (the forms by which he brings all encosmic beings into existence).

44. However, this argument is not sufficient even to persuade itself of its truth, as it often shifts towards contrary conclusions. But if we assert that evil is perpetual and, admitting that the causes of perpetual beings are immobile, refuse to accept such a cause to be evil, there should be no reason for surprise. For we call 'eternal' that which has a progression towards being according to nature, but not what comes to be in any way whatever. Hence this 'revolving about'[322] must apply to evils, not insofar as each is evil, but in that these evils too are adorned by the order of the universe and especially by the heaven: it gives a share of eternity to things generated, of circular periodicity to rectilinear motions,[323] of order to disorderly things, of boundary to indeterminate things, of goodness to evil things. Everything, therefore, that exists according to nature and exists always, is generated from a definite cause, but evil is not according to nature. For there is no rational principle of limping in nature, just as there is no principle of artlessness in art.[324]

Why then should we look for an immobile principle in their case? And what could be a rational principle of evils in the forms, if all things that come about in accordance with them are forms and limits, whereas the nature of evil things is unlimited and indeterminate in itself?

45. In the third place, therefore, we have to consider the soul, and ask ourselves if that soul, which we call maleficent,[325] is to be blamed as the cause of all evils. Is it either the essence of this soul to generate evil and to infect with malice all things to which it comes close, just like it is the essence of fire to warm and not to refrigerate anything – and just as other things each have their own function? Or does this soul, though invariably good by nature, nevertheless in its activities behave now in this way, then in another way, projecting now this, then that kind of life? If the latter should be the reason it is called maleficent, not <only> the irrational soul must be called maleficent, but also the soul that is superior to it and from which it derives its good, for this soul, too, can change to better and worse states. If, on the other hand, it is maleficent in its essence and by its very being, as some maintain, from where shall we say that it derives this being? From any other source than from the demiurgic cause and the encosmic gods? And how is it possible that it should not proceed from these causes,[326] from which the species of mortal life originates? But if it

proceeds from these, how can it be evil in substance? Indeed, these
15   causes and their offspring are good. And in general all evil is outside
the substance and is not substance. For nothing is contrary to substance,[327] but good is contrary to evil. Substance is an image of being;
being, on the other hand, is situated in the good and generates all
things according to the good; and nothing that comes from there is
evil.

If however the Athenian stranger[328] calls 'maleficent' such a soul on
20   account of the evil in its powers and activities, [we must say that] even
that soul does not always remain, [but is now in this, then in that
state. If the irrational soul persists,] whereas this soul can somehow
also be made good and can adapt its own activities to a superior soul,
why wonder? There is indeed a kind of soul that is disposed to
preserve itself, whereas another is incapable of reverting to itself. And
25   the soul that has made itself evil but then takes on a good aspect
possesses measure and reason [in itself], whereas the other has them
from elsewhere,[329] because body, too, and all things that receive
movement from something else, have being and goodness of being
because of something else and as something from the outside.

46. But it would be absurd and sacrilegious,[330] so to speak, to make
such a soul the cause of evils, since it is neither for the body the cause
of all evils that are in it, nor for a superior soul. Indeed for the latter,
evil and weakness come from the soul itself, as the mortal life-form is
5   woven onto the soul when it descends; but weakness is already there
before the soul has been allotted generation, as the downward fall of
the soul is not to be imputed to anything else than to its weakness and
incapacity for contemplation.[331] We do not flee from the contemplation
of being nor does disorder affect our contemplation when we are both
capable of and agreeable to being established in the intellective
realm. Nor is it in any way possible for those who are capable [of
seeing] not to see what is in the superior realm merely because they
10   do not want to see. Indeed, even at a distance 'all souls aspire to what
is above'; 'but,' Plato says, 'when they are impotent they are carried
around in a submerged condition'.[332]

Hence, weakness alone remains as an explanation. For 'the eyes of
the soul cannot bear to look' at truth itself and at 'the brightness' of
the higher world.[333] Therefore, evil is present in the soul, not as a
consequence of its 'secondary life'[334] but from much earlier on.[335]

15   But the way in which evil is present in this soul and why Plato has
called this soul maleficent has been explained sufficiently for the
present. For its unmeasuredness and indeterminateness are contrary
to measure and the limits that proceed from reason. And not only is
this soul deprived of these; it does not even desire to attain them. If
one looks at all of this, then, one will call that soul maleficent and
20   contrary to reason, not because it would be something which has been
allotted this kind of nature, but rather something that has this

inclination,[336] although it is capable of being drawn away from itself towards better things.

47. But if these are not the causes of evils, what then will we ourselves claim to be the cause of their coming to be?[337] By no means should we posit one cause that is a unique, *per se* cause of evils. For if there is one cause of good things, there are many causes of evils, and not one single cause.[338] If all good things are commensurate with, similar to, and friendly with one another, with evils it is the complete opposite: neither among themselves nor in relation to good beings do they have a common measure. Indeed, if things that are similar to one another must have one antecedent cause, but things that are dissimilar a multitude of causes – for all things that stem from one cause are friendly and sympathetic to each other and 'affable',[339] some to a greater, others to a lesser degree – we have to posit not one cause of evils, but a multitude of causes, some for souls, others for bodies, and examine evil from these causes and in these causes.[340]

And it seems to me that Socrates in the *Republic* intimates this, when he says that the divinity is not to be held responsible: 'we must look for some other causes of evils.'[341] For by these words he signifies that these causes are many and indefinite, and that they are particular. For what monad or what boundary or what eternal principle could there be for evils, the very being of which, down to the level of individual beings, is naturally defined by dissimilitude and indefiniteness? The whole, on the contrary, is everywhere without badness.

48. These, then, are the efficient causes of evil, and such are certain souls and the forms that exist in matter. For the former [i.e. the souls] throw themselves into evil, whereas the latter [i.e. the forms in matter], being adverse to each other, create room for the coming to be of the unnatural, since that which is according to nature for one thing is unnatural for another. If you wish to have a paradigm of evils as well, you might refer to 'that godless and dark thing', revealed by Socrates in the *Theaetetus*,[342] a form of badness 'revolving with necessity around the mortal nature'. Indeed, souls assimilate themselves to evil beings and exchange the assimilation to what is better for the life of these evil beings. For the soul does behold the paradigms of good things when it is converted to itself and to beings superior to itself; there the primarily good things and the summits of beings 'seated on their holy seat'[343] exist, in separation. But when it beholds paradigms of evil things it looks at things external to and inferior to itself, things that are particular and external to themselves, disorderly and indefinite and irregular by their own nature. These things are deprived of the good things and the things by which 'the eye of the soul'[344] is 'nourished' and 'watered'[345] so that it can lead its own life.

Hence, the efficient causes of evils are not reasons and powers, but lack of power, weakness, and a discordant communion and mixture of dissimilar things. Nor are they some immobile paradigms that always

20   remain the same, but rather such as are unlimited and indeterminate
      and are borne along in other things – unlimited things, that is.

      49. Certainly one must not put the final cause of all among the
      causes of evil. Indeed, it would not be suitable that the good were the
      goal of evils. But since souls pursue what is in every way good and do
      everything, including evil things, for its sake, someone might perhaps
      think that for evils, too, the good is the final cause. For all things are
5   for the sake of this good, all the good and all the contrary things alike.
      Indeed, when we act badly, we do so out of ignorance as to the nature
      of these deeds, despite our desire for the good. And perhaps it will be
      better to make neither the efficient cause, nor the natural paradigm,
      nor the *per se* final cause the principal cause of evils. For the form of
10   evils, their nature, is a kind of defect, an indeterminateness and a
      privation; their [mode of existence, or] *hupostasis*, is, as it is usually
      said, more like a kind of [parasitic existence, or] *parupostasis*.[346]

      Therefore, evil is often said to be involuntary.[347] Indeed, how could
      it be voluntary if it is done for the sake of the good, whereas according
      to what it actually is, it is that which is neither desirable to nor willed
      by any being? We shall, however, discuss these things elsewhere.

15   But from what has been said it is evident that the evil in souls
      arises from weakness and from the pull of the inferior – for, as Plato
      says, the horse that participates in evil becomes heavy, and verges to
      the earth[348] – and that evil in bodies arises from the mixture of
      dissimilar things, I mean form and the formless, or from the mixture
      of contrary rational principles.[349]

[The mode of existence and the nature of evil]

      50. We must next consider what the mode of evil is and how it comes
      into existence from the above-mentioned causes and non-causes. Here
      we have to bring in the aforementioned *parupostasis* [i.e. parasitic
      existence]. For there is no other way of existing for that which neither
      is produced, in any way whatever, from a principal cause, nor has a
5   relation to a definite goal and a final cause, nor has received in its own
      right an entry into being, since anything whatever that exists prop-
      erly must come from a cause in accordance with nature – indeed,
      without a cause it is impossible for anything to come about[350] – and
      must relate the order of its coming about to some goal.[351]

      In which class of things should we, then, place evil? It would belong
10   to the beings that have their being accidentally and on account of
      something else, and not from a principle of their own, would it not?
      For we do everything and we act in our own right for the sake of
      participation in the good, gazing on it, and, as it were, being in labour
      for it and always desiring it. The resulting [action] is in some respect
      right, and in another not right: insofar as we consider what is not good
15   as good, it is not right; but insofar as we endeavour to obtain the good

through our action, it is right.[352] We are also right insofar as we envisage the good in its universality, but as considering the good in particular, we are wrong. What is desirable to us is thus something other than that which happens and which is attained, the first being the nature of the good, the latter the contrary.

Therefore, if generation of the contrary takes place, in whichever way this comes about, because of the weakness of the agent or because of the incommensurability with that which actually happens, would we be right in saying that it exists rather than that it exists parasitically upon what happens? Or is it not rather the case that existence belongs to those beings that proceed from causes towards a goal, but parasitic existence to beings that neither appear through causes in accordance with nature nor result in a definite end?

Evils, then, do not have a principal cause for their generation, a so-called efficient cause – for neither is nature the cause of what happens contrary to nature, nor is reason the cause of what happens contrary to reason – nor do evils attain the final goal, for the sake of which everything that comes about exists. Therefore it is appropriate to call such generation a parasitic existence [*parupostasis*], in that it is without end and unintended, uncaused in a way and indefinite. For neither is there one cause for it, nor does that which is a cause in its own right and a principal cause produce effects for the sake of evil itself and the nature of evil, nor [is this the case for] anything which is not a principal cause nor a cause in its own right. No, it is the exact opposite: everything that is produced, is produced for the sake of the good; but evil, coming from outside and being adventitious,[353] consists in the non-attainment of that which is the appropriate goal of each thing.

The non-attainment is due to the weakness of the agent, since the agent has received a nature of such a kind that a part of it is better, a part worse, each part being separate from the other. For where the One is, there at the same time is the good. But evil is – and the One is not – present in a split nature. For incommensurability, disharmony and contrariety are in multitude; and from these weakness and indigence proceed. Indeed, in the gods, too, are to be found the 'winged nature' and 'both horses';[354] but there 'these are all good, consist of good things' and not 'of contrary things'.[355] But in other beings these are mixed; in them there is multitude and diversity of powers, and each [of these powers] pulls towards different things. In the superior realm multitude looks at the One and is determined according to one kind of life. But where multitude and diversity appear because of a decrease in union, there lack of power appears – for all power is what it is by the One and from the One –, as well as disharmony and dissidence of one thing from the other, each being drawn by its own desires.

50   So we have explained the way in which evils are produced, what
the so-called *parupostasis* is, and where it comes from.

51. Now we have to say what the nature of evil itself is.[356] It will
appear, however, to be the most difficult of all things to know the
nature of evil in itself, since all knowledge is contact with form and is
a form,[357] whereas evil is formless and like a kind of privation. But
5   perhaps even this will become clear, if we look at the good itself and
at the number of good things and thus consider what evil is.[358] For just
as the primary good surpasses all things, so evil itself is destitute of
all good things – I mean insofar as it is evil – and is a lack and
privation of these.

Regarding the good, we have remarked elsewhere[359] on its exten-
sion, on the manner in which it exists, and on the orders it possesses.
With respect to evil, on the other hand, we should say the following.
10   From the fact that *qua* evil it is a complete privation of goodness, it
follows that:

(1)   as evil it is deprived of the fount of good things;
(2.1.1) as unlimited [it is deprived] of the first limit;[360]
(2.1.2) as weakness [it is deprived] of the power that resides there;[361]
(2.1.3) as incommensurate and false and ugly [it is deprived] of
         'beauty', 'truth' and 'measure'[362] – by which the mixed is
         produced, and in which the henads of beings reside;[363]
15   (2.2)   as being unfounded in its own nature, and unstable, it is
         deprived of 'eternity which remains in one'[364] – and of the
         power of eternity; for 'not in the same way' is typically said of
         impotence;
(2.3)   as privation[365] and lifelessness it is deprived of the first
         monad of forms and of the life that is there.

And if evil is destructive, and the cause of division for any being to
which it is present,[366] and imperfect, it is deprived of (3) the goodness
that perfects complete beings. For the destructive leads from (3.1)
20   being to non-being; the divisive destroys (3.2) the continuity and
union of being; and the imperfect prevents each thing from obtaining
(3.3) its perfection and natural order.

Moreover, the indefiniteness of the nature of evil is a failure and a
deprivation of the (4.1) unitary summit; its barrenness is deprivation
of (4.2) the summit of fertility; and its inactivity is deprivation of (4.3)
25   the summit of demiurgy. Withdrawal, and weakness, and indeterminateness, then, consist in the privation of these goods, privation, that
is, of the monadic cause, of generative power, and of efficient creation.

But if evil is also the cause of dissimilitude, division, and disorder,
it is clearly necessary that it is deprived of (5) assimilative goods, and
of (5.1) the indivisible providence of divisible beings, and of the order
30   that exists in the divided beings. Since, however, the good is not

limited to this level, but there is also (6) the immaculate class, and the effective and the splendid in its accomplishments, evil then will be ineffectual, dark and material. Or from where will it obtain each of these and similar properties, if not from privations of these good things? For in the higher realm the good things exist primarily; and it is of these higher goods that also the good in us is a part and an image; and the privation of the good in us is evil. As a consequence it is also a privation of those goods, to which, as we claim, the good bears a resemblance. 35

And why say more, since it is obvious that evil in bodies is not only privation of the good that resides in them, but also of the good that prior to them resides in souls? For the good in bodies consists in being the image of the good in souls. Destruction, therefore, and the privation of form will be nothing other than the falling from intellective power, for form, too, is the offspring of Intellect, and that which produces forms is intellective in substance. 40

Now, about that which is in every sense evil this much has been said: it is a privation of goods and a deficiency.

52. From where does evil, its nature being such as we have explained, derive its opposition to the good? Let us explain this now.[367] Evil is indeed privation, though not complete privation.[368] For being coexistent with the very disposition of which it is privation, it not only weakens this disposition by its presence, but also derives power and form from it. Hence, whereas privations of forms, being complete privations, are mere absences of dispositions, and do not actively oppose them, privations of goods actively oppose the corresponding dispositions and are somehow contrary to them. For they are not altogether impotent and inefficacious; no, they are both coexistent with the powers of their dispositions, and, as it were, led by them to form and activity. 5

Plato, too, acknowledged this when he said that on its own injustice is weak and inactive,[369] but that through the presence of justice it acquires power and is led towards activity, not abiding in its own nature nor in mere lifelessness, because that which brings forth injustice, being vital, imparts even to evil a participation in life. All life, however, is essentially power. And once evil has established itself in a power that belongs to something else, evil is contrary to the good, and it uses the power proper to the latter in order to combat it. And the stronger the power is that inheres in evil, the greater will be the actions and works of evil; and the weaker its power, the more meagre its actions and works. 15

In fact, even in bodies the activity contrary to nature ceases proportionally to their physical powers, although when order is entirely dissolved the unnatural exists in greater degree.[370] Therefore, in souls, too, greater effects are produced from lesser vices, and lesser from greater.[371] For when a vice becomes isolated from its contrary, it 20

increases in ugliness and deformity, but diminishes in strength and
activity, becoming weak and ineffectual. For a vice does not have
25   power from itself, – such that an increase in power would be a
transition to more – but derives power from the presence of its
contrary. This would be as if, for instance, coldness could use the
power of warmth for its own purposes, vanquishing and subduing the
power of warmth. Hence, when the nature that is the contrary [of
some vice][372] is deficient, as far as privation is concerned the vice will
be greater as the deficiency increases; but as far as action is con-
30   cerned, it will be weaker as the power diminishes. It will be a greater
evil, but less effective.

53. If, then, we are right in our claims, we must assert that evil is
neither active nor powerful, but that it gets its capacity for acting and
its power from its contrary. Indeed, the good grows weak and ineffectual through its admixture with evil, and evil participates in power
and activity because of the presence of the good. Both indeed are
together in one [subject].
5   In bodies the contrary becomes matter for its contrary, and the
natural strengthens the unnatural – or from where come its measure,
cycles, and the order of its cycles, if not from natural numbers and
from its natural disposition?[373] – but the unnatural weakens the
natural, whereby [the body's] natural [capacity] to act disappears and
10   the order in which the well-being of nature consists is dissolved.
Likewise in souls, evil, when it vanquishes good, uses the power of the
latter on behalf of itself. That is, it uses the power of reason and its
inventions on behalf of the desires. And they communicate to each
other a part of their nature, the one giving a share of its power, the
other of its weakness, since evil in itself is not able to act or to have
15   power. For all power is something good, and all activity is the exten-
sion of some power. And how could evil still be a power, being evil to
those who [allegedly] possess this power, if it is the function of all
power to preserve the being that possesses it and in which it resides,
whereas evil dissolves everything of which it is the evil?[374]

54. Hence evil is ineffectual and impotent on its own. But if it is
also involuntary, as Plato says,[375] and unwilled,[376] it will also for this
reason be a privation of the foremost triad of the good: will, power and
activity.[377] For the good is willed, and powerful and efficacious on
5   account of its own nature, whereas evil is unwilled, weak and inefficacious. For no thing would desire that which may destroy it, nor does
it belong to a power to destroy what possesses it, nor does it belong to
an activity to have an existence that would not correspond to its
power.
But just as people desire evils which to them appear to be good, and
the evil appears to them as willed – for we call it thus on account of
10   its admixture with the good – likewise both power and productivity
exist only apparently in evil, because evil does not exist in its own

right nor *qua* evil, but is external to that upon which it is parasitic and in relation to which it is said to be evil. It seems to me that this is also shown by Socrates in the *Theaetetus*, to those who are capable of following him more or less, when he calls evil neither a privation nor contrary to the good. For privation is not capable of producing anything, and has indeed no capacity at all. Nor does the contrary of itself possess a power or activity. But Socrates calls evil a 'subcontrary' (*hupenantion*) somehow, since in itself it is a privation indeed, though not an absolutely complete privation, but a privation that, together with a disposition and participating in the power and activity of this disposition, assumes 'the part of the contrary'.[378] And it is neither a complete privation, nor contrary to the good, but subcontrary to it. And to those who are accustomed to listen attentively to what he says it is clear that *parupostasis* [i.e. a parasitic existence][379] is what is really meant. From what we have said it is clear what evil is, which nature it has, how and whence it exists.

[Different types of evils]

55. Let us speak next of the [specific] differences in evil and determine how many they are and what they are. We have said earlier already that one kind of evil is in the souls, another in bodies, and that evil in souls is twofold, one residing in the irrational type of life, the other in reason. Let us repeat once again: there are three things in which evil exists, namely, the particular soul, the image of the soul, and the body of individual beings.[380] Now for the soul that is above, the good consists in being according to intellect – because intellect is prior to it. For the irrational soul it consists in being according to reason – because for each thing being good comes from the thing immediately superior to it. And for the body again it is being in accordance with nature, because nature is the principle of motion and rest for it.[381] If this is the case, it is necessary that evil for the first is being contrary to intellect, as being subcontrary to what is according to intellect; for the second it is being contrary to reason, as in its case being good means being according to reason; and for the third it is being contrary to nature. These three species of evil inhere in the three natures that are liable to weaken because of the decline into partial being. For wholes, as we have often asserted, are in permanent possession of their own good, whereas evil resides down here, I mean in particular and individual beings; in these latter beings lack of power occurs because of the decline in their very being, as well as an increase of division, when their union is weakened.[382]

56. In general there is one [type of] evil in souls and another in bodies; of these evils, that in souls is again twofold, with 'disease' on the one hand, and 'foulness' on the other,[383] as the Eleatic Stranger somewhere says.[384] Foulness is 'ignorance' and privation of intellect;

disease, on the other hand, is 'discord' inside the soul and deficiency in the life according to reason. In this respect, too, evil will be threefold,[385] and each of these kinds will in its turn be twofold. Foulness indeed differs according to whether it concerns discursive thinking or opinion[386] – as in these cases also the [mode of] cognition is different – and may be either lack of knowledge or lack of skill.[387]

10 And also disease differs according to whether it affects cognitions or impulses[388] (appetites are not according to reason, just like many of the sense-perceptions and precipitate sense-images[389]). For those whose life consists in practical activity, [disturbance comes about] because of opposing appetites; for those whose life consists in contemplation, the intervention of sense-images destroys the purity and

15 immaterial character of their contemplations. That which is contrary to nature,[390] too, may be twofold: foulness in the body is contrary to nature, as it, too, is a weakness and a deficiency with respect to form; in the case of disease, the order and proportion inherent in the body are dissolved.

57. In so many ways, therefore, is evil to be divided. Since the measures of beings are also to be found in the same three principles – nature, soul, and intellect – likewise unmeasuredness is privation either of the reasons inherent in nature, or of those inherent in soul,

5 or of those inherent in and generated from intellect. For that which imparts order to each thing is better than what is ordered by it primarily – I mean what primarily imparts order to each [of them]. Such is nature in bodies, reason in the irrational kinds of life, and in the rational souls the good that is prior to them[391] And for images [of souls] [the good] exists because of the superior soul, insofar as all

10 these images also depend on such a soul, or because of that which is an external principle, providing good for the beings over which it exercises its providence. Finally, the good for bodies comes from a particular for some; for others, from a universal nature.

[Providence and evil]

58. Perhaps someone may raise the question of how evils can exist and where they come from, given the existence of providence. [For there seem to be only two possibilities:] if there is evil, how will it not stand in the way of that which is providential towards the good? On the other hand, if providence fills the universe, how can there be evil in beings? Some thinkers indeed yield to one of the two lines of reasoning: either they admit that not everything comes from provi-

5 dence, and <acknowledge there is evil, or they> deny the existence of evil, and maintain that everything comes from providence and the good. And this indeed is a troubling problem. But perhaps one may find a perspective from which both points of view do not conflict.[392]

Let us consider first this evil in souls in itself: if it were unmixed with its contrary and totally deprived of it, if it were utter darkness and nothing but darkness, then perhaps it would be an obstruction to the works of providence, from which come 'all the good things and nothing bad'.[393] But if, as we have already repeatedly stated, this evil is also good, if it is not an unmixed and absolute evil, but evil in a certain sense and not unqualifiedly evil,[394] then we must not, because of its participation in the good, deny that it exists, nor because of the wickedness that resides in it, deny that all things, including this [evil] itself, are good and become good.

After all, saying that god is the cause of all things is not the same as saying that he is the only cause of all things. The former statement is correct, the latter is not. For intellect, too, is the cause of all things that are posterior to it, and soul of the things that follow it, and nature of bodies and all things pertaining to bodies. Each of these produces in a different way, the one primordially and unitarily, the other eternally, the next by self-movement and the last through necessity.[395] And neither is that which produces intellectively the same as that which is prior to it, nor as that which is posterior *qua* posterior. If then all things come from providence and no thing is evil insofar as it is through providence that it exists and comes to be, why would it be absurd to admit that evil may have a place among beings insofar as it gets its existence from soul? And the same thing will be evil to particular things, but good for the whole. Or rather, is it not the case that even for particular things it will only be evil insofar as it stems from those things themselves, but not evil insofar as it stems from the whole?[396] For not only activity has its goodness from providence, but also the agent.

How then is there good in them, I mean in the evils inherent in souls? For only thus does providence keep its credibility and does not leave any of these evils in the soul deprived of itself. Now, these evils, too, must be held to be twofold: some internal, belonging to and affecting the soul itself, for instance in the case of inappropriate impressions or wrong assents or choices that are base in some way; others exterior and manifesting themselves in various actions that are done out of anger or desire.[397]

59. Now, all such things have in many ways good effects. For they happen for the punishment of other beings, and the action performs what is deserved.[398] Moreover, acting badly towards a being that needs suffering is not the same thing as acting badly towards any being whatever. These actions are totally good as well to the one who suffers them as to the one who performs them, insofar as the latter follows the designs of the whole. But insofar as he does not follow these, but performs such an action for his own motives, he does evil, and he gives in to the woes of his soul that are not appropriate to him nor grand. For the sufferer, it is nevertheless the beginning of salvation.[399] For many people conceal the evil which they contrive and

which stays inside the soul, and make it [appear] good, as it [really]
is shameful and inappropriate, but when the evil is performed its
10   nature becomes evident. This is shown by the repentance and remorse
of the soul that reproaches itself, as it were, for the evil deed. In
medicine, too, doctors open ulcers and thus make evident the ailment
and the inwardly concealed cause of the disease. [In so doing,] they
display an image of the workings of providence, that hands [souls]
over to shameful doings and passions in order that they may be freed
15   from their pain,[400] as well as this festering condition, swollen up with
evils, and then begin a better cycle and a better [type of] life.[401]

And all the internal passions of a soul that make the soul evil
possess goodness, in the sense that they always lead the soul towards
what is appropriate to it. For it is not possible for the soul to choose
the inferior and still remain among superior things. No, the soul will
soon be dragged towards darkness and baseness. And not only the
20   actions of the soul, but also its choices, even without action, are
punished. For every choice leads the soul towards a state similar [to
what has been chosen]. If then anything that is depraved, base and
godless in the soul will bring it to a like condition, the soul will soon
have what is good for it, namely that which it deserves according to
providence.[402] Such is the law [implanted] in the souls,[403] which guides
each soul to what is appropriate to it, one soul projecting [some type
25   of] life, while another attaches itself to things similar to it;[404] this is
tantamount to the soul getting either what it deserves, or what is just,
[in other words], either what is according to providence, or what is
good.

If it were the fortune of the souls that act unjustly to remain above
– what an awful thing to say! – their choice would in no way exhibit
30   well-being. For their choice, being nothing but evil, would be utterly
godless and unjust. But if the choice removes the soul immediately
from the superior realities, then it possesses the good from there,
mixed with evil: for every soul by nature strives for that which is
superior. Hence, when souls fall, the shamefulness of their life becomes manifest to them. But every soul that does not operate
35   according to intellect necessarily falls, and for some the fall is steeper,
for others less, since the choices that they make are different too.

60. But how is the evil inherent in bodies at the same time good?
Is it because it is according to nature for the whole, but contrary to
nature for the part? Or rather, is it even for the part according to
nature insofar as it operates for the benefit of the whole, and contrary
to nature when cut from the whole?[405]

5   The evil inherent in bodies, as well, is twofold, one kind existing as
foulness, the other as disease[406] – I call foul all things contrary to
nature that are not diseases, for monsters, too, are foulnesses of
nature. Of these two kinds, [let us first consider] foulness. Foulness
is in accordance with universal nature, as reason and form are to be

found in it, <yet not in accordance with particular nature.> Indeed, in
a particular nature there is one rational principle, and what is 10
contrary to it is for this thing against nature, but in universal nature
all the rational principles and forms exist naturally. And (1) sometimes one thing only is generated out of one form – for 'man is
begotten by man', properly speaking;[407] (2) sometimes many things
are generated out of one thing – for of a [certain] figure [there is only]
one formula, but [there are] many figures [that exist] in accordance
with this formula;[408] (3) sometimes one thing is generated out of many, 15
as in the case of mixtures of matter-related forms – these mixtures
seem to be monsters with respect to the individual nature, which
desires to be dominated by and exist according to a single form; (4)
sometimes many things are generated from many things – equality
and inequality indeed are in many things. All the forms then, both
unmixed and mixed, are according to nature, and depend on the 20
rational principles in nature, that are all from the higher realm.

As to diseases, they are according to nature in another way, for each
of those evils is generated, as we say, in a twofold manner, according
to both the universal and the particular nature. What is perishable is
in accordance with the universal but contrary to the particular nature. For the species into which that which perishes is transformed
possesses a rational principle from universal nature, a rational principle that is contrary to the nature of the former thing [i.e. the thing
that perishes], and it has this rational principle not from the former 25
thing but from the whole. Insofar as transmutation is from above, it
is according to nature. It destroys some things and gives generation
to others. Insofar as there is a single rational principle in the thing
that changes, it is unnatural – indeed, when it concerns [the thing] as
a whole, the change is unnatural, for every being is a whole according 30
to the rational principle inherent in it; however, when it concerns [the
thing as] a portion of a whole, it is in accordance with nature, because
for the whole it is produced from another thing that is destroyed, and
its destruction again leads to the generation of another thing.[409]

61. Hence the evil in bodies is not evil without admixture. But in a
sense it is evil, insofar as it does not stem from the higher realm,
whereas in another sense it is good, insofar as it stems from natural
providence. And in general, how could one say that things that come
to be because of the good are completely divested of the good and 5
remain deprived of the nature of the good? For it is not possible that
evil exists without taking the appearance of its contrary, the good,
since everything is for the sake of the good,[410] even evil itself. But then
all things are for the sake of the good, and divinity is not the cause of
evils.[411] For never is evil *qua* evil derived from there; it stems from
other causes, which, as we have said, are able to be productive not on
account of power but on account of weakness. That is the reason, I 10
think, why Plato arranges everything there is around the king of

everything, and asserts that everything is because of him, including the things that are not good, for they appear as good and are part of the beings. In the same spirit he names this the cause of all good things; he does not just say 'all things', for it is not the cause of evil things.[412] But while it is not the cause of evils, nonetheless it is the cause of all being. Indeed it is a cause of evils only in that they are beings and insofar as each of them is good.

Now, if we are right in stating this, all things will be from Providence *and* evil has its place among beings. Therefore the gods also produce evil, but *qua* good. The gods know[413] evil, since they possess a unitary knowledge of everything, an undivided knowledge of divisibles, a good knowledge of evils, a unitary knowledge of plurality. For the knowledge of the soul differs from that of intellect, which again differs from that of the gods themselves. For the knowledge of the soul is self-moving, that of intellect is eternal, and that of the gods is ineffable and unitary, knowing and producing everything by the One itself.

Notes

1. Proclus' opening question is clearly reminiscent of the title and opening phrases of Plotinus *Ennead* 1,8[51]: 'On what are and whence come evils. Those who enquire whence evils come [...] would make an appropriate beginning of their inquiry if they proposed the question first, what evil is and what is its nature. In this way one would know whence it came and where it is founded and to what it belongs as an accident, and one would be able to decide the general question whether it belongs to beings' (1,8, title; 1,1-6, transl. after A.H. Armstrong). Of the last question (*ei estin en tois ousin*), Proclus at 2,1-2 says it should be the very first. Plotinus' question as to what it is that evil belongs to as an accident (*hotôi sumbebêke*) will be taken up by Proclus at 30,3. On the similarity between the opening words of *DMS* and the ancient title(s) of *Enn.* 1,8, see also Henry (1961 [=1938]), p. 8.

2. Perhaps a reminiscence of the *Seventh Letter* (341D12).

3. *kat'aitian proêgoumenên*. See chs 40-9 for a causal analysis of evil. Proclus will argue that there are only accidental causes and no principal cause of evil(s).

4. i.e. different from the principle of being. Plotinus claims that there is a *principle* for evil, namely at 1,8[51],6,33-4: 'there are two principles (*arkhai*), one of good things, the other of evils.' Plotinus does not want to say that matter is a selfsubsisting principle – he actually holds the view that matter is generated by something else, a lower soul –, but rather a principle in the sense that it is the absolute starting-point for all evils: there are no evils prior to matter. See Opsomer (2001b), pp. 4-8.

5. In this paragraph the structure of the whole treatise is set out. The question whether evils exist or not will be dealt with in chs 2-9; in chs 10-39 Proclus looks at the different ontological levels (in much more detail than suggested by the dichotomy intelligible-sensible) in order to see where evil first occurs; chs 40-9 contain a causal analysis of evil; its mode of existence and the question 'how it can exist if its being is insubstantial' is dealt with in chs 50-4 [its characteristics are discussed in ch. 51; chs 52-4 deal with the question how evil can be opposed to the good]; the question 'where it begins and up to which point it proceeds' is explicitly mentioned in ch. 39 and also discussed in chs 55-7, where the different forms of evils are explained (those of bodies and those of souls); the traditional problem of providence and evil is discussed in chs 58-61. See our Introduction, 3. Analysis.

6. In the extant commentaries, Proclus discusses evil at *in Tim.* 1,372,25-381,21; *in Remp.* 1,37,37,2-39,1; 1,96,1-100,20; 2,89,6-91,18; *in Parm.* 829,23-831,24. See also the other *opuscula*. Also *TP*, written after *DMS*, contains a discussion of evil (1.18, pp. 83,12-88,10). Cf. our Introduction, 1.1.

7. Plotinus deals with this question only at the end of *Ennead* 1,8: cf. 1,8[51],15,5, but see also 1,8[51],3,2. Proclus at *in Tim.* 1,227,18-22 explicitly states that methodology requires that the question 'if it is' precede the question 'what it is'. Cf. Arist. *An. Post.* 2.1, 33b34.

8. The examples and metaphors of darkness and light throughout the treatise are reminiscent of the Platonic analogy between the the the sun and the good (*Resp.* 6, 508A-509C).

9. cf. Aristotle *Metaph.* 12.7, 1072b14; *EN* 1.1, 1094a3; Plot. 1,8[51],2,1-3, Procl. *ET* prop. 8. In metaphysical terms, this 'striving for' and 'desire for' the good is called the 'reversion' (*epistrophê*), that is the 'return' of everything towards its principle.

10. Literally 'subcontrary' (*hupenantion*), as at *Theaet.* 176A6. In the present chapter, where Proclus only presents the view of others, 'subcontrary' is not being used in the technical sense that it will receive in ch. 54.

11. *Theaet.* 176A6. Those philosophers who deny the existence of evil – whose view Proclus here presents – are forced to reject what Socrates says in the *Theaetetus*, namely that there must be something contrary to the good.

12. The argument actually is Syrianus': cf. Procl. *in Tim.* 1,374,15-18; *TP* 1.18, p. 86,20-1. Plotinus, on the contrary, does not appear to distinguish between what is contrary to the forms and what is contrary to what is beyond the forms: cf. 1,8[51],6,27-8.

13. *amenênoteron*, from *amenênos*, a poetic word (e.g. *Iliad* 5,887; *Odyssey* 10,521; 536; 19,562), used in prose texts: Tim. Locr. 100C; Arist. *HA* 628b4; *Probl.* 899a31; Plot. 3,6[26],7,30; 6,6[34],8,11; Procl. *in Parm.* 823,8; 834,23; 1098,34; *in Tim.* 3,95,11 ('*amenênon* and closest to non-being'). 'As the saying goes' (*ut pronuntiavit sermo*) could be a reference to the Chaldean Oracles (as in *De prov.* 42,15-16 *qui a deo traditi sermones*); see also 38,28.

14. Proclus is thinking of people committing suicide to escape from a miserable life; in doing so they prefer non-being to something that is worse (the argument seems to require that death indeed is the end of everything, at least in the mind of the people who argue along these lines). Cf. *in Alc.* 144,4-7; 337,12-14; *in Remp.* 89,24-8; 90,25-6. Steel (1997), pp. 98-9.

15. *Tim.* 30A2-3 (see Introduction, 2.1, T3): 'God wanted (*boulêtheis*) that all things should be good and nothing bad (*agatha men panta, phlauron de mêden*), so far as this was attainable (*kata dunamin*).' The restriction at the end has conveniently been left out from the argument as presented by Proclus. Cf. *in Tim.* 1,372,19-373,21. The demiurge is called 'maker and father' at *Tim.* 28C3 (cf. 41A7; *Polit.* 273B2-3) and 'father' at 37C7. On the title 'father' according to Proclus, see *in Tim.* 1,311,25-313,2 and *TP* 5.16, and Opsomer (2000b).

16. The demiurge of the Timaeus creates 'by his very being' (*autôi to einai*). Cf. Opsomer *Les jeunes dieux* (forthcoming).

17. This is a standard phrase to denote the activity of the subordinate creators, i.e. the lower levels of production. See *Tim.* 41A7-D3. The universal demiurge creates everything directly and 'by his very being', but uses the lower creators as intermediaries. Cf. *TP* 5,69,20-1. The latter produce in a quasi-independent way (*hoion autourgountôn*). The lower creatures are then created directly by the universal demiurge *qua* beings, and by the subordinate demiurges *qua* lower. Cf. Opsomer (2000b).

18. A reference to the argument of chs 2-3.

19. For the idea of the fighting (the discord or 'civil war') that goes on between the different parts of the soul, see bk 4 of the *Republic* and the *Phaedrus* myth (246A-256E).

20. Proclus is referring to *akrasia* or incontinence.

21. On the disease of the soul see below, ch. 56 and Plato *Soph.* 227C10-228E5.

22. The word for vice (*kakia*, 'badness') is derived from *kakos*, 'evil', 'bad'.

23. Plotinus (1,8[51],5,6-8) seems to be in agreement with Proclus on this point. See however also 2,9[33],13,27-9.

24. cf. 6,11-35.

25. *Resp.* 10, 608E3-4: 'that which destroys and corrupts in every case is the evil; that which preserves and benefits is the good' (*to men apolluon kai diaphtheiron pan to kakon einai, to de sôizon kai ôpheloun to agathon*). As he is developing his argument, Socrates indeed also says that the soul yearns (*ephietai*) for what is truly good for it (611E1-3).

26. *Phaedr.* 245E1 (*pasan te genesin sumpesousan stênai*). Cf. *in Parm.* 998,29.

27. *Tim.* 41B7-C2 (the speech to the young gods): 'Three classes of mortal beings (*thnêta genê*) remain to be created. Without them the universe will be incomplete (*atelês*), for it will not contain all the classes of living beings which it ought to contain, if it is to be sufficiently perfect (*teleos hikanôs*).'

28. *Tim.* 34B8-9: 'he created the world a blessed god (*eudaimona theon*).'

29. *Tim.* 31B1 (*homoion tôi pantelei zôiôi*).

30. The words 'in which it exists primarily and per se' (*en hoî prôtôs esti kath' hauto*) are strongly reminiscent of Aristotle's definition of nature as a thing's internal principle of motion and rest. 'Nature,' Aristotle says (*Phys.* 2.1, 292b21-3), 'is a principle or cause of being moved and of being at rest in that to which it belongs primarily, in virtue of itself and not accidentally' (*en hôi huparkhei prôtos kath' hauto kai mê kata sumbebêkos*). Proclus obviously alludes to the view of Plotinus, who posited a *nature* of evil (e.g. 1,8[51] 1,4; 2,1; 6,33). Proclus himself will insist that evil is always accidental, denying that it can be something natural. For the notion of an evil *inhering in* a thing, compare already Plato *Resp.* 609A9 (*to sumphuton kakon hekastou*). Commenting on this text (*in Remp.* 2,89,18-24), Proclus explains that a thing can only be destroyed by its own evil, that is a corruptive principle proper to it. 'Corruptive' is then to be taken as 'not accidentally corruptive' (*dei mê kata sumbebêkos lambanein to phthartikon*). If injustice were *per se* (*kath'hauto*) corruptive, it would invariably destroy all things in which it is present (*pantakhou kai en pasin*).

31. On the evils of bodies and those of souls see chs 39 and 55-6. It is not immediately clear what Proclus means here, and the text is probably corrupt (compare, however, 51,19-20). Some light may be shed on this obscure passage by looking at the tenth book of the *Republic*. There, following on the passage referred to at the beginning of this chapter, Socrates explains why the soul can never be destroyed. In doing so, he argues that whereas the evil of the body destroys the body (*apollumi*), 'leads it to no longer being a body' (*agei eis to mêde sôma einai*, 609C7) and 'to non-being' (*eis to mê einai*, D2), the soul is not destroyed by the evils proper to it (and neither by the evils alien to itself). The evils of the soul – Plato sums them up: injustice, licentiousness, cowardice, and ignorance (*adikia, akolasia, deilia, amathia*, 609B11-C1) – are not lethal, which makes them even worse (610D5-7): if injustice were fatal to its possessor, that would be a release from all evils (an idea Proclus will take up at 39,38-40). But it is quite the contrary: injustice could perhaps kill others, but renders its possessor very lively indeed (*mala zôtikon*) and wakeful (*agrupnon*), and makes him or her dwell far away from deadliness (610D5-E4). Commenting on this text (*in Remp.* 2,91,6-18), Proclus remarks that in the case of the soul, too, something is destroyed, viz. the activities of the rational soul. Now, the vices of the soul are actually only contrary to the rational soul; for the irrational soul they are perfectly natural. That is why the vices create a kind of separation of the irrational and the rational soul. A *complete* separation (*pantelês khôrismos*) extinguishes (*aposbennusin*) the life (*zôên*) of the rational soul. Probably this is what Proclus at *DMS* 5,24-6 means by 'vital corruption'.

32. i.e. from the highest principle of the order to which it belongs. The highest principle in any series is always monadic. The monad of the equal, e.g., is absolute equality.

33. In other words, from bad to good there is no continuum; injustice does not belong somewhere on a scale between good and bad, but is merely a gradation on the scale of the evil. Likewise, contrary to modern intuitions, hot and cold, being contraries, are here thought of as separate principles, each with their proper activity: decrease of warmth does not make something cold, only the principle of cold has that power. Cold, then, is a positive force in its own right. Cf. Plutarch of Chaeronea, *De primo frigido* (transl. W.C. Helmbold), e.g. 945F: 'Is there [...] an active principle or substance of cold (as fire is of heat) through the presence of which and through participation in which everything else becomes cold? Or is coldness rather a negation of warmth, as they say darkness is of light and rest of motion?' 946B-D: 'It is the nature of coldness, however, to produce affects and alterations in bodies that it enters no less than those caused by heat. [...] Moreover, the property whereby coldness promotes rest and resists motion is not inert, but acts by pressure and resistance [...]; since there are many other effects which may be seen to be produced through the agency of cold, we are not justified in regarding it as a negation. Besides, a negation does not permit degrees of less or more.'

34. i.e. the *locus classicus*, *Theaet.* 176A5-8: 'It is impossible, Theodorus, that evil things will cease to exist (*out'apolesthai ta kaka dunaton*), for it is necessary (*anankê*) that the good always has its contrary (*hupenantion ti tôi agathôi aei einai*); nor have they any place in the divine world, but by necessity (*ex anankês*) they revolve about our mortal nature and this place.' See Introduction, 2.1, T1.

35. On the necessity of corruption in order to have generation, see below ch. 60.

36. *Theaet.* 176A5-8. See n. 34; Introduction 2.1, T1.

37. e.g. *ET* 63; *in Alc.* 117,22-118,25, pp. 97-8.

38. i.e. their productive activity.

39. i.e. the so-called unparticipated Forms (*ET* 23), which are called unparticipated in order to emphasise their transcendence; they 'transcend all properties in others' (in this they differ from 'forms in matter', *enula eidê*). By 'overflowing' they nonetheless produce orders which 'in a sense' participate in them, and which are themselves 'participated in' by the lower orders. But the transcendent forms are not 'participated in' in the sense that this would diminish their power ('unparticipated', then, does not imply that nothing participates in them; it really means 'transcendent' or 'prior'; cf. Festugière (1967), tome II, pp. 51-2 n. 1). The 'unparticipated' forms of *ET* 23 are here called 'participated only' to differentiate them from the intermittent participants, which participate in the eternal participants, and the eternal participants, which participate and are participated. In short, Proclus distinguishes three levels: transcendent Forms, eternal participants, intermittent participants.

40. cf. *De dec. dub.* V, 28,5-6: in order for the universe to be perfect, as Plato says in the *Timaeus* (41B7-8), the first things should not also be the last. In *De dec. dub.* III, 10,12-14, Proclus explains that matter is inefficacious and sterile because there is nothing lower than it, whereas providence is most efficacious and fertile because everything is lower than it. See Procl., *in Alc.* 117,22-118,25, with Segonds's excellent *notes complémentaires* (1985, t. 1, p. 97 n. 5 and 6, pp. 189-190).

41. cf. *in Tim.* 1,372,19-373,21.

42. The problem with this reasoning is that a lesser participation in the good does not imply the existence of evil, since 'less good' is not yet evil, as has been pointed out in the previous chapter. Or, to look at it from a different angle, the argument does not explain why the mere existence of something that is not the good itself (being itself, the eternal participants) is not already evil (a view that is also strongly rejected by Plotinus). However, Proclus' own argument will be more subtle: the existence of intermittent participants (i.e. partial beings, which sometimes fail to participate in the good) is indeed necessary, but is in itself not yet evil; it is, however, a necessary condition and the ultimate metaphysical reason for the existence of evils. See Introduction, 2.4.1.

43. In the remainder of this chapter, Proclus anticipates his account of the special kind of privation that evil is. See chs 52-4.

44. i.e. privations of forms, not of the good.

45. Even before 'being', the One or the Good created the first limit and the first unlimitedness (i.e. the first power). Cf. *ET* 92, 82,31-5; *TP* 3.8, p. 32,2-5; 3.14, p. 51,6-7.

46. *amenênon*. See n. 13.

47. Proclus gives some examples, first of evils of the soul, then of bodily evils (the same distinction as in 5,23-6), which show that they cannot be complete privations of the good. Instead they are empowered by the good (in other words, they are parasitical upon the good).

48. The world of change is measured by days, seasons, years – cycles determined by number. Cf. 53,6-8.

49. chs 52-4. Also 38,13-31.

50. This discussion of non-being is ultimately dependent on the *Sophist*. Proclus refers to the interpretation of Plotinus (1,8[51],3), who wants to use the *Sophist* in order to argue that evil does not belong to beings, but somehow to non-beings. Cf. O'Brien 1999, pp. 56-66, esp. 62 n. 49. Non-being, then, is not to be taken in the sense of absolute non-being (*pantelôs mê on*), claims Plotinus, but as something merely different from being (*heteron monon tou ontos*). It is not the non-being of rest and motion (two of the 'greatest forms'), but as it were an image of being or even more non-being, a 'form which is of what is not' (*eidos ti tou mê ontos on*). It has to do with the sensible and is as it were its accident or one of its constituents (6-12).Yet prior to evil as an accident, there must be evil itself, as it were an essence or nature of evil. Proclus rejects this very notion of 'evil itself': it would have even less being than absolute non-being. Or in other words (cf. 8,19-22), there is no 'nature' lower than the lowest nature, 'whose being is accidental'.

51. *Parm.* 160D8.

52. *Soph.* 258B1-2. Difference (from being) is itself one of the 'greatest forms'.

53. *mesiteian*. This is a *hapax legomenon* in the extant works of Proclus. Moreover, in this context the word does not occur anywhere else in pagan Neoplatonic literature. Christian authors use this term for the mediation of angels and saints in the process of salvation. We suspect that *mesiteian* is a corruption for *metousian*. The phrase should then be translated as 'because of the participation in the good.'

54. *hupenantion*. *Theaet.* 176A6. See n. 34.

55. Evil never affects wholes (universal beings), but only particular beings. Cf. Introduction, 2.4.1; *TP* 1.18, p. 86,10-14.

56. An allusion to a popular quotation from Euripides, *Troad.* 887-8 (addressing Zeus): *panta ... kata dikên ... ageis* ('you guide everything in accordance with justice').

57. *Tim.* 30A2-3: 'God wanted (*boulêtheis*) that all things should be good and nothing bad (*agatha men panta, phlauron de mêden*), so far as this was attainable (*kata dunamin*).' Cf. n. 15.

58. *Theaet.* 176A5: 'it is not possible that evil things would cease to exist, Theodorus' (*all' out' apolesthai ta kaka dunaton, ô Theodôre*). The 'geometer' mentioned by Proclus is Theodorus, the interlocutor of Socrates.

59. *Theaet.* 176A8 (cf. 176A6).

60. All things are good from the perspective of the gods / the demiurge – *qua* created by the demiurge, things are good. See also ch. 61. Evil is never due to a deficiency of power in the cause, but always to the weakness of the participants. Cf. *TP* 1.18, pp. 83,24-84,15.

61. See n. 8. What Proclus here says about darkness may be regarded as his reply to the way in which Plotinus uses the metaphor of evil as darkness.

62. In speaking of the intellective essence over which the gods preside, Proclus refers to the demiurgic function of the gods, as can be inferred from the ensuing description of their providential activities.

63. cf. *ET* 122; Steel 1996.

64. Proclus is speaking about the henads, the direct manifestations of the One that completely transcend being.

65. A quotation from the Chaldean Oracles, as appears from ps.-Dion., *De div. nom.* 2,7, p. 132,3 Suchla. This fragment is not included in the collection by Des Places.

66. i.e. *ipsius visibilis*, sc. *autou tou horatou*, literally, 'the visible itself'. It is the sun that in our world bestows visibility on things. For the expression, cf. *in Tim.* 1,430,13.

67. The analogy between the sun and the good has an old pedigree in Greek philosophy, and figures prominently in Plato's *Republic*. Proclus dwells on it in his commentary: *in Remp.* 1,276,23-287,18.

68. A similar distinction is made in ps.-Plato, *Epist.* 2, 310E8. The term 'conversations' (*sunousiai*) refers to philosophical dialogues, that is, conversations as reported in 'the' dialogues (cf. *in Parm.* 1,624,29-625,36), or even 'unwritten teachings' (*TP* 1,10, p. 42,13). Here Proclus obviously has in mind Plato's dialogues. In ch. 12 Proclus will adduce a number of examples from Homer and Plato.

69. A reference to the Homeric expression *theoi rheia zôontes* (*Il.* 6,138; *Od.* 4,805).

70. The 'souls of good fortune' are those that have chosen a better life; cf. *in Tim.* 1,201,1-2; *in Remp.* 2,172,15; 2,254,13-22. The reading of the manuscripts, 'ephemeral souls', cannot be correct, as the 'ephemeral souls' are those souls that long for mortal and ephemeral things, and not for things divine. Cf. *in Remp.* 2,270,14-6; *Resp.* 617D7.

71. Plato *Phaedr.* 251C and 255D. See our Philological Appendix.

72. cf. *TP* 1.24, p. 107,4 (*tês theias euphrosunês*); 108,11-12 (*met'euphrosunês kai tês theias rhâistônês*).

73. cf. *TP* 4.4, p. 18,18-19; Plot. 6,9 [9], 11,17.

74. *Phaedr.* 247A8: *pros daita kai epi thoinên*.

75. This passage echoes Platonist polemics against Gnosticism. The *Corpus Hermeticum* mentions boldness (*tolma*, fr. 23, 24,2), excess (*hubris*, 10,21, p. 123,23) and satiation (*koros*, 10,21, p. 123,26) in relation to the soul's descent. In its overproudness, resulting from its heavenly condition, the soul desires to become a creator itself (1,13, p. 10,20-1). Perhaps even the occurrence of 'to vanquish' (*kratein*) in our text may be related to the same context, where man envies the Demiurge's power (*kratos*, ibid., p. 11,4-5). Boldness (*tolma*) is also mentioned by Plotinus as a cause for the fall of the soul (cf. Armstrong [1967], pp. 242-5). Excess (*hubris*) is linked by Proclus to procession (*proödos*) and declension (*huphesis*): *in Tim.* 1,175,2-18.

76. cf. *Phaedo* 103C-D; Procl. *in Tim.* 1,375,22-5; Plot. 5,4[7],1,31.

77. cf., e.g., *ET* 174 and 189.

78. This is a fundamental metaphysical law. Cf. *ET* 29.

79. cf. 51,15 (*anidruton*). Plot. 1,8[51],1,5.

80. For the sake of clarity, we have reversed the order of the clauses in the Latin text.

81. cf. 5,1-4, citing the *Republic* (10, 608E3-4).

82. cf. 5,21-6.

83. The souls are literally said to 'project' different kind of lives during their different reincarnations.

84. Proclus may be referring to *Timaeus*, esp. 37D6-7 (where eternity is said to 'remain in / according to one') and 38C1-2. From these and some other passages Proclus manages to derive the three intelligible triads: that which 'is eternal' depends from 'eternity itself', which in its turn depends from 'the one-being' (the third, second and first intelligible triads, respectively). Cf. Opsomer (2000a), pp. 360-8. See also *ET* 53 (Dodds, p. 52,5-7). However, the expression 'what is before eternity' in our text refers to the One itself (the transcendent One, not the one-being), and the expressions 'in accordance with the one' and 'eternal' probably refer to the entire intelligible realm.

85. The activity of intellective and intelligible gods is immobile, and therefore prior to the activity in our world, which is not immobile. But prior to immobile activity is the One, which transcends being and activity.

86. Eternity is the second intelligible triad, and everything which participates in it is posterior to it. Time is an image of eternity and comes much lower in the divine hierarchy. The intelligible triads still belong to being, whereas the gods themselves – the henads, that is – transcend being.

87. cf. *in Parm.* 833,9-10: 'For ignorance is something evil, not the knowledge of ignorance'.

88. Cf. *ET* 29.

89. 'The portals of the good' is a famous expression from the *Philebus* (64C1: *epi tois tou agathou prothurois*). See, e.g., *TP* 3.18, p. 64,6-12. For the image of beings emerging from a sanctuary (*prokuptô*), see *TP* 1.24, 108,17; 3,52,9; 5.11, 36,4; *in Crat.* 107,12.

90. cf. Psellus, *OD* 98,5-8: 'The more wise among the Greeks believe that the angels stand in the portals of God [...]. For they reveal the divine silence.'

91. Cf. *De dec. dub.* 65,23-8.

92. This can also be inferred from *ET* 22.

93. i.e. angels, demons, heroes. These 'superior kinds' receive an extensive treatment in Iamblichus' *De mysteriis*. However, Iamblichus uses the term 'superior kinds' also for other higher beings, such as gods, archangels, and divine souls. See also Stob., *Ecl.* 1,455,3-4; Steel (1978), p. 27.

94. One of the many examples of the triad being-power/potency-activity (*ousia-dunamis-energeia*), where goodness can be substituted for being, life (fertility) for power, and intellect for activity. The third position in a triad is always that of reversion (the fundamental triadic structure remaining-procession-reversion maps onto the triad being-power-activity).

95. Evil and mortal demons were part of the popular tradition, and were also incorporated in philosophical systems, such as the Stoics'. Porphyry (cf. *De abst.* 2,38-40) and Iamblichus (*De myst.* 2,7; 3,31; 4,7; 9,7), too, believed in evil demons.

96. Demons are responsible for the punishment of souls after death in a subterranean place. The punishment of souls in a place under the earth is well attested in the Platonic myths, e.g. in the story of Er the Pamphylian (*Resp.* 10, 614B-621D) or in the *Phaedrus* myth (249A6-7).

97. *Theaet.* 176E3-5: 'There are two paradigms set up in reality, my friend. One is divine and supremely happy (*tou men theiou eudaimonestatou*); the other is ungodly and is the paradigm of the greatest misery (*tou de atheou athliôtatou*).' Cf. Introduction, 2.1, T1′. See also below, 40,13-14; 48,5-7.

98. cf. *Resp.* 10, 615D-E. The mouth of the cave constitutes the border between the earth and the subterranean place of punishment. Cf. *in Remp.* 2,94,5-7; 2,179,28-180,8; 2,181,15-27.

99. Cf. *Resp.* 10, 615E4-616A4. Proclus considers the 'bellowing mouth' and the 'fiery and savage men' as belonging to the demonic realm. Cf. *in Remp.* 2,94,5-8; 2,180,20-2.

100. However, initially (16,4-7) these 'Platonic' demons were presented as allegedly evil by choice only (as opposed to the demons of popular belief, who are supposed to be evil by nature).

101. Presumably, Proclus has Iamblichus in mind (see n. 95), and possibly even the Theurgists (cf. *in Tim.* 3,157,27-8; the Theurgists are a father and a son, both called Julian, the latter being the author of the Chaldean oracles). Proclus does not usually call Porphyry divine.

102. On the creation of the demons, see *in Tim.* 3,157,27-158,11.

103. Proclus here distinguishes beings who are by nature (*phusei*) demons from those who are only dispositionally (*skhesei*) demons. The latter are souls that have succeeded in ascending to a demonic pattern of life. Whereas someone's nature is unalterable, one's acquired behaviour may very well change. Cf. *in Tim.* 3,158,22-159,7; *in Crat.* 117, p. 68,13-19 Pasq.; 74, pp. 35,27-36,6; *in Remp.* 1,41,11-25. Theodorus of Asine is said to have made the same distinction at *in Tim.* 3,154,19-24. At *in Alc.* 73,21-3 Proclus adds yet another category to the distinction 'by nature' and 'by relation', to wit 'by analogy'.

104. i.e., they take on various kinds of life. Cf. 18,8.

105. cf. 51,15-16.

106. See n. 103.

107. Or 'and other so-called vices' (cf. the Philological Appendix). See n. 22.

108. cf. 51,12; 53,16-18.

109. Intellective beings should act according to intellect (*nous*), which surpasses discursive reason (*logos*).

110. cf. *in Remp.* 2,125,8-9 (*tên neusin kai tên pros ton desmon sumpatheian*). The 'bonds of the body' are mentioned at *Phaedo* 67D2; see also *Resp.* 7, 514A6. For the downward inclination, see *Phaedr.* 246C; 247B; 248A.

111. An alternative interpretation would be: 'as food for human beings'. In order to support the 'active' interpretation one may refer to *De dec. dub.* VII (esp. 43,11; 15); Plot. 3,2[47],15,17-33; *SVF* II 1173 (Orig. *Contra Celsum* 4,75; 78).

112. cf. *in Parm.* 735,17-19.

113. cf. *Resp.* 10, 615D-616A; above, 16,13.

114. cf. *Tim.* 42E5-8.

115. Or: 'after the heroes'.

116. The words 'this place', just like 'the mortal nature' a few lines below, refer to the famous *Theaetetus* passage (176A7-8) and are also discussed by Plotinus, 1,8 [51],6,4-9. See Introduction, 2.1, T1.

117. i.e. after the gods and the angels, demons and heroes. Proclus will now be speaking about the souls, although he does not use the word until 21,16. It is important to notice that Proclus in *DMS* 21-4 only discusses particular souls, not universal divine souls (who are, just as the gods, unaffected by evil, and who are superior to the two classes discussed in these chapters; cf. *Phaedr.* 247D-248A). His description of the different classes of souls is mainly based on the *Phaedrus* myth: after the gods who enjoy an easy contemplation, Socrates tells the story of 'the other souls' (248A1), distinguishing three categories: those that follow a god most closely and are able – with some difficulty – to raise 'the head of the charioteer' up to the place outside , where it can contemplate the higher world; those that rise at one time and fall at another; the remaining souls that are all eagerly straining to keep up, but are unable to rise (248AB). Then Socrates announces the law of destiny (the law of Adrasteia) that determines the fate of the souls: any soul that becomes a companion of a god will be unharmed until the next cycle (248C2-5); a soul that is unable to keep up will lose its wings and fall to earth, where it enters the cycle of reincarnations (248C5-249C4). The two classes that Proclus distinguishes in the present text correspond to the two basic conditions determined by the law of destiny. Proclus, however, maintains that *both* classes descend, and that they all, to some extent, suffer oblivion (the immaculate souls, however, will never lose their internal disposition). See 21,14-16 and 22,2-3, with our nn. 128 and 137.

118. *Tim.* 43E1 (*klaseis kai diaphoras tôn kuklôn*). See also 90D. According to Plato's account of the generation of the world-soul in the *Timaeus*, the soul is made to consist of circles (the circle of Sameness and the circle of Difference). Since the other souls resemble the world-soul, this account holds for them, too. A soul does well when its circles turn smoothly, but is diseased when its circles are shattered and irregular. See also 39,5-7, with our n. 281.

119. *lêthê.* Cf. 21,15-16; 22,10, with our nn. 128 and 137.

120. Socrates polemicises against the tragic poets and Pindar who had told the story that Asclepius, the son of Apollo, was bribed by a rich man, and had thus represented a child of god as greedy (*Republic* 3, 408BC). Cf. also *in Remp.* 1,143,18-46,5, on the Homeric heroes' love of money. *Tim.* 40D-41A was considered to contain information on the 'children of the gods', for there Timaeus mentions 'those figures of the past who claim to be the offspring of the gods' and who inform us about the divine genealogies. Proclus explains (*in Tim.* 3,159,13-160,12) that all souls are in fact children of the gods, but not all recognise the god from which they depend; only those who do and accordingly make their choice of life are *called* children of the gods. 'Those we ought to trust' (*Tim.* 40D7-E2) are, according to Proclus, the souls which unfailingly follow their presiding gods (contrary to most humans, who forget their divine provenance) and whose information is therefore trustworthy. Proclus has in mind special human beings like Orpheus, Pythagoras, the Sibyls, but also Heracles, Hermes, Asclepius, Dionysos (sc., the human beings who have kept the names of the gods at the top of the 'chain' to which they belong – not to be confused with the gods themselves). They come here to fulfil a special task, such as prophecy or medicine, depending on the series to which they belong. Cf. *in Crat.* 81, p. 38,5-18; Hermias *in Phaedr.* p. 94,18-28.

121. *Phaedr.* 248C2-5 (transl. A. Nehamas and P. Woodruff): 'Besides, the law of Destiny is this: If any soul becomes a companion to a god and catches sight of any true thing, it will be unharmed until the next circuit (*mekhri tês heteras periodou apêmona*); and if it is able to do this every time, it will always be safe (*ablabê*).' See also 248D. Hermias in his commentary (*in Phaedr.* pp. 162,30-163,19) equates immunity from harm with not descending to generation, whereas Proclus (21,14) maintains that these fortunate souls, too, descend.

122. These souls closely follow their leader gods and assist them, carrying out specialised tasks.

123. cf. *in Crat.* 81, p. 38,13 (*ep' euergesiâi tôn têide topôn*).

124. cf. *in Parm.* 719,22.

125. *sun theôn pompêi.* Cf. *in Crat.* 81, p. 38,14 Pasq.; *in Tim.* 1,134,33. Cf. Festugière (1953), pp. 69-96, esp. p. 77, on Iamblichus ap. Stob. 1,379,1-6.

126. cf. *in Alc.* 60,15; 80,15-16; Hermias, *in Phaedr.* pp. 162,30-163,19 (demons and heroes assist in keeping these souls free from harm).

127. Plotinus, too, denies that generation is in itself evil. Cf. O'Brien (1971), pp. 130-1; (1993), p. 48.

128. *to poma tês lêthes,* Plato *Resp.* 10, 621A6-7 (all had to drink, with the exception of Er; some drink more, others less). The word *poma* is not used by Plato; cf., however, *in Tim.* 3,323,20; *in Alc.* 189,7. According to Eustathius the expression *poma tês lêthês* was coined or at least used by the Homeric poets (*Comm. ad Hom. Odyss.* 1,399,13). Oblivion is also mentioned in the *Phaedrus* (248C7; 250A4), but there it is used only for the souls that do not remain unharmed. Proclus needs the quotation from the *Republic* to prove that *every* soul, including the class mentioned in *DMS* 21 and *Phaedr.* 248C3-5, suffers from oblivion. The difference for the divine souls is that they do not forget their true nature; it is just their functioning that is, as it were, put to sleep. Cf. Van den Berg (1997), p. 160.

129. cf. *Phaedr.* 248B1; *Phaedo* 66D6 (the body intrudes in our investigations by causing disturbance, *thorubon*); *Tim.* 43B6. The closest parallel is Plot. 3,4[15],6,6: *dia ton thorubon ton ek tês geneseôs.*

130. cf. *in Tim.* 1,52,25-7 (*ta ourania psukhôn genê kai akhranta*); 2,112,23-5; *in Crat.* 117, p. 68,25-30.

131. At *in Tim.* 1,111,14-28 Proclus distinguishes three kinds of souls: the first remain immaculate and are rightly called 'children of the gods'; the second descend without being perverted; they are children of the gods, but also become children of humans; the third descend and are filled with all sorts of evil; they are bastard children of the gods. However, besides the fact that Proclus here posits an intermediate kind, this description does not seem to be exactly the same as the one we find in *DMS*. In our text the best souls also come down to this world. However, at *in Tim.* 2,112,12-13 Proclus implies that they, too, descend. See also Van den Berg (1997), pp. 159-60. The threefold division may be inspired by *Phaedr.* 248AB. At *in Tim.* 3,259,1-27 Proclus distinguishes *four* classes: the first two do not figure in *DMS*: they are those who are truly divine and those that always follow the gods (presumably the truly divine souls whose fate is described at *Phaedr.* 247D1-248A1 *before* that of the 'other souls'; some of the latter are called divine, e.g. in *DMS* 21, but they are actually *children* of the gods; cf. Herm. *in Phaedr.* 152,27-8; 157,5-19); the third corresponds to the first class of *DMS* (the souls that descend but remain unharmed), the fourth to the last class of our text (those that descend and become perverted).

132. In the *Phaedrus* the souls that come down to earth are mentioned after the divine souls that Proclus has discussed in the previous chapter. The souls that descend to earth have lost their wings and are replete with oblivion and evil (248C5-8). Proclus will discuss their fate in chs 23-4 (see also 22,9-12). At *Polit.* 272E1-3 Plato speaks about the souls that are sown in the earth (cf. *in Tim.* 3,233,9-10).

133. e.g. the souls that abide in the heavenly bodies; cf. *Tim.* 42D4-5 (the demiurge sows souls in the heavenly bodies); *in Tim.* 3,233,4-22; *in Parm.* 817,4-819,29.

134. Proclus maintains that all souls descend, even the divine souls, and that there is no part of them that always remains in the intelligible world. Cf. *in Parm.* 948,18-24 (against Plotinus).

135. cf. *in Remp.* 2,350,9-10 (*skotos – lêthê*). For the imagery of darkness in the soul, see *Resp.* 518AB; *Leg.* 875C2. For the image of light that remains unaffected by the surrounding darkness see Plot. 3.6[21],5,21-2.

136. *Phaedr.* 248C7.

137. *pterorruêsis*, *Phaedr.* 246C2; (D4); 248C8. Cf. *in Tim.* 3,325,15: 'oblivion (*lêthên*) and shedding of wings (*pterorruêsin*) and what follows from these'. Also 3,43,7.

138. The gods and the superior kinds.

139. The souls of chs 23-4.

140. *Phaedr.* 248B3-4: *khôleuontai – polun ekhousai ponon*.

141. cf. *in Tim.* 3,349,14-15: 'lameness (*khôleia*) and shedding of wings (*pterorruêsis*) and oblivion (*lêthê*) and mischance (*suntukhia*) and heaviness (*barutês*)'; 3,334,25.

142. *Phaedr.* 246C1-2: *meteôroporei te kai panta ton kosmon dioikei*.

143. cf. *Phaedr.* 247D5-E2.

144. cf. *Phaedr.* 248A3 (*sumperiênekhthê*) and 8 (*sumperipherontai*), with Herm. *in Phaedr.* 158,1-2; 158,21.

145. *Phaedr.* 247A8 (*pros daita kai epi thoinên*). Cf. *in Parm.* 629,2-5; *in Tim.* 1,18,8-10; 1,52,26-7.

146. *Phaedr.* 247E6: the charioteer feeding ambrosia and nectar to the horses – said with respect to (the souls of) the gods. Nectar is nutriment for the souls (cf. *TP* 4.6, p. 24,3-12) and it strengthens them in their providential activity (ib. 4,15, pp. 46,14-47,6). Cf. Hermias *in Phaedr.* 156,17-157,3.

147. cf. Arist. *EE* 1.1, 1214a32-3. Proclus argues that a perfect life for the soul cannot be restricted to self-centered contemplation, but has to go outwards and benefit other things (i.e. bodily nature). Cf. *De dec. dub.* 65.

148. cf. *Or. Chald.* 8 (transl. R. Majercik): 'besides this one sits a dyad. [...] For it has a double function: it both possesses the intelligibles in its mind and brings sense-perception to the worlds.'

149. cf. *Tim.* 36BC.

150. cf. *in Parm.* 660,22; 668,25; 718,31-3; 954,9; 1022,9; 1028,20; 1118,22; *in Tim.* 1,84,19; 1,332,26; 3,7,25; 3,26,3; 3,27,29; 3,71,22 etc. At *in Parm.* 719,20-3 Proclus gives examples of opportune gifts from the gods: good offspring, medical art, divine prophecy, mystical initiation.

151. cf. *Phaedr.* 247A7; *Tim.* 29E1-2.

152. cf. *Tim.* 29E3.

153. *Resp.* 10, 617D7: *arkhê allês periodou*.

154. *TP* 1.18, p. 84,16-24.

155. cf. *in Tim.* 1,44,8-12, 2,90,2-3; 2,109,3.

156. The banquet mentioned at *Phaedr.* 247A8.

157. cf. Psellus, *OD* 197,6-7.

158. The power that regulates bodies is called nature. Cf. below, ch. 27.

159. Proclus combines two passages: *Phaedr.* 248C6-7 (transl. A. Nehamas & P. Woodruff): 'if [...] by some accident (*tini suntukhiâi khrêsamenê*) [the soul] takes on a burden of forgetfulness and wrongdoing (*lêthês te kai kakias plêstheisa*), then it is weighed down (*baruntheisa*), sheds its wings and falls to earth (*epi tên gên pesêi*)' and *Resp.* 10, 617D7: 'the mortal, death-bringing kind' (*thnêtou genous thanatêphorou*). The phrase that Proclus here quotes from the *Phaedrus* introduces the description of the fate of the fallen souls that enter the cycle of generation.

160. *Tim.* 42C4-D2 (part of a description of successive reincarnations; transl. D.J. Zeyl): 'And he would have no rest from these toilsome transformations (*alla tôn te ou proteron ponôn lêxoi*) until he had dragged that massive accretion (*ton polun okhlon kai husteron prosphunta*) of fire-water-air-earth into conformity with the revolution of the Same and uniform within him, and so subdued that turbulent, irrational mass (*thorubôdê kai alogon onta*) by means of reason. This would return him to his original condition of excellence.' Cf. *in Tim.* 3,296,1-300,20; *in Alc.* 57,11-15. See also *Resp.* 10, 611D2-7.

161. *Resp.* 7, 518C9: *eis to on kai tou ontos to phanotaton.*

162. Proclus refers to the 'demonic region', the ethereal region 'between heaven and earth'. 'Meadow' (*leimôn*) is one of its names, taken from *Gorgias* 524A2 and *Resp.* 614E2-3. Cf. *in Remp.* 2,128,3-136,16; esp. 2,128,17-19; 132,26-133,2. It must be distinguished from the higher meadow mentioned at line 16, which is that of *Phaedr.* 248B5-C1 (transl. P. Woodruff, slightly adapted): 'The reason there is so much eagerness to see the plain where truth stands (*to alêtheias pedion hou estin*) is that this upper meadow (*tou ekei leimônos*) has the grass that is the right food for the best part of the soul.' The upper meadow is part of the supracelestial region and forms a triad together with the 'plain of truth' and the 'nutriment of the gods'. Cf. *TP* 4.15, pp. 45,17-46,6; 4.16, pp. 48,24-49,21.

163. *Resp.* 10, 620E6-621A1: 'it passed beneath the Throne of Necessity' (*hupo ton tês Anankês iënai thronon*).

164. *Resp.* 10, 621A2-3: 'the plain of oblivion' (*to tês lêthês pedion*). This place is of course the complete opposite of the 'plain of truth' from the *Phaedrus* (248B5); cf. *in Remp.* 2,346,19-25.

165. cf. Psellus *OD* 197,8-10.

166. cf. *Phaedr.* 248B5-C1.

167. *Phaedr.* 248B7.

168. *Phaedr.* 248B5: *trophêi doxastêi khrôntai* (i.e. they use their opinions for food).

169. cf. *Resp.* 10, 621C1-2: *ton tês lêthês potamon.*

170. e.g. *Theaet.* 177A1; *Phaedo* 81A6; 93B9; *Resp.* 2, 382C9; *Leg.* 10, 897B3.

171. *puthmên*; cf. *Phaedo* 109C5: we are like someone who lives deep down in the middle of the ocean – 'the pit of the ocean' (*tôi puthmêni tou pelagous*) – but thinks he is living on its surface, for we dwell in the hollows of the earth but are unaware of this and think we live above. The 'pit of the universe' became a metaphorical expression designating the deepest point of the world: cf. *in Tim.* 1,189,11; 1,445,11. It also stands for 'the place where we live' (*in Tim.* 1,353,6-7). As in the *Phaedo*, its smallness is often contrasted with the greatness of the whole (*in Tim.* 2,268,11). On the darkness in the pit of the universe, see *in Remp.* 2,347,20-348,2. The term 'pit' also figures in an Orphic fragment, where Zeus is called *puthmên* of the earth and the starry sky (ps.-Arist. *De mundo* 401b1; Orph. fr. 21A3, and also 168). Proclus interprets the Orphic fragment in the same way: Zeus encompasses everything, including the pit of the world (*in Tim.* 1,313,17-314,2).

172. cf. *Resp.* 611D4-7; see also *Tim.* 42C4-D2 (quoted at 24,9-11).

173. cf. *Tim.* 43E1-4; *DMS* 20,11 (with n. 118); *in Tim.* 3,322,31-323,5; 338,11; 343,1-3.

174. cf. *Phaedr.* 249A3.

175. e.g. *Phaedrus* 249A6-7; *Resp.* 10, 614B-621D.

176. cf. Plato *Gorg.* 524D5; Plot. 1,6[1],7,5-7; *Or. Chald.* 116 (= Procl. *in Crat.* 155, p. 88,4-5); *ET* 209. Proclus usually refers to the oracles when using this image: cf. *in Alc.* 138,18; 180,2; *TP* 1.3, p. 16,5-6 (with Saffrey & Westerink [1968], p. 16 n. 3). See also Porph. *De abst.* 1,31,3 (without reference to the oracles), with Bouffartigue & Patillon (1977), pp. 37-41. Psellus *OD* 197,10-13; Plot. 1,6[1],7,5-7.

177. cf. Plot. 1,6[1],9.

178. cf. Plot. 1,8[51],4,17-32.

179. cf. *Theaet.* 176A8-B3 (following on the idea that evil will always haunt 'this place'; transl. M.J. Levett & M.F. Burnyeat): 'That is why a man should make all haste to escape from earth to heaven; and escape means becoming as like God as possible *(phugê de homoiôsis theôi kata to dunaton)*; and a man becomes like God when he becomes just and pure, with understanding'. Cf. Introduction, 2.1, T1.

180. cf. *Phaedr.* 250C1-6.

181. The 'images of souls' are the irrational souls. According to Proclus, among souls there are those that are rational and free-standing, which are with some right called 'souls'; and there are the images of souls, the irrational souls, that is, which are the correlates of that which is ensouled (the soul as *entelekheia* of the body). Cf. *De dec. dub.* 63,29-34; *TP* 3.6, p. 23,21-3; *ET* 64; *in Tim.* 3,330,9-24. See Blumenthal (1996), ch. 7.

182. *kakergetis.* Cf. *Leg.* 10, 896E5-6: (we must assume two souls,) one beneficent and the other capable of the contrary effect' *(tês te euergetidos kai tês tanantia dunamenês exergazesthai)*; and 897D1: 'the evil (soul)' *(tên kakên)*. Plato does not use the word *kakergetis*, but Proclus ascribes the doctrine of a maleficent soul to Plutarch of Chaeronea and Atticus and their adherents *(in Tim.* 1,382,2-11). This so-called maleficent soul is the precosmic soul that receives order in the cosmogonic process. See also 1,391,10; *TP* 1.18, p. 87,24 (with Saffrey & Westerink [1968], p. 87 n. 3). *DMS* 40,15-17 provides some more details about the doctrine of the two souls: see n. 293, and Opsomer (2001a), pp. 191-3. In ch. 45 Proclus will examine the possibility that the maleficent soul is the cause of evil. But here, in ch. 25, he deals with the irrational souls, which appear to be parts of this maleficent soul.

183. Proclus is here speaking of irrational souls as they can be found in animals. They are themselves images of the so-called irrational soul discussed in ch. 45. These irrational souls are inferior to the irrational soul that exists in us ('the mortal life-form' that is 'woven onto the descending soul', 46,4-5, and that is not really discussed here, but merely used as a point of reference), and therefore it would be very unlikely that they would not run the risk of becoming evil as well. Now, if such an 'image' belonged to the rational soul of an individual (as is the case with the irrational soul of human persons), its evil would consist in not conforming itself to reason. But in the case of animals, who have only an irrational soul, evil arises when they lack the appropriate virtue, that is, when they are not true to their kind. Animals do not need to be rational, they should just be what they are. Cf. 18,22-3. Proclus rejects the view that the souls of animals are reincarnated human souls, yet admits that human souls can enter animals. What Plato means by the reincarnation of human souls in animals, Proclus claims, is not that human souls enter into the *bodies* of animals, but rather that they enter into the *life* of an animal, i.e. into the body of an animal that already has an (irrational) soul. By making this distinction, Proclus can claim that the rational soul is fundamentally different from the images of soul, and always remains what it is: cf. *in Tim.* 3,294,22-295,14; *in Remp.* 2,310,29-311,22; see also Iamblichus ap. Nemes. p. 35,8-11 Morani.

184. Cf. *TP* 1.18, p. 85,6-10.

185. cf. *ET* 45, p. 46,15-17; *in Tim.* 3,322,5-8.

186. cf. Arist. *Metaph.* 5.2, 1013b25-7; *Phys.* 2.3, 195a23-5.

187. cf. 21,17-18.

188. Proclus argues that the things that are not by nature virtuous, but become virtuous by their behaviour, become perverted when their behaviour is bad (when they lack a virtuous 'disposition'). Through a process of habituation this badness may attain their nature so that it becomes itself evil.

189. Nature is the principle that governs body. Universal nature does so in an invariable way.

190. This is a quotation from *Leg.* 10, 897B2-3. However, whereas our Plato manuscripts read *ortha kai eudaimona paidagôgei*, Proclus here and at *in Tim.* 1,382,6 cites this phrase slighly differently as *ortha kai emphrona paidagôgei*.

191. cf. *TP* 3,94,15-21.

192. cf. Plot. 1,8[51],3,35-6.

193. Isaac (1982), 64 n. 2 (pp. 118-19) argues against the interpretation of *etiam in totis* as referring to wholes, since wholes are said to be outside the realm of matter (§27) and do not have evil (§47). But *kai mên en tois holois* cannot mean 'même aux yeux de tous'. In our view, Proclus is probably thinking of wholes which may be of a material nature, such as the four elements. Cf. 28,24-6. See also *Tim.* 33A7.

194. Proclus may be thinking of the Presocratics, who failed to offer an analysis of matter, though some of them did posit material, or rather bodily principles. The first philosophical discussion of matter according to Proclus, will have been the *Timaeus* or its supposed model, Timaeus Locrus.

195. cf. *Or. Chald.* 34 = *in Tim.* 1,451,19-22.

196. cf. Plot. 4,4 [28], 13,3-4 and 19-20.

197. For this distinction, see also 56,15-18; 60,4-6; Plot. 1,8[51],5,21-4.

198. cf. *in Parm.* 855,10-11.

199. So far Proclus has discussed ordinary, individual and material bodies, which are liable to become evil. Now he turns to universal bodies (e.g. the four elements), which cannot become evil, and immaterial bodies, whose nature cannot become evil. Among the immaterial bodies he distinguishes those that enjoy an invariable activity, and hence remain entirely free from evil, and those that have a varying activity, such as pneumatic vehicles following the vicissitudes of their soul, and can therefore be affected in their activities. For the concept of 'immaterial bodies' (e.g. light, the celestial bodies) or bodies that are 'halfway between the material and the immaterial' (e.g. 'pneumatic vehicles'), see *in Remp.* 2,162,24-163,8; *In Tim.* 2,10,4-9; Siorvanes (1996), pp. 250-2.

200. cf. Plot. 1,8[51],3; 1,8[51],8,38-40 *et passim*.

201. cf. 5,10-13, with n. 27.

202. For the expression, see Arist. *Metaph.* 5.7, 1016b31-5.

203. i.e. the instrumental body or pneumatic vehicle. See *in Tim.* 3,236,31-237,9, *ET* 209 and Dodds (1963), p. 320.

204. Proclus summarises the distinctions made in the previous chapter between ordinary material bodies and immaterial bodies. When he says that the latter can get corrupted in their activities, he is speaking only of partial immaterial bodies (the instruments of the soul, i.e. pneumatic vehicles). Then he mentions universal bodies (without specifying whether they are material or immaterial) and seemingly introduces a new distinction, that between those possessing order unproblematically and those whose order is due to a perpetual, yet always victorious, struggle against disorder. Yet from what follows one may infer that Proclus takes this distinction to correspond to that between material (sensible) and immaterial bodies, whose 'matter' is sensible or intelligible respectively (in the intelligible realm, it is however preferable to speak of 'power', rather than matter; cf. the assessment of Plotinus' view in *TP* 3.9, pp. 39,24-40,8). Of course, in principle it can not be excluded that Proclus only later inserted some of these cross-references into his texts.

205. cf. *Tim.* 30A3-5: *pan ... kinoumenon plêmmelôs kai ataktôs*. The demiurge takes over 'that which moves in an irregular and disorderly fashion', introducing order into it. Proclus here takes this expression as referring to matter in the broad sense as that which serves as a substrate.

206. Disorder consists in the deprivation of the quality that is the essence of the next higher level. In earthly bodies the substrate is matter, and order comes from the imposition of form, form being bestowed by nature, the governing principle of (material) body. In heavenly bodies, form is the substrate, and order comes from the higher principle, Life. Note that Nature as a principle is not to be confused with 'the nature' – the essence, that is – of matter, mentioned some lines below.

207. cf. *in Tim.* 1,39,4.

208. Three *hapax legomena*: *autoäoristia, autoämetria, autoskotos*. See however Plotinus' description of matter at 3,4[15],1,11-12 (*aoristian pantelê*); 3,9[13],3,12-13 (*to aoriston pantê skoteinon*); 1,8[51],3,27; 6,41-4.

209. For Proclus' criticism of Plotinus' conception of matter-evil see Introduction, 2.3, and Opsomer (2001b).

210. Accidents are predicated not of substrates, but of individuals and of species. Cf. Porph. *Isag.* 13,10-21. One of the questions that Plotinus posits at the outset of his treatise on the origin of evil is: 'to what does it belong as an accident?' (*hotôi sumbebêke*, 1,8[51],1,5). See also 1,8[51],3,16-24.

211. The opinion of Plotinus, but also of Numenius, who made it a positively evil force (ap. *Calc.* c. 294), and also Cronius and Celsus (Orig. *Cels.* 4,65; 8,55) and Moderatus (Simpl. *in Phys.* 231,21). Harpocration is said to have derived evil rather 'from the bodies'. For Numenius, Cronius and Harpocration see Iamblichus, *De anima*, ap. Stob. 1, p. 37,12-16 Wachsmuth-Hense.

212. Hom. *Iliad* 20,65. See also Plotinus 5,1[10],2,27.

213. Proclus closely follows the argument of *Ennead* 1,8[51],3: ll. 12-16: evil is all kinds of privations of the good (cf. *DMS* 30,9-12); ll. 16-22: these do not belong to evil as accidents, they *are* evil itself (cf. *DMS* 30,12-14); ll. 21-4: the difference between evils that participate, and the absolute evil in which evils participate (cf. *DMS* 30,14-22); ll. 35-40: the description of this first evil as that which underlies all forms and measures, but is incapable of receiving them (cf. *DMS* 30,22-4). Only later, in §4, does Plotinus explicitly identify this nature as matter.

214. *autokakon* (see also 30,24 and 58,13), the word used by Plotinus 1,8[51],8,42.

215. 28,9-10; 29,12-21.

216. cf. Plot. 1,8[51],14,49-51: 'matter, then, is the cause of weakness for the soul, and the cause of [its] vice. So matter is evil first, and is the first evil.' Proclus ignores the subtle distinctions between the soul's weakness and its vices. Cf. 33,1-3.

217. cf. *Phaedo* 79C7-8.

218. This is exactly what Plotinus does in 1,8[51],14,17-24: he argues that the fact that weakness only occurs in souls that are near matter is an indication that matter is the cause of this weakness.

219. In his treatise on matter Plotinus rejects this coarse, Numenian-styled, dualism: 2,4[12],2,9-10.

220. *sc.* than the evils generated by it.

221. cf. Philop. *De aet. mundi* 445,28-446,2.

222. *Tim.* 34B8-9.

223. In ch. 52, however, Proclus will explain that privation of being/form differs from privation of the good. But here he just wants to highlight the contrast with the necessary as a condition of *existence*.

224. *Tim.* 49A6; cf. also 51A4; 52D4-5.

225. *Tim.* 50D3 and 51A4.

226. Proclus is using Plotinus' own conception in a dialectical way against him. Cf. Plot. 1,8[51],3,35-40; 3,6[26],11,29-36; 3,6[26],11,43-5. See also Porph. *Sent.* 21 (p. 12,8-9).

227. *to endeës.* Plotinus included measurelessness (*ametria*) and need among the characteristics of evil: 1,8[51],3,12-15. He even gives a vivid description of matter begging the soul, making a nuisance of itself and trying to worm its way inside (1,8[51],14,35-6; cf. 3,6[26],14,5-15 where the metaphor of begging is explicitly related to Plato *Symp.* 203B4).

228. This idea is entertained, as a mere hypothesis, by Plotinus: 1,8[51],5,4. He deals with the objection that refers to the weakness of the soul in 1,8[51],14, maintaining that matter is the cause both of the weakness of the soul (which is not yet evil) and of its evil.

229. cf. *Phaedr.* 248A1-B1. See n. 117.

230. See our nn. 141 and 159 for 'mischance' (*suntukhia*) and 'oblivion' (*lêthê*). For 'oblivion' see also 20,11-12; 21,15-16; 22,10, with our notes.

231. *Phaedr.* 247B3-4, also cited below: 49,16-17.

232. cf. Plato *Resp.* 10, 621A6-7. See n. 128.

233. *a-poion*, 'without quality', with the familiar pun on *poiein*, 'to do'. See Plot. 1,8[51],10.

234. The souls are themselves responsible for their vices. Cf. *in Tim.* 3,313,18-21; 3,302,24-303,12.

235. i.e. the mode *kat'enantiôsin*, that moves from the negation of a predicate to the affirmation of its contrary. Cf. Anon. *in Parm.* V,26.

236. see, however, 37,1-6.

237. *Tim.* 50D3 and 51A4.

238. *Tim.* 49A6; 52D4-5.

239. *Tim.* 46C7; 76D6; cf. also *Phaedo* 99B; *Polit.* 281DE.

240. *Tim.* 34B8-9.

241. *Polit.* 273B4-C2 (transl. C.J. Rowe): 'the cause of this was the bodily element in its mixture (*to sômatoeides tês sunkraseôs aition*), its companion since its origins long in the past (*to tês palai pote phuseôs suntrophon*), because this element was marked by a great disorder (*pollês metekhon ataxias*) before it entered into the present world-order. For from the one who put it together the world possesses all fine things (*para tou sunthentos panta kala kektêtai*); from its previous condition (*para tês emprosthen hexeôs*), on the other hand, it both has for itself from that source everything that is bad and unjust in the heavens, and produces it in its turn in living things.'

242. *Phil.* 26C4-27C1. Socrates here first distinguishes three elements: the limit, the unlimited, the product resulting from their mixture (i.e. 'coming-into-being', *genesis eis ousian*). Then he adds a fourth, which he calls the cause (*aitia, aition*) of the generation, that which makes (*to poioun*) or fabricates (*to dêmiourgoun*) the mixture. He even says that 'that which makes' and 'the cause' are 'one', which Proclus may have taken as a reference to the One. At 27A5-6 Socrates affirms the priority of the 'fourth' principle. That the cause produces limit and the unlimited is derived from 23C9-10: 'we agreed earlier that the god (*ton theon*) had revealed a division of what is into the unlimited and the limit', where 'to reveal' (*deixai*) is interpreted as 'to produce'. Cf. De Haas (1997), p. 8 n. 30. Proclus' wrote a commentary on the *Philebus*, which is unfortunately no longer extant.

243. *Resp.* 2, 379C6-7: *tôn kakôn all'atta khrênai zêtein ta aitia, kai ou theon.*

Cf. Introduction, 2.1, T2; *DMS* 41,10-11; 47,13-14; *TP* 3.7-9, esp. pp. 30,19-21; 32,2-7; 36,10-24; *in Tim.* 1,375,25-376,1; *in Remp* 1,38,3-9.

244. *Tim.* 30A4-5: *to plêmmelôs kai ataktôs kinoumenon*, one of the phrases to indicate the precosmic disorderly motion (i.e. that which is in motion). The demiurge takes over this 'mass', that is 'visible' and contains already some 'traces' (*ikhnê*, 53B2) of the forms. The traces of the forms refer to the causal influence of the principles that are ontologically prior to the demiurge, and therefore already exert their influence 'before' the demiurge (not to be understood in a chronological sense). These forms are partial – for that is how they are received in the realm of the sensible – and hence conflicting. Proclus then does not equate the 'disorderly moving mass' of the *Timaeus* or 'the bodily nature' of the *Politicus* with matter. Cf. *in Tim.* 1,387,8-30; *in Parm.* 844,24-6. Plotinus, on the contrary, glosses 'the world's ancient nature' from the *Politicus* as 'the underlying matter, not yet set in order by some god' (1,8[51],7,6-7).

245. *Polit.* 273B4: *to sômatoeides*. See n. 241.

246. *Tim.* 30A3.

247. *Tim.* 53B2 (*ikhnê*).

248. *Polit.* 273B8. See n. 241.

249. See n. 244.

250. See n. 242. Proclus holds that matter is the lowest manifestation of unlimitedness, which itself as a principle is the immediate manifestation of the One (*ET* prop. 92), as being the infinite power of the One (*TP* 3.8, p. 32,15-23; *in Tim.* 1,384,30-385,17). Matter is in a sense directly produced by the One, which is an application of the general rules that higher causes are to a higher degree causative of a given product than its immediate cause, and that their influence extends further down the ontological scale. Cf. *ET* props. 56-7; 70-2; Siorvanes (1996), p. 183; De Haas (1997), p. 15.

251. Proclus' argument in the present text can then be rephrased and explained as follows: if one simply calls all unlimitedness matter, as Plotinus does (cf. Procl. *TP* 3.9, pp. 39,24-40,8), then matter is from god, for in the *Philebus* it is said that god produces the unlimited. The One, according to Proclus, indeed produces the first unlimited, that is the henad of the unlimited which is prior to being. But there are many forms of unlimitedness: the first unlimited is followed by substantial unlimitedness (the unlimited 'belonging to being'; cf. ibid., p. 38,22-7), and the unlimited extends over all levels of reality, down to sensible matter, the lowest manifestation of unlimitedness (*TP* 3.12, p. 45,3-6; the unlimited in the realm of generation should according to Proclus no longer be called 'power', but 'matter', because it needs to receive from elsewhere the power to become limited; conversely, one should not call substantial unlimitedness matter, but rather power: *TP* 3.10, pp. 10-20). Even this lowest form of unlimitedness, that according to Plotinus is evil itself, is produced by god, for all the forms of unlimitedness derive from one single cause. Especially in the case of sensible matter, god's power is necessary, as matter can not out of itself, taking the initiative, engage in any mixture. Especially then, even more than at the higher levels, god is needed a second time, since he is the cause of both the existence of limit and the unlimited, and their mixture (*TP* 3.9, p. 36,20-4). This means that both matter and material bodies are produced by god: matter as the expression of his unlimitedness, body as a mixture, produced by god, of constituents (viz. matter/unlimited, and form/limit) equally produced by him. Hence neither of them can be evil.

252. *Phil.* 27A11-12. See n. 242.

253. cf. *TP* 3.8, p. 34,1-3.

254. *Phil.* 27A11.

255. *Phil.* 27B1-2; cf. also 27B6-C1.

256. cf. *Resp.* 335D.

257. *to hou heneka*, an expression that already in *Gorg.* 467D-468C is related to the notion of the good and is contrasted with *to heneka tou*, 'that which is for the sake of [something else]'.

258. cf. *Leg.* 1, 636D7-E1. See also Hom. *Iliad* 24,527-8, quoted by Plato, *Resp.* 2, 379D3-4.

259. cf. 28,28.

260. We would almost call matter good, were it not that it is the last in the hierarchy: there is no being lower than it for which matter would be the goal. Matter is then neither good nor bad, but, as something necessary, intermediate.

261. cf. *in Remp.* 1,37,30-38,3. See Philoponus' criticism: *Contra Procl.* 9, 403,22-404,1; De Haas (1997), p. 2.

262. Matter is necessary for the immanent ('enmattered') forms, not for the transcendent, freestanding forms.

263. cf. *ET* prop. 8.

264. Plot. 1,8[51],7,19-20: 'and this last, after which nothing else could come into being, is evil.'

265. Again Plotinus' view: 1,8[51],6,36-59.

266. cf. chs 8-9.

267. If evil does not exist on its own, it cannot be identified with matter, since matter exists on its own, and not in something else, as also Plotinus affirms (1,8[51],10,8-9). But of course Plotinus does not concede that evil has no separate existence.

268. cf. *Phaedo* 60B8-C1; *In Parm.* 741,3.

269. See Aristotle's definition of 'contrary': *Cat.* 6, 6a17-18. In order to make the claim that a contrary of substance is possible and indeed exists (namely, matter-evil), Plotinus had to truncate Aristotle's definition of contraries as 'things which stand furthest apart in the same genus' to 'things which stand furthest apart'. An extreme contrariety would imply, so he claims, that the contraries have nothing at all in common, not even their genus (1,8[51],6,54-9). This construction is here rejected by Proclus. See also 45,15-17, with n. 327.

270. In the etymological sense of 'belonging to the same genus'.

271. i.e. common to both the good and the principle allegedly homogeneous to it.

272. cf. 7,28-50.

273. According to Calcidius *in Tim.* 288, this is Aristotle's view. Compare Plot. 1,8[51],11,1.

274. This passage is reminiscent of Aristotle *Phys.* 1.9, 192a13-25, who criticises 'certain thinkers' (Platonists unfortunately) for not distinguishing matter and privation. Privation, which is the contrary of the form and in its own nature does not exist, is different from the substrate, which desires form and only accidentally does not exist. Aristotle says that if one considers privation ('the other part of the contrariety', i.e. 'that which is contrary' and hence the destruction of the form) as an evil agent (*kakopoios*, the same word is used by Proclus – *malificam* in Moerbeke's translation: 38,4; also 38,29), it may almost seem not to exist at all. He explains that privation is contrary to what is divine, good, and desirable, whereas matter desires this and yearns for it. Now, if one conflates matter and privation, the consequence is that the contrary desires its own extinction, 'as contraries are mutually destructive' (cf. *DMS* 37,17). Next Aristotle compares matter's desire of form to the female desiring the male, an example that does not fit his account (the female does not disappear as a result of the fulfilment of its desire) but which Plotinus uses for his own theory of matter (2,4[12],16,14-17) in order to show that change does not necessarily entail the disappearance of privation. From there Plotinus argues – against Aristotle – that in the case of both change and desire, the privation, i.e. non-being, does not disappear, but persists. Hence the substrate – matter – can be identified with privation, complete absence of form and light, and therefore evil. This also is why he claims that matter can never truly receive form (cf. *DMS* 32,13-14, with n. 226): the privation remains. Cf. O'Brien (1999), sect. XIV-XV. In upholding the distinction between privation and matter (see also 32,15-16), Proclus again sides with Aristotle against Plotinus. On the other hand, he does not concede that privation is evil. Cf. Introduction, 2.3.

275. cf. Arist. *Phys.* 1.9, 192a4-6.

276. cf. above 7,47-8; ch. 52.

277. cf. 32,10-12.

278. In other words, Proclus distinguishes between privation of form (i.e. 'Aristotelian' privation), which is a mere absence and in no way evil, and the so-called privation of the good, i.e. that which actively opposes the good and is therefore evil. The latter kind of 'privation' derives its power from the good, and should therefore be called not a contrary, but a subcontrary of the good, as he will argue later (chs 52-3). Here he claims that opposition to the good should not be called privation. See however also 39,42. Cf. Introduction, 2.4.5.

279. *amenênon*, cf. 3,5-6, with n. 13.

280. *TP* 1.18, p. 85,6-10.

281. cf. *Tim.* 43E1 (*klaseis*); Procl. *in Tim.* 3,348,29-349,19; *DMS* 20,11. For *quietatio* we have found no direct parallel; *galêne* (*Tim.* 44B3), suggested by Boese, is a positive concept; *paula* at *Phaedr.* 245C6-7 (suggested by D. Isaac) is not applicable to the soul itself (yet perhaps to some of its powers). Doubtlessly, the difference between 'fractures' and *quietatio* is to be traced back to the two circles of the soul (see n. 118): when the soul fares badly, the circle of the Same is merely shackled or hindered in its motion (*pedasthai*), while that of Difference is fractured. In other words, the former is never distorted (*diastrephesthai*), but only paralysed; the latter can be distorted. Cf. *in Tim.* 2,314,26-7; 3,333,2-9; Dam. *in Parm.* 2,254,12-19; Herm. *in Phaedr.* 122,13-14; Steel (1978), p. 38; 54, n. 2. Perhaps *quietatio* corresponds to *pedê* or *pedêsis*.

282. Against Boese, Erler, and Isaac, we believe Proclus' text here to be sane, as Proclus rejects the possibility that the substance of a soul gets corrupted. Hence there is no need to speak of substantial (*ousiôdês*) corruption, as a third kind of corruption next to the corruptions of activity (*energeia*) and of potency/power (*dunamis*).

283. cf. chs 20-2, 23-4, and 27-9, respectively.

284. Although Proclus denies the possibility of a contrary of substance, here he probably entertains the idea – in a dialectical context – that what destroys a particular substance is the contrary of that substance.

285. Intellect and nature are the principles governing – i.e. immediately superior to – soul and body respectively.

286. *Resp.* 10, 610D5-7: 'By god, if injustice were actually fatal (*thanasimon*) to those who contracted it, it wouldn't seem so terrible (*pandeinon*), for it would be an escape from their troubles.' See also n. 31.

287. cf. *in Remp.* 15, 2,89,25-90,1.

288. Possibly the Manicheans. Cf. Simpl. *in Ench.* 70,28-71,5; Ascl. *in Metaph.* 292,26-9, and Erler (1978), p. 144, n. 1; I. Hadot, pp. 117-18; see also Introduction, p. 50 n. 57. However, there must also have been Platonists who endorsed the view that there is a fount of evils, as is suggested by 41,16-24, and especially 42,3-4 (with n. 304). See also Maximus of Tyre *Or.* 41,58-60 Trapp: in a rhetorical comparison, Maximus argues that instead of searching the sources of the Nile, one would do better to look for the sources, or founts (*pêgai*), of good and evils. Eusebius speaks of 'the much discussed source of vice' (*kakias pêgê*), which he situates in human freedom (*Praep. ev.* 6,6,47). See also Calcidius *in Tim.* 297, p. 299,14.

289. Plutarch of Chaeronea, Atticus and their adherents: see *in Tim.* 1,382,2-11 and our nn. 182 and 329.

290. Intermediate in that their principle of evil, the intellective forms, is situated between the level of the first principle(s) and that of the soul. The view that there are forms of evils was presumably Amelius': cf. Ascl. *in Nic. arithm.* 1,44; Saffrey & Westerink (1968), p. 87 n. 2 (at p. 153). See ch. 43 with our notes.

291. In *TP* 1.18, pp. 87,22-88,10 Proclus claims that these three doctrines – evil as being caused by gods, by a soul, or by forms – are in complete disagreement with Plato's thought. In the next chapters of *DMS* he will make the same claim.

292. *Theaet.* 176E4. See also above,16,8-10, with n. 97; Introduction, 2.1, T1'.

293. *Leg.* 10, 896E5-897D1. See n. 182. Proclus may be thinking of Plutarch of Chaeronea and Atticus. Whatever the view of Atticus was, Plutarch for one did not hold that there are two different souls governing the sublunary realm, neither at the precosmic nor at the cosmic stage. See Opsomer (2001a), pp. 191-7.

294. These are the three main hypostases that function as principles. Proclus uses this simple scheme (most notably in the *Elements of Theology*) next to the more complex hierarchy that figures in the *Platonic Theology* (see also ch. 51), and is thus prepared to operate at different levels of complexity depending on the occasion.

295. chs 11-13.

296. *Phaedr.* 246D8-E1: *to de theion kalon, sophon, agathon.*

297. Goodness does not produce by means of an external activity. That is why it remains in itself. Often the image of overflowing is used. Also is reversion a crucial feature of the causal process: beings become good by turning towards goodness.

298. *Resp.* 335D; cf. above 35,26-7.

299. chs 4-7; 11,2-3.

300. *Resp.* 2, 379C6-7: *tôn kakôn all'atta khrênai zêtein ta aitia, kai ou theon*; cf. 34,13-14 with n. 243; 47,13-14; Introduction, 2.1, T2.

301. cf. Erler (1978), p. 149 n. 1, with references to *Or. Chald.* fr. 53 Des Places = Procl. *in Remp.* 2,220,14; *Hymn.* 1,5; *in Remp.* 2,104,18.

302. cf. *in Tim.* 1,374,8-12.

303. Presumably the Chaldaeans.

304. This could be an allusion to Aristotle, who in *DA* 3.6 claims that the intellect knows evil, namely by means of its contrary (430b22-3; compare Plato *Phaed.* 97D; *Leg.* 7, 816D; Arist. *Metaph.* 4.2, 1004a10). See also n. 357; Philop. *On Aristotle on Intellect* 82,27-31 (transl. Charlton, p. 97): 'It is not when we are asleep or mad, because it is not functioning, that it knows lacks of forms, but because the knowledge of contraries or opposites is the same. Plainly when it knows light it also knows the lack of this; similarly with good and rest.' See also Themistius *in DA* 111,26-112,1, who denies knowledge of evil to the *divine* intellect.

305. Knowledge and production coincide for the gods. See 42,14-16, and also 61,17-24, Proclus' final words on this matter.

306. At *TP* 1.18, p. 88,1-7 Proclus refers to authors of esoteric writings who seem to suggest that the gods cause evil *qua* evil. This view amounts to positing a maleficent cause (*kakopoion aitian*) among the gods and is condemned by Proclus as bordering on the absurdities of the barbarians and the fictional tales of the war of the Giants. Cf. Saffrey & Westerink (1968), p. 88 n. 1 (at p. 154): 'Ce sont évidemment les Gnostiques en général et les Manichéens en particulier qui supposent un dieu mauvais, qui n'est autre que la matière.' See also ibid., p. 88 n. 2.

307. *TP* 1.18, p. 85,6-10.

308. Evils are *necessary* for the whole; see chs 7 and 60. For the whole there is only good: cf. *TP* 1.18, p. 84,20-4; 27.

309. Proclus manages to uphold the view expressed in *Resp.* 2, 379B15-16, according to which the good is the cause of everything (is 'responsible for', *aition*, everything) yet is responsible for good things only, not for bad things (*tôn de kakôn anaition*).

310. The forms are causes *for* the sensible, yet *of* form. The forms transcend the sensible and are not themselves formless. Likewise the gods are causes *for* the evils, but *of* good.

311. The same question is treated, with similar arguments, at *in Parm.* 829,23-831,24. See also Syrianus *in Metaph.* 107,8-9.

312. Compare *ET* prop. 76 (and the more general propositions 28-30).

313. *Theaet.* 176A7-8. See Introduction, 2.1, T1.

314. This passage is loosely inspired by *Theaet.* 176A-177A.

315. *Pol.* 269D5-6.

316. cf. 40,13-14.

317. *Theaet.* 176E3-4.

318. From the Neoplatonic doctrine of demiurgy Proclus derives an additional argument against the view that the forms are causes of evil. When it is said in the *Timaeus* that the demiurge looks at the intelligible model (*Tim.* 28A6, 29A3), Proclus takes this to mean that the demiurge interiorises the forms: they are contained in him in an intellective way (and display a greater diversity than at the purely intelligible level). By these forms the demiurge creates. And his creatures assimilate themselves to the demiurge, that is to the forms contained in and constituting his being. Now, if the forms – or at least some forms – caused evil, the demiurge would produce evil effects. *Quod non.*

319. *Tim.* 29E3.

320. *Tim.* 30A2-3. See n. 16.

321. The demiurge in the *Timaeus* acts 'by his very being' (by consequence, in an unchanging and atemporal way) and in a universal way, by which features he is to be distinguished from the lower demiurges (such as the young gods). See nn. 16 and 17.

322. This whole passage refers to *Theaet.* 176A1-4.

323. cf. *in Eucl.* 144,16-17: the circular stems from limit, the rectilinear from the unlimited.

324. cf. Plot. 5,9[5],10,2-5; ps.-Dion. *De div. nom.* 4,30, pp. 175,16-176,1 Suchla.

325. See 25,2-3 with n. 182; 40,6; and 40,15-17, with n. 293.

326. i.e. from the demiurge and the young gods (the encosmic gods).

327. Plotinus had claimed, against Aristotle (*Cat.* 3b24-25; *Phys.* 1.6, 189a32-3), that there is a contrary to substance as such, namely matter, and that the contrary of substance is evil, since substance is good (1,8 [51], 6). Simplicius *in Cat.* 5, pp. 109,5-110,25 gives a refutation of Plotinus – partly with the same arguments as those found in Proclus' section on matter (esp. *DMS* 37,6-25) – followed by a summary of the Proclean doctrine of evil. Cf. Opsomer (2001b), pp. 31-5.

328. *Leg.* 10, 896E5-6; see nn. 182 and 293.

329. 'The soul that is disposed to preserve itself' is the soul that can correct itself, because it has within itself measure and reason; it is this soul that can 'adapt its activities to a superior soul.' The other kind of soul cannot correct itself, because it lacks an internal measure; it must receive this from elsewhere. In this it resembles bodies (cf. *ET* 44). It always remains what it is. The latter kind of soul must probably be equated with the 'images of souls', i.e. the irrational souls of ch. 25 (the irrational souls of animals, but also the irrational soul that gets attached to the human soul when the latter descends; see 46,4-5). The former soul is the soul that the Athenian Stranger calls maleficent (see n. 182), the meaning of which Proclus tries to minimize by saying that it can merely be hindered in its activities and powers; in itself it remains good. Indeed, Proclus maintains that no soul can be affected in its substance. The so-called irrational soul can, but only because it is not really a soul: it is an 'image of a soul', 'the mortal life' (*ET* 64, p. 62,11-12; 209, p. 182,19-20). Proclus nowhere explains what the maleficent soul according to him is. In his extant works he merely rejects the view of Plutarch of Chaeronea and Atticus, who equate the maleficent soul of the *Laws* with the precosmic soul, say that the irrational precedes the rational and make the irrational soul a principle of evil (cf. *in Tim.* 1,381,26-384,1; 1,391,6-17). Proclus himself probably considered the maleficent soul a cosmic soul, yet one that is clearly inferior to the rational soul of the *Laws* and, moreover, can adapt itself to that superior soul. It apparently also is the principle from which the irrational life is derived, as in 25,2 Proclus calls the irrational souls part of this maleficent soul. See also *TP* 1.14, pp. 63,21-64,13.

330. cf. *Leg.* 10, 898C6.

331. cf. ch. 33, with our n. 228, referring to the view of Plotinus.

332. *Phaedr.* 248A6-8: *glikhomenai men hapasai tou anô* [...], *adunatousai de hupobrukhiai sumperipherontai.*

333. *Soph.* 254A9-B1: '[The form Being] isn't at all easy to see because that area is so bright (*dia to lampron tês khôras*) and the eyes of most people's souls (*ta tês tôn pollôn psukhês ommata*) can't bear to look at what's divine (*karterein pros to theion aphorônta adunata*).'

334. i.e. the mortal life forms that it acquires on its descent (see 46,4-5), and which stem from the principle of irrational life (the so-called maleficent soul). Cf. 25,2; 45,19-27, with our notes.

335. *Phaedr.* 248C5-8.

336. The term inclination, *rhopê*, is derived from *Phaedr.* 247B, cited at 33,7-8 and 49,16-17.

337. A summary of Proclus' causal analysis of evil can be found at *in Remp.* 1,37,23-39,1.

338. cf. Iambl. *De myst.* 4,7; Orig. *Contra Cels.* IV 64 vol. I, p. 334,33 Kö., p. 552 Delarue.

339. The expression is taken from *Theaet.* 146A8. See also Porphyry *De abst.* 2,53,1.

340. Cf. Iambl. *De myst.* 4,7,1-5.

341. *Resp.* 2, 379C6-7 (*alla atta aitia*), quoted at 34,14 (see n. 243; Introduction, 2.1, T2) and 41,10-11. Proclus insists on the fact that Plato here uses the plural and an indefinite pronoun (*atta*).

342. A combination of *Theaet.* 176A en 176E; see nn. 97 and 34; Introd. 2.1, T1 & 1'; see also 40,13-14.

343. *Phaedr.* 254B7: *en hagnôi bathrôi.*

344. *Resp.* 7, 533D2; *Soph.* 254A10.

345. *Phaedr.* 246E2; 251B3; C8; 255D1, *Resp.* 8, 550B2. Cf. Erler (1978), p. 170, n. 1.

346. See ch. 50.

347. *Leg.* 9, 860D (Socrates); *Tim.* 86DE; *Meno* 77A-78B. See also Procl. *De prov.* 57,12-13: 'We claim that evil is unwilled by all. And it will seem good to those who choose it.' Cf. *in Parm.* 1024,28-33 (and compare Arist. *EN* 3.1, 1111a22-4), *in Remp.* 2,355,11-352,2.

348. *Phaedr.* 247B3-4. Cf. above, 33,7-8.

349. cf. 60,9-21; *TP* 1.18, p. 85,24.

350. cf. *Tim.* 28C2-3 (transl. D.J. Zeyl): 'Further we maintain that, necessarily, that which comes to be (*tôi genomenôi*) must come to be by the agency of some cause (*hup'aitiou tinos anagkên einai genesthai*).'

351. i.e., everything that exists is produced by an efficient cause, but must also revert to this cause, which then simultaneously functions as its final cause. Anything that is not caused by a cause operating *per se*, but merely by a cause producing it accidentally, does not have a true existence (*hupostasis*), but merely a parasitical existence (*parupostasis*), as a side-effect. The origin of this idea can be traced back to Plato's *Sophist*, 288C1-5: 'when things that participate in motion, putting forth some goal (*skopon*) and trying to achieve it, at each attempt are deflected (*paraphora*) from it and fail to achieve it (*apotunkhanei*), shall we say that this is the effect of symmetry among them, or of the want of symmetry?' For a more extensive explanation see the Introduction, 2.4.3, and Opsomer & Steel (1999), pp. 244-60.

352. cf. Arist. *EN* 3.4, 1113a15-22; *EE* 4.13, 1127a21-2.

353. *epeisodiôdes*. See also *in Remp.* 1,38,26-9; *in Tim.* 3,303,22; Simpl. *in Cat.* 109,29-110,5; *De dec. dub.* 15,2; 20,3; *De prov.* 34,11. Already Plutarch of Chaeronea used the term in a similar context: *De an. procr.* 1015BC; *Quaest. conv.* 734C (where it is linked to causes operating 'from outside', just as in the present text). The metaphor derives from Aristotle: *Poet.* 1451b33-5. See Opsomer & Steel (1999), p. 256 n. 145.

354. cf. *Phaedr.* 246A6-B1 (transl. A. Nehamas & P. Woodruff, slightly adapted): 'Let us then liken the soul to the natural union of a team of winged horses and their charioteer. The gods have horses and charioteers that are themselves all good and consist of good things, while everyone else has a mixture'. Ordinary souls, Plato continues, have one good and one bad horse. (Proclus mentions the bad horse at 33,7-8 and 49,16-17). For the different meaning of the 'horses' with respect to gods, on the one, and humans, on the other hand, see Hermias *in Phaedr.* 127,8-13 and esp. 121,35-122,24, where Hermias explains that the human soul differs from the divine in that the former can become evil in its powers, the latter not. No soul, however, can be affected in its substance (compare *DMS* 21,15-28; 39,16-26). All souls are 'winged', but only non-divine souls shed their wings (*Phaedr.* 246B7-C8).

355. *Phaedr.* 246A8 (*autoi te agathoi kai ex agathôn*) and B3 (*ho d'ex enantiôn kai enantios*). Plato probably means that the horses are good or bad, respectively, and come from (*ex*) a good or bad stock. But for Proclus, *ex* refers not to their bloodline, but to the powers of which they consist and which are either good or 'contrary' (not only to the good, but to one another). Cf. *in Alc.* 227,12-15 Segonds; Steel (1978), p. 69 n. 68.

356. In this chapter Proclus explains the 'properties' of evil as privations of the good at different levels of reality. What we get here then is a summary of his metaphysical hierarchy, with all of its attributes negated. For the reader's convenience, we briefly explain the levels to which Proclus makes allusion.

(1) the highest good.

(2.1) the first intelligible triad, consisting of (2.1.1) limit, (2.1.2) unlimited, and (2.1.3) the first mixture. Proclus also refers to an internal triadic organisation of (2.1.3) : beauty – truth – measure. The first intelligible triad (2.1) is the level of One-Being. Since being shines forth for the first time in the third term of this triad (2.1.3), Proclus can say that it contains the monads of beings. (Since Proclus speaks of the first limit, he could also be referring to limit and the unlimited as henads, that is above the level of being; more probably he does not want to distinguish here between limit and unlimited as henads, and limit and the unlimited as the constituents of the first being).

(2.2) the second intelligible triad, 'eternity', 'life' or 'power'. Power holds the middle position of the intelligible triads (2.1-2.2-2.3), just as it did at a higher level, within the triad (2.1.1-2.1.2-2.1.3). Borrowing a phrase from the *Timaeus* (37D), level 2.2 is designated as 'eternity remaining in one', that is, it 'remains in' and is dependent upon the One-Being (2.1). Note that Plato does not say that it remains in *the* one (which would be the highest one), but in one. Cf. Opsomer (2000a), p. 367.

(2.3) the third intelligible triad, or the *autozôon* or the very first living being (participating immediately in life [2.2]). As the universal paradigm it contains all the forms, but still in a hidden and undivided way.

(3) the three intelligible-intellective triads, consisting of (3.1.) the triad of being, (3.2) the triad of power (the continuity and power of being), and (3.3) the perfecting (*telesiourgos*) triad. This reflects the structure remaining-procession-reversion.

(4) the intellective realm, of which only the first triad – that of the 'parents' – is mentioned here : (4.1) the 'unitary summit', 'monadic cause' or Kronos, (4.2) the 'summit of fertility' or 'generative power' or Rhea, and (4.3) the summit of demiurgy or efficient creation, or Zeus (the universal demiurge, creating universal things in a universal way, *tôn holôn holikôs*).

(5) the hypercosmic or 'assimilative' gods. Among these is a demiurgic triad (5.1) that *orders* and exercises *providence* over divisible beings, yet in a universal way (*tôn merôn holikôs*).

(6) the hypercosmic-encosmic or 'immaculate' gods.

357. cf. Plot. 1,8[51],1,9; Arist. *DA* 3.8, 431b29-432a3.

358. This introduction echoes Plot. 1,8[51],1,7-15. See also1,8[51],9. The idea may well go back to *Phaed.* 97D. Cf. *Leg.* 7, 816D; Arist. *DA* 430b22-3.

359. In the (lost) commentary on the *Philebus*, according to Westerink (1962), pp. 167-8. But one can also think of the extant commentary on the *Parmenides*, or, with Boese, of *ET* prop. 8ff., or *in Remp.* 1,269ff.

360. cf. 35,5-8, with our notes.

361. Westerink (1962 p. 168) points out that Isaak Sebastokrator has christianised the text: 'the power that resides in Him'.

362. cf. *Phil.* 64A6-65A7.

363. cf. *TP* 3.9, p. 38,5-7; 3.11, pp. 43,19-44,20. This triad is operative in the production of any mixture, and stands 'in the portal of the good' (cf. *Phil.* 64C1), which for Proclus means that it consists of pre-essential henads.

364. *Tim.* 37D6: *menontos aiônos en heni*.

365. What is meant is privation of form. See ch. 38, and esp. ch. 52.

366. cf. *Resp.* 10, 608E3-4; *DMS* 5,1-4.

367. See also ch. 7.

368. Compare Plot. 1,8[51],5,12-14.

369. cf. *Resp.* 352C (the discussion with Thrasymachus). See Proclus' commentary: *in Remp.* 1,20,27-21,7.

370. cf. 38,13-14.

371. A remark apparently first made by Amelius: cf. Procl. *in Remp.* 1,24,7-9.

372. i.e. the corresponding virtue.

373. cf. 7,48-50.

374. i.e. evil destroys everything to which it inheres (e.g. the disease dwelling in a body).

375. *Leg.* 9, 860D; *Tim.* 86DE.

376. cf. 49,11-14, with n. 347.

377. There is no exact parallel for the triad will-power-activity (*boulêsis-dunamis-energeia*). At *in Tim.* 1,171,10-25, Proclus explains that the hyperessential triad is goodness-will-providence (*agathotês-boulêsis-pronoia*), and its intelligible counterpart being-power-activity (*ousia-dunamis-energeia*). The triad in the present passage corresponds to the latter threesome, with its first term being replaced by the middle term of the highest triad (which is above being). In a number of texts, power is treated as being posterior to will, e.g. *TP* 1,103,3-5. In the *Timaeus* (29E1-30A6) Proclus discerns the triad will-power-providence (*boulêsis-dunamis-pronoia*), while the triad will-power-knowledge (*boulêsis-dunamis-gnôsis*) is found in the *Laws* (901D1-902A5); cf. *TP* 1,72,21-74,6. Providence and *gnôsis* could easily both be seen as forms of activity, which would give us the same triad as that of the present text. This structure is actually underlying Proclus' account in *TP* 1,72.21-74,6. See also *in Alc.* 125,8-12; Olymp. *in Gorg.* 59, pp. 65,20-66,2 (the triad good [i.e. good will]-power-activity, and the 'Proclean' idea that evil is due not to power, but to weakness).

378. Arist. *Phys.* 1.9, 192a14 (*hê hetera moira tês enantiôseôs*). In this passage Aristotle distinguishes privation from the substrate (192a14-16, transl. R.P. Hardie & R.K. Gaye, ed. J. Barnes): 'For the one which persists [i.e. the substrate] is a joint cause, with the form, of what comes to be – a mother as it were. But *the other part of the contrariety* may often seem, if you concentrate your attention on it as an evil agent (*kakopoios*), not to exist at all.' In privation, according to Aristotle, one part of the contrariety destroys the other, as contraries are mutually destructive. Proclus sides with Aristotle against Plotinus in upholding the difference between privation and the substrate, yet refuses to admit that privation would be evil (cf. ch. 38,1-9, and also 32,14-16).

379. cf. ch. 50.

380. These beings have in common that they are partial natures capable of change with respect to their rank, by letting themselves be guided or ruled either by what is superior or by the inferior. See also *TP* 3.27, p. 94,15-21; *in Tim.* 1,380,24-381,6; *in Alc.* 117,22-5. Cf. Segonds (1985), t. 1, *notes complémentaires* 5 and 6 for p. 97 (pp. 189-90).

381. cf., e.g., *in Parm.* 1045,30-1. For the readers' convenience we present this in the form of a table:

beings in which evil exists	their governing principle
(particular) souls	intellect
irrational souls (the images of the soul)	reason
(particular) bodies	nature

382. See *TP* 1.18, p. 86,14-16: the gods are not responsible for evil, but the weakness of the receiving natures.

383. *nosos* and *aiskhos*, respectively.

384. This whole section is based on *Soph.* 227C10-228E5. Disease of the soul is defined as 'sedition among things naturally akin', such as opinions at variance with desires, courage with pleasures, reason with pain. Under this heading are ranked vices such as cowardice, intemperance and injustice. Foulness, on the other hand, is due to lack of proportion causing a failure to 'hit the mark'. In the soul this consists in ignorance. Cf. Cornford (1935), p. 179: 'Ignorance (*agnoia*) is the swerving aside of the soul's impulse towards truth, and (as Socrates has taught) is always 'involuntary' – against the true wish for the right end.'

385. Namely, evil of the body, disease of the soul, foulness of the soul. At 56,15-18, however, Proclus also divides the evil of the body into disease and foulness. The same distinction is applied in the section on providence, where it is moreover paralleled with the division of the evils of the soul (cf. 60,4-6). See also 28,10-11. Cf. Plotinus 1,8[51],5,21-4.

386. *dianoia* and *doxa*, respectively.

387. *epistême* and *doxa*, respectively. Cf. *Soph.* 228E6-230E4: the Stranger explains that ignorance may be subdivided in two categories: (1) 'one large and grievous kind of ignorance' or complete stupidity, in which case one thinks one knows a thing when one does not know it; and (2) forms of partial ignorance. To these apply different remedies, 'education' for the former kind of ignorance, 'instruction in handicraft' for the latter (229D1-3). Education is later subdivided into admonition (*nouthetêsis*) and refutation through cross-questioning (*elenkhos*).

388. *gnôseis* and *hormai*.

389. *orexeis, aisthêseis* and *phantasiai* are all non-rational. See, e.g., *in Parm.* 893,6-7.

390. i.e. the bodily evil.

391. The text is sound: nature governs body, the principle of life (soul) governs irrational soul, and what is prior to rational soul (i.e. intellect) governs the rational soul.

392. On this dilemma , its history and Proclus' solution, see Opsomer & Steel (1999), esp. pp. 229-31 and 259-60.

393. *Tim.* 30A2-3. See n. 15; Introduction, 2.1, T3.

394. cf. 8,6-9, 9,5-6, 37,6-8, 42,7-20 *et passim*.

395. god, intellect, soul, and nature, respectively.

396. cf. *in Tim.* 1,377,22-4. See already Max. Tyr. *Or.* 41,125-131 Trapp.

397. The transition is somewhat abrupt, yet the parallel text *in Tim.* 1,377,7-378,29 shows that this idea belongs in the same context. Proclus has argued that the necessary existence of a realm where evils occur is reconcilable with the existence of providence. Vices of the soul are partial and only from a partial perspective evil: they are not evil to the whole, but only to the partial soul. A further distinction consists in the difference between evils that affect only the *choices* of the soul (impression, consent and choice, but not yet impulse), and those that are also expressed in *deeds*. Proclus makes his point in the next chapter (59): providence is concerned with both choices and deeds, and punishes the soul for both in case they are bad.

398. cf. Simpl. *in Phys.* 9,361,4.

399. Proclus is thinking of the case of a person who is prepared to harm another for the sake of his own interest, but unknowingly contributes to the well-being of the other, thus promoting the good from a universal perspective.

400. *ôdis*, as in 59,6 ('woes').

401. cf. *in Tim.* 1,380,8-20.

402. It is a good thing for a soul to be punished when it needs to be: cf. *Gorg.* 477A.

403. A more elaborate account can be found at *in Tim.* 3,302,4-31. The laws of the souls are implanted in the souls themselves, so that they have the full responsibility for the kind of life they lead and the punishments they incur.

404. i.e. the soul is either incarnated (it 'projects' a specific life) or it clings to the heavenly sights and is carried around, as is described in the *Phaedrus*. See n. 117.

405. cf. *De dec. dub.* 29, where Proclus is arguing that both generation and corruption are necessary. Generation is according to nature, but the thing destroyed seems to suffer corruption contrary to its nature; one could however say that even destruction is for that thing *according to* its nature, and therefore in a sense good. See also *in Tim.* 1,376,28-377,7.

406. *Soph.* 228A1-2; 228E6-229A1.

407. A stock phrase since Aristotle (*Phys.* 2.1, 193b8; 2.2, 194b13; 2.7, 198a27; *Metaph.* 7.7, 1032a25; 12.3, 1070a8). Cf. Procl. *in Parm.* 884,1.

408. Proclus is probably thinking of the many different geometrical figures which can be derived from the same formula: many triangles (right-angled, equilateral, different scalenes, etc.) share the same definition of 'the triangle'.

409. Proclus considers a thing in which a change occurs from two different perspectives: the thing taken as being itself a whole, and then a change is unnatural, as it entails the alteration of the rational principle inherent in the thing; or the thing taken as part of another whole, and then the change is natural from the perspective of the encompassing whole.

410. cf. 36,5-7.

411. *Resp.* 2, 379B16. See also *in Remp.* 1,36,25-9.

412. *Epist.* 2, 312E1-3: 'all things are around the king of all, and they all exist for his sake, and that is the cause of all things beautiful.' This passage is also cited by Plotinus: 1,8 [51], 2,28-30. For the history of the interpretation of the second Letter see Saffrey & Westerink (1974), pp. XX-LIX.

413. In the gods knowledge and production coincide: see 42,14-20, with our notes ad loc. For knowledge of evil, see 51,1-6, with n. 357, and n. 304.

Philological Appendix

We follow some of the conventions set out in Charlton - Bossier 1991, p. 27: 'read' introduces readings found in one or more Latin MSS but not accepted by Boese; 'conjecture' introduces readings not found in the MSS which, it is suggested, restore Moerbeke's original Latin; 'understand' introduces words corresponding, it is suggested, to words in Proclus' original Greek which were either not in Moerbeke's manuscript or which he misread or misinterpreted; 'sc.' signals the presumable Greek equivalent for a Latin term.

1,5-6	*Nichil autem deterius ... scribere*: Proclus must have written οὐδὲν δὲ χεῖρον καὶ ἡμᾶς ... ἀναγράψαι (Westerink 1962, p. 165).
2,6	The text is sound: *ut non* stands for ἵνα μή, 'because otherwise' (Westerink 1962, p. 165), 'unless'.
2,19	Perhaps delete the first *et* (lacking in Isaak Seb.). Yet *et ... et* (καὶ ... καί) is also possible.
2,21	Do not delete *malum aut* in *aut neque esse malum aut neque factum esse malum*, contrary to what Boese suggests. Cf. 2,30-1, *omnia enim entia et facta sunt et sunt*.
2,24	For *fontem* 'beyond the source' understand *fons* (Westerink 1962, p. 166). The good is indeed equated with, and not beyond the source of beings. E.g. *DMS* 14,15-16.
2,27	*multo ergo opus est*, sc. πολλοῦ οὖν δεῖ.
3,4	It is clear that something is missing after *alterum*. The lacuna has been completed by C. Steel, based on the parallel passage in ps.-Dionysius: <*aut non ens est nullatenus ens aut quod superessentiale; sed impossibile le malum esse ultra non esse superessentiale, quod bonum est;*>. Cf. Steel 1997, p. 98 n. 17.
3,6-8	The text is sound (Westerink 1962, p. 166). There is no lacuna in line 8.
3,20	*ypostato* stands for ὑποστάτου, from the noun ὑποστάτης.
3,21	For *operantibus* understand or conjecture *ex se operantibus* αὐτουργούντων, as in Isaak Seb. (Pépin 2000, p. 9 n. 33). Cf. *Theol Plat.* 5,69,20-1 and 5,62,17.
4,11	For *semper* understand πάντως (Isaak Seb.).
4,18	After *vincitur quidem* (μὲν) *melius a deteriori* a clause is missing. It is preserved, however, in Isaak Sebastokrator's paraphrase: ποτὲ δὲ τὸ χεῖρον ὑπὸ τοῦ κρείττονος.
4,30	For *ad ipsam* (πρὸς αὐτὴν) understand *ad se ipsam* (πρὸς αὐτήν).

5,6 To supply the lacuna after *aut*, we suggest with Boese adding *malum esse aut*.

5,10-11 *simul omnis*, sc. σύμπας.

5,19-20 For *generibus* (γένεσιν, from γένος) understand *generationem* (γένεσιν, from γένεσις) (Boese).

5,21 Before *esse* add *oportet* (Boese).

5,25 *ducente*. One would rather expect *ducta*. Probably Moerbeke interpreted the passive form ἀγομένης as a medium.

5,25 For *ut esse* conjecture or understand *ad non esse* (εἰς τὸ μὴ εἶναι). Boese suggests that Moerbeke may have read ὡς for εἰς and left out the negation.

5,26 The text is corrupt: *ab ente* fits better in the previous line, before *esse* (cf. 51,19-20), but probably much more is lacking after *fugiente*. For *non ens* (μὴ ὄν) perhaps understand *non vivens* (μὴ ζῶν or μὴ ζῷον), or maybe μεῖον, or perhaps even for *ad aliud non ens* (ἐπ' ἄλλο μὴ ὄν) understand *ad amenenon* (ἐπ' ἀμενηνόν, cf. 3,5; 7,37; *in Parm.* 834,22-3: ἄζωον καὶ ἀμενηνόν).

5,29 For *ipsi esse* understand *ipso esse* (αὐτῷ τῷ εἶναι).

6,6 Punctuate *imperfectius factum propter defectum, distat*. Cf. the Greek of Isaak Sebastokrator (ἀτελέστερον διὰ τὴν ἔλλειψιν γινόμενον).

6,7 For *sue unitatis* understand *sua unitate*. Moerbeke failed to see that the genitive in the Greek should be interpreted as a comparative genitive, the Latin equivalent of which is an ablative.

6,10 After *et pulcrum* add *et turpe* (Cousin).

6,14 Conjecture or understand *eius que magis et minus <iniustitia, que quidem minus> quanto minus est iniustitia*.

6,28 *enuntiative* probably stands for ἀποφαντικῶς or even ὑφηγητικῶς. Cf. *Theol. Plat.* 1,9,20-10,5; *in Tim* 1,21,18-26.

6,36 *transitum*, sc. πάροδον.

7,6 For *potentibus* understand *potentia* (neuter plural). Boese suspects that Moerbeke has misinterpreted the genitive δυναμένων as being congruent with αὐτῶν (7,5, *ipsis*), whereas it is presumably governed by μέχρι (7,5, *usque ad*).

7,7 *virtutis* most probably stands for δυνάμεως.

7,9 *monoydaliter*, sc. μονοειδῶς.

7,11 For *ex causis* (ἐξ αἰτιῶν) understand *ex ipsis* (ἐξ αὐτῶν) (Thillet, cited by D. Isaac).

7,11-12 *nata sunt*, sc. πέφυκεν.

7,21 *ante*, sc. ἀντί.

7,22 For *autem que* (δ'ἅ) understand *propter* (διά) (Boese).

7,22-3   *omnis potentie et omnis bonitatis*, sc. παντοδύναμον καὶ πανάγαθον.

7,26-7   *illius coexistentiam negligens*, sc. τῆς ἐκείνου μετουσίας στερούμενον.

7,27   *transumptionis*, sc. μεταλήψεως.

7,32-3   *autem ergo* stands for δ'ἄρα. Cf., e.g., *in Crat.* 71, p. 31,8; 88, p. 43,12 Pasquali.

7,37   The syntactic value of *le impermanens* is unclear. Our translation corresponds to Isaak Sebastokrator's version: τὸ ἑαυτῆς ἀμενηνὸν τῇ ἐκείνου ῥώσασα δυνάμει. For Moerbeke's translation of ἀμενηνόν, compare 3,5-6: *amenenoteron (id est immansivius)*.

7,40   For *idem ... passio* understand *eandem ... passionem* (Moerbeke mistook τὸ αὐτὸ ... πάθος for a nominative) (Boese).

7,41   For *abscendentis habitus* understand *abscendente habitu* (corresponding to a Greek genetivus absolutus) (D. Isaac).

7,41-2   Punctuate *abscendente bono penitus, non est* etc.

8,2   *ex Platonis narratione*, sc. ἀπὸ τῆς Πλάτωνος ὑφηγήσεως.

8,14   *insinuat coimplicationem non boni*, sc. ἀναπίμπλαται τῆς παρεμπλοκῆς τοῦ μὴ ἀγαθοῦ.

8,28   *obtentum*, sc. κρατούμενον.

9,4   For *amanti* (ἐρωμένῳ) understand *qu(a)erenti* (ἐρομένῳ, Isaak Seb.).

9,8   For *mesiteiam* perhaps understand μετουσίαν. See our note *ad loc.*

10,6   *non diffugit*, sc. οὐ διαφεύγει + inf. (cf. *in Tim.* 3,254,25).

10,10-12   For *sole*, *aere*, and *patre* understand *soli*, *aeri*, and *patri*, respectively. The ablatives translate Greek datives, which should presumably be interpreted as expressing the perspective from which something is the case.

10,13   For *quod autem* (τὸ δέ) understand *hoc* (τόδε).

10,19   For *scire* (εἰδέναι) understand *esse* (εἶναι, as in Isaak Seb.). Moerbeke, or a scribe in the textual tradition preceding Moerbeke, presumably misread εἶναι as εἰδέναι. If one does not accept the correction, one has to translate: 'as we do not know evil that ...'

11,7   For *incidentes* read *insidentes* (with V, Westerink 1962, p. 166), a translation of ἐποχούμενοι, literally 'riding on' (cf. *Prov.* 17,2).

11,20   *enter deorum*. For the expression ὄντως θεοί see *in Tim.* 3,73,2; 3,225,25; *in Parm.* 1070,28; *Theol. Plat.* 1,2,27.

11,36   *Sustinentium*, sc. ὑποδεχομένων (cf. Alex. *in Meteor.* 90,65) in the sense of 'to give ear to'.

11,36-7   Punctuate *imbuunt, dicentes igitur* (taking up *dicentes* of line 34).

12,3   *indeflexis.* D. Isaac suggests to conjecture *indeflexa* (ἀτρεμῆ): 'we possess these ideas about the gods fixed in our minds.' This could be a reference to the ἀτρεμῆ φάσματα of *Phaedr.* 250C3, also cited, in the context of intellective knowledge, at *in Tim.* 1,302,7-8.

12,4   For *anime efimere* (ψυχαὶ ἐφήμεροι, as in Plato *Resp.* 10, 617D6-7) understand *anime eumoire* (ψυχαὶ εὔμοιραι, Taylor, but better ψυχαὶ εὔμοιροι), which refers to the undefiled souls. Cf. *in Tim.* 1,201,1-2, *in Remp.* 2,172,15; 2,254,13-22, and see Erler 1978, p. 45 n. 4 and Baltes 1982, col. 171.

12,5   *alatum inflantes.* Cf. Plato *Phaedr.* 251C5, φύουσα τὰ πτερά, 251C4 and 255D2, πτεροφυεῖν. As Boese cleverly points out, Moerbeke probably mistook φύσασαι ('having grown wings') for a form of φυσάω, 'to inflate'.

12,7   *innocua vita,* sc. ἀπήμων βίος. Cf. 36,10 (*vita innocua* = βίος ἀπήμων); *Theol. Plat.* 1,74,23.

12,12   *iniuriationis,* sc. ὕβρεως.

13,7   For *neque* (οὐδέ) understand *neque aliud* (as in 13,6) or *nihil* (οὐδέν) (Boese).

13,12   For *ad hec* read *adhuc* (with *O*).

13,21   For *et* (καὶ) understand *secundum* (κατά).

13,24   *nam quod similitudinis secundum unum et eternaliter ens,* sc. τὸ γὰρ ὁμοιότητος κατὰ τὸ ἓν καὶ αἰωνίως ὄν, which cannot be correct. Our translation is *ad sensum.* One could conjecture τὸ γὰρ <δι'> ὁμοιότητος κατὰ τὸ ἓν καὶ αἰωνίως ὄν (the expression δι'ὁμοιότητος is standardly used to emphasise the continuity of the procession; cf. *ET* 29). Another possibility is to conjecture τὸ γὰρ ὅμοιον τούτῳ ('that which is similar to this' [sc. to the One]).

14,17   *procedentium et procidentium* is a double translation of προκυψάντων, as appears from the marginal note in MS Vat. lat. 4568.

14,20   For *sed* conjecture or understand *et* (cf. Isaak Seb.).

14,24   *differenter,* sc. διαφερόντως.

17,15   *fluctuose,* sc. πλημμελῶς.

17,17   For *male* (κακῶς) understand *malos* (κακούς) (Cousin, Boese).

18,2-4   Punctuate *existentia, deinde et* and *aliorum providentiis?* (Baltes 1982, col. 171).

18,7   Conjecture or understand *potentia enim le <non> semper.* Cf. *De decem dub.* 23,11.

18,10   For *deus* understand *heros* (Taylor).

18,14   For *dictis malis* understand *dictorum malorum.* Moerbeke has probably mistaken a Greek *genitivus partitivus* for a *genitivus absolutus.* Plausibly one should even understand *dictarum malitiarum* (κακῶν for κακιῶν).

18,18   For *ipsam* (αὐτήν) understand *se ipsam* (αὐτήν) (Boese).

18,19   *desinentiam*, sc. λῆξιν.

19,9   *hominum devorationem*, sc. ἀνθρώπων ἐδωδήν.

19,18   *consummantium*, sc. τελευτώντων or τελευτησάντων.

19,19   For *cuius* understand *quorum* (ὧν – i.e. *consummantium*). Cf. 19,26: *talium custodes.*

19,20   Very corrupt. We suggest to understand *preterite vite* (παρελθούσης ζωῆς) for *preter ipsarum vitam* (παρὰ ἑαυτῶν ζωὴν).

19,29-31   *Que quidem igitur de diis et de melioribus generibus misericorditer aliqualiter nobis facta esse dicimus.* According to a marginal note in MS Vat. lat. 4568, *misericorditer* stands for ἵλεω. The prototype of the sentence is *Phaedo* 95A4-5. Westerink (1962, p. 166) has reconstructed the Greek as follows: τὰ μὲν δὴ παρὰ θεῶν καὶ παρὰ τῶν κρειττόνων γενῶν ἵλεά πως ἡμῖν γεγονέναι φαμέν, with παρά for περί and ἵλεα for ἵλεω.

20,1   After *autem* add *hic* (τὰ δὲ τῇδε) (Westerink, 1962, p. 166).

20,2   For *si autem* conjecture or understand *si autem <non>* (Westerink 1962, p. 166).

21,10   *hee ... hee ... hee ... hee*: a sudden transition from the neuter plural (cf. 21,1-2: 'superior beings') to the feminine plural ('divine souls'). D. Isaac's suggestion to conjecture *hec* for *hee* is, however, unnecessary, as the shift to souls is made anyway, at the latest by 21,20 (*illarum animarum*, prepared by 21,16 *animam* – in a reference to Plato).

21,12   *cum diis gloriatione* stands for the standard expression σὺν θεῶν πομπῇ. Cf. *in Crat.* 81,19.

21,16   For *facere* (ποιεῖν) understand *bibere* (πιεῖν), as in the text cited by Proclus (Plato, *Resp.* 10, 621A6-7) (Boese).

21,20   Westerink (1962, p. 167), remarking that a finite verb is missing, suggests to add *<dic>*.

21,21-6   The syntax is difficult. *Hee autem* in 26 takes up *hee autem* of 20-1. The reading of *OSV* may contain a trace of the original.

21,26   *in dependentibus*, sc. ἐν τοῖς ἐξηρτημένοις (σώμασι). Cf. *in Tim.* 3,135,19; 3,268,1-3.

21,27   For *animal, effulget* read *animal, facto autem* (γενομένου δὲ [i.e. ἐν ἠρεμίᾳ τοῦ ζῴου]) *effulget* (with *OSV*, Westerink, 1962, p. 167). Perhaps also conjecture *silent* for *silentes*.

22,6   For *ipsum* (αὐτό) understand *se ipsum* (ἑαυτό) (Boese). Otherwise translate 'that which is even incapable of preserving the light'.

22,11   *insatiabilitas et alarum defluentia.* Cf. the marginal gloss in MS
         Vat. lat. 4568, ἡ ἄτη καὶ ἡ πτερορρύησις. It is doubtful whether
         the original indeed read ἄτη. Yet ἄτη is mentioned by Proclus a
         few times in a quotation from Empedocles: 'the meadow of Ate' is
         the realm of sublunary generation and is called 'replete with
         evils' at *in Remp.* 2,257,25-8.

23,1   *habitum,* sc. ἐχόμενον (Boese).

23,6   For *quidem entibus* (μὲν οὔσαις) *ipsis* understand *manentibus*
         (μενούσαις) *ipsis.*

23,21   For *aliter* (ἄλλως) understand *alterius* (ἄλλης). Cf. *Resp.* 10,
         617D7: ἀρχὴ ἄλλης περιόδου. Punctuate *principium hic et peri-
         odi animabus alterius, et impotentia* etc.

24,1   *intuitione* stands for ἑστιάσεως (P. Thillet, see the app. crit. of D.
         Isaac). See the marginal note ἑστιασ in MS Vat. lat. 4568, and
         Psellus *OD* 197,3-5. Moerbeke always has difficulties translat-
         ing ἑστία and cognate forms, as can be gathered from the index
         in *Proclus. Commentaire sur la Parménide de Platon. Traduc-
         tion de Guillaume de Moerbeke,* edited by C. Steel, tome II, Leu-
         ven, 1985, p. 727.

24,10   *suborientia,* sc. ὑποφύοντα. Presumably one should understand
         προσφύ(ο)ντα as in *Tim.* 42C6 (cf. Boese's *app. fontium*).

24,12   For *ad continens vel portum* understand *ad pratum* (εἰς τὸν
         λειμῶνα). The marginal gloss in MS Vat. lat. 4568 reads λειμῶνα.
         Moerbeke presumably did not know the meaning of λειμῶνα,
         which he will have found in his Greek text, so he put *continens
         vel portum.* The second guess, *portum,* is based on his confusing
         λειμῶν with λιμήν. At l. 16 he translates ὁ ἐκεῖ λειμών (cf. *Phaedr.*
         248B7-C1) as *qui ibi continens.* The emendation is confirmed by
         the parallel in Psellus *OD* 197,8-10: κατιοῦσα δὲ ἀπὸ τῆς πρώτης
         τοῦ θεοῦ θεωρίας ἥξει δηλαδὴ εἰς τὸν λειμῶνα, περὶ οὗ Πλάτων
         πολὺν ποιεῖται λόγον (*Resp.* 10, 614E), καὶ θεάσεται τὰς ἐκεῖ
         ψυχάς. ἥξει δὲ καὶ ὑπὸ τῶν τῆς Ἀνάγκης ὅρων.

24,13-14 For *sub necessitatis terminum* understand *sub necessitatis
         thronum* (Cousin, Boese). Moerbeke may indeed have found ὑπὸ
         τὸν τῆς ἀνάγκης ὅρον ('beneath the limit of Necessity') in his
         manuscript. Psellus' paraphrasis (*OD* 197,10: ἥξει δὲ καὶ ὑπὸ
         τῶν τῆς Ἀνάγκης ὅρων) stands in the same tradition. But Pro-
         clus himself most probably wrote θρόνον, as in the passage in
         the *State* to which he is alluding (620E6-621A1: ὑπὸ τὸν τῆς
         Ἀνάγκης ἰέναι θρόνον, 'it passed beneath the Throne of Neces-
         sity') and which he quotes correctly at *in Remp.* 2,341,12;
         2,344,6; 2,344,20-6; 2,346,1; 2,346,15; *in Tim.* 3,277,30; *in Parm.*
         692,22.

24,16   For *et enim* conjecture *etenim.*

24,16   For *qui ibi continens* understand *quod ibi pratum*. See our note on 24,12.

24,20   For *anime* conjecture *omne*. Punctuate *ducit ad simile omne, anoian* etc. (D. Isaac).

24,30   For *nudi* perhaps understand or conjecture *nudis* (Boese, cf. Isaak Seb.).

24,35   For *bonos* conjecture or understand *boni* (Boese).

25,4   For *aliter* (ἄλλως) one should probably understand *totaliter* (ὅλως, with the value of 'actually', 'really').

25,17   The text is corrupt. We suggest for *unumquodque* to understand *unicuique*, and to supply *<bonum>*. Another lacuna is to be assumed after *eius autem que secundum ipsam*, which is probably the *pendant* of 25,12 *irrationalitate quidem enim ad rationem dependente*. Because of the lacuna Moerbeke failed to understand *eius* etc. as another *genitivus absolutus*. Therefore we suggest to understand ἑκάστῳ <ἀγαθόν>· τῆς δὲ καθ' αὑτὴν <ὑφεστώσης οὐκ ἐν τῷ ἐνεργεῖν καθ' αὑτὴν> κακὸν, ἀλλὰ κτλ. Cf. 26,1, *omni enim cui le secundum naturam agere non est.*

25,24   *elatum et virile,* τό τε γαῦρον καὶ αδρὸν (marginal gloss in MS Vat. lat. 4568). See also *in Tim.* 1,62,9.

25,25   *laxans,* sc. ἀμύσσων.

26,4   For *anima tali presente sortiente demone* understand *anima tali presentem sortiente demonem,* sc. ψυχῆς τοιαύτης ἡγουμένου λαχούσης δαίμονος. Moerbeke presumably failed to recognise the construction λαγχάνω + genitive.

26,11   After *operari,* read *aut in* (with *O*).

26,13   For *ante naturam* conjecture or understand *ante operationem*.

26,20   *superbum,* sc. γαῦρον (marginal gloss in MS Vat. lat. 4568).

27,5   After *manentem* read *autem* with *OSV,* and punctuate *aliquando, manentem autem, quod equidem est ducere corpus secundum naturam.*

27,7   *hoc autem in causis omnibus*: possibly a gloss added by Moerbeke.

27,25-6   Punctuate *et impressio, et ratio partita inde et in corpus defluxa neque pura manere potens – et rursum* etc.

27,32   Punctuate *quod turpe, nature ratione non obtinente, passio est* (Westerink, 1962, p. 167).

28,15-16 For *sed non²* read *neque* (with *O*).

28,17   For *ex ipsa* (ἔξω τῆς) *materia* understand *extra* (ἐξ αὑτῆς) *materiam* (Boese).

28,28   *difficultate,* sc. δυσχερείας. Cf. 36.10: *neque extra mortalem difficultatem* = οὐδὲ ἔξω τῆς θνητῆς δυσχερείας (Isaak Seb.).

29,6   For *apparet* understand *repleta sunt*. See the marginal gloss in
            MS Vat. lat. 4568: αναπιπλαται. *Apparet* (ἀναφαίνεται?) makes
            no sense; *repleta sunt* gives the required meaning and syntax.

29,7   *victa*: the perfect participle probably renders a Greek present
            participle.

29,19-20   For *ipsum immensuratio* (αὐτὸ ἀμετρία) understand *autoimmen-
            suratio* (αὐτοαμετρία) (Baltes 1982, col. 171).

30,8   *odiunt*, sc. στυγέουσιν, as specified in a marginal gloss in MS
            Vat. lat. 4568 and as in Hom. *Ilias* 20,65.

33,2-3   *preerat...materia* (ablative): 'was prior to matter' (Boese).

33,4-5   For *tollere quidem ad eum qui extra locum aurige caput le impo-
            tentes occumbere* conjecture and punctuate *has quidem tollere
            ad eum qui extra locum aurige caput, has de impotentes occum-
            bere*. Cf. *Phaedr.* 248A1-B1.

33,7   *exorbitatio* and *exorbitat*, sc. τὸ ἐμβριθές and βρίθει (*Phaedr.*
            247B3). Cf. the marginal glosses in MS Vat. lat. 4568.

33,12   *affectamus*, presumably a translation for γλιχόμεθα (as in
            Phaedr. 248A6). Cf. *in Parm.* 135,39 (Steel): 'hoc addiscere affec-
            tantibus' = 785,3-4, τοῖς τοῦτο μαθεῖν γλιχομένοις.

33,14   For *nullam* (οὐδέν) understand *non deum* (οὐ θεόν) (Boese), as
            in the passage quoted (*Resp.* 379C6-7).

34,20-1   Punctuate *compositum – visibile enim est, ut ait Timeus; quod
            autem apoion non visibile – sed cum emfasi* etc. (Baltes 1982,
            col. 171).

35,6   *ex se*, sc. αὐτόθεν.

35,7   For *sive* (εἴτε) understand *siquidem* (εἴ γε, as in Isaak Seb.)
            (Boese).

35,7   After *infinitum* add *et* (cf. *Theol. Plat.* 3,45,3-6).

35,11   For *ducere* understand *ducit*, as in Isaak Seb. ἄγει.

36,8-9   For *fabulati* understand μεθειμέναι (see Isaak Seb., as well as
            the marginal gloss in MS Vat. lat. 4568, and Plato *Leg.* 636D7),
            which may have been misread at some point as μυθούμεναι.
            Delete *in*, with *OV*.

36,12   For *ipsam* (αὐτήν) understand *seipsam* (αὑτήν) (Boese).

36,13   Punctuate *dicendum.* (full stop instead of question mark). 36,13
            aut (ἤ) introduces the answer (Baltes 1982, col. 171).

36,19   *Si itaque generatio gratia huius † aliud autem.* The text is cor-
            rupted. On the basis of the Greek and the sense we conjecture,
            e.g.: *si itaque generationis gratia illa, aliud autem.* ταύτης
            (*huius*) could be a corruption of αὕτη, or perhaps even of ὕλη.
            Compare H. Boese and D. Isaac, app. crit.

36,27   *ab ipsa*. The Greek tradition has ἐπ' αὐτῆς.

37,7	For *facere* (ποιεῖν) understand *esse* or *alicubi esse* (που εἶναι) (Boese).
37,9	For *ens* understand *ente*. Moerbeke wrongly made ὄντος depend on πρό (*ante*), whereas it formed an absolute genitive with ἀγαθοῦ (*bono*, 37,8) (Boese).
37,21	For *circa* (περί) understand *ante* (πρό) (Boese).
37,21-2	For *erit aliquod illorum* understand *erunt illa* (Boese). Cf. Isaak Seb. ἂν ὑπάρχοι ἐκεῖνα.
38,12	After *secundum se* add *bonum*. At 38,11 *OSV* have *bonum bonum*, a duplication which makes no sense. We suspect that the second *bonum* may have been transposed.
38,13	Perhaps emend *privatio simpliciter* <*non malum*>.
38,14	For *facta* conjecture or understand *tota facta*. Cf. Isaak Seb. παντελοῦς δὲ γενομένης.
38,17	For *nondum genitum non privatio quidem est* understand or conjecture *nondum genitum privatio quidem est* (Isaac).
38,24	For *magis que* perhaps understand *magisque* or *magis autem* (Boese).
39,7-8	Read and punctuate *ut qui illius sermo*. Against Boese and Isaac, we believe Proclus' text is sound, with the possible exception of *quas* instead of 39,6 *has* (cf. Westerink, 1962, p. 167).
39,21-2	For *quod autem potentie substantie contrarium* conjecture *quod autem potentie* <*aut substantie corruptivum potentie aut*> *substantie contrarium*.
39,32	Before *mirabile* add *quid* (Boese).
39,34-5	Delete *et alterius* with *OSV*.
39,46-7	For *propinquius enim corpus quam materia animarum* understand *propinquius enim corpus materiae quam animae*. The Greek can be plausibly reconstructed as: ἐγγύτερον γὰρ τὸ σῶμα τῆς ὕλης (genit. ruled by ἐγγύτερον) τῶν ψυχῶν (genit. comparationis).
39,51-2	Conjecture *hee autem ad* <*operationem* [sc. *suscipientes malitiam*], *quibus*> *malum operationis privatio* (Baltes 1982, col. 171).
41,10	For *alia ... causa* understand *alie ... cause*, as in Isaak Seb., Plat. *Resp.* 2, 379C6-7, and DMS 34,13-14; 47,13-14. Moreover, the context requires the plural.
43,9	For *illa* understand *illas* (sc. *species*, corresponding to the Greek neuter εἴδη).
43,29	For *alia et* (ἄλλα καί) understand *sed et* (ἀλλὰ καί).
44,8	For *maximum* read *maxime* (with *V*, Erler).
45,8	For *non quod* Boese suggests to understand *non solum*. The source of the corruption is unclear. Boese thinks that Moerbeke

may have written *non quidem*, misreading οὐ μέν for οὐ μόνον.
Westerink, on the contrary (1962, p. 167), claims that nothing is
wrong with the text: *non quod ... sed et* stands for οὐχ ὅτι ... ἀλλὰ
καί, as in 33,28.

45,20-3   The text is corrupt and probably has a large lacuna. In lines 23-
            7 two souls are compared, one having, the other lacking, the
            capacity of self-reflection and self-improvement. The first must
            be the maleficent soul, that is capable of improving itself (*huic
            malignate a se ipsa boniformi facte*); the second must be the
            irrational soul tied to the body (the so-called image of the soul;
            cf. ch. 25; *in Remp.* 2,70,7; *ET* 42,10-11; 44,7-8). The last type of
            soul, however, has not been introduced in the previous lines, as
            we have them. Also from the parallel in ps-Dion. *De div. nom.*
            4.30, 176,1-8 Suchla (not in Boese), it is obvious that something
            is missing. A lacuna should be assumed before 21-2 *hac boni-
            formi*. There is also a problem with 21 *sed quod aliquando dic-
            tum est a me*, as Proclus almost always uses the first person
            plural to refer to his own work and person, and never the
            expression ὑπ' ἐμοῦ. Moreover, the expression *neque hanc* (l. 20),
            sc. οὐδὲ ταύτην, often introduces an apodosis qualifying the con-
            ditional clause (e.g. *in Parm.* 877,23). *Sed quod aliquando dic-
            tum est a me* could correspond to a corrupted version of ἀλλ'
            ἄλλοτε ἄλλως γενομένην (for λεγομένην) λεκτέον. This could have
            been followed by something as <εἰ δὲ ἡ ἄλογος ψυχὴ διαμένει>,
            ταύτης ἀγαθοειδοῦς πως γενομένης κτλ.

46,1   *intutum*, sc. ἀνόσιον. We think that the reading *in totum*, found
            in two families of manuscripts (*OSV*), is closer to the original,
            although it makes no sense in Latin. It probably renders ανολον,
            itself a corruption of ἀνόσιον. Proclus is probably alluding to
            Leg. 10, 898C6: οὐδ' ὅσιον ἄλλως λέγειν (i.e. one should say about
            the soul governing the heavens that it is virtuous).

46,4   For *ipsam* (αὐτήν) understand *se ipsam* (αὑτήν) (Boese).

46,4   *cooritur*, probably προσυφαίνεται (προυφαίνεται according to the
            marginal gloss in MS Vat. lat. 4568). See *Tim.* 41D1-2 and, e.g.,
            Procl. *in Tim.* 1,236,6-8.

46,19   For *hanc* read *hec* with *OSV*.

47,4   For *multa* (πολλὰ, sc. αἴτια) and *unum* (ἓν, sc. αἴτιον) understand
            multe (sc. *cause*) and *una* (sc. *causa*) (Boese).

47,6-7   For *si itaque* (εἰ δὲ δή) understand *si oportet* (εἰ δὲ δεῖ) (Wester-
            ink, 1962, p. 167).

47,12-13   For *quoniam divinum non causas negavit horum dicere* probably
            understand τὸ θεῖον μὴ αἴτιον (*causas* for *causans*) ἀπέφηνε
            (Moerbeke probably read or misunderstood ἀπέφησε) τούτων
            λέγειν, combining suggestions made by Westerink 1962, p. 167
            and Baltes 1982, col. 171. The text as printed by Boese is diffi-

cult to translate: 'since he denied that a divine nature is not <?>
the cause[s] of evils' or perhaps 'since the divinity did not refuse
to admit that there are causes for these things.'

48,3 For *ipsas* (αὐτάς) understand *se ipsas* (αὐτάς).

48,6 *atheon illud et tenebrosum* is sound. Boese wants to understand
atheos illa et tenebrosa (sc. *species*). Boese argues that the original had indeed τὸ ἄθεον καὶ σκοτεινόν, but that this was congruent with εἶδος, and not with παράδειγμα. When Moerbeke
translated εἶδος by *species*, he should have put the quoted
expression in the feminine. However, Baltes (1982, col. 171) has
pointed out that Moerbeke probably understood τὸ ἄθεον καὶ
σκοτεινόν as a phrase on its own: 'this godless and dark thing',
whereas τῆς κακίας εἶδος is a mere apposition.

48,6-7 Punctuate *ostendit, malitie species* etc. (Baltes 1982, col. 171).

48,18-19 For *similium <in>commensurata communio* conjecture *dissimil-
ium incommensurata communio et mixtio* (τῶν ἀνομοίων
ἀσύμμετρος κοινωνία καὶ μίξις). Compare Steel 1997, p. 103.

49,16 For *victoriam*, sc. την ἀλκήν (marginal gloss in *v*) understand
tractum, sc. τὴν ὀλκήν (Westerink, D. Isaac).

50,6-9 Punctuate, with Westerink, D. Isaac and in accordance with the
Greek of Isaak Seb.: *oportune ipsum principaliter substans et
quodcumque ex causa fieri secundum naturam – omni enim
impossibile sine causa generationem habere – et ad aliquem
finem ordinem generationis ipsius referre.*

50,9 For *utrum igitur malum ponendum, aut* understand ποτέρων
(instead of πότερον) οὖν τὸ κακὸν θετέον; ἤ (ἤ *dubitativum*). For
the expression see *Theaet.* 186A2; *Hipp. Maj.* 303B1; B2
(ποτέρων δὴ τιθεῖς τὸ καλόν).

50,12 For *parientes* (τίκτοντες) conjecture *parturientes* (ὠδίνοντες)
(Taylor).

50,18 For *Igitur* (οὐκοῦν) understand *Nonne ...?* (οὔκουν;).

50,22 Punctuate *utique?*

50,38 For *qua* understand *cuius*. Isaak Seb. has ἦς, a *genitivus partitivus*, mistaken by Moerbeke for a *genitivus comparationis*.

50,43 After *non* add *ex* (with *OSV)*.

52,4 For *ipsius* (αὐτῆς) understand *sui ipsius* (αὐτῆς) (Boese).

52,13 For *azoia privatione* conjecture *azoia <id est, vitae> privatione*
('in mere lifeless<ness, that is> in privation <of life>'): a translit-
eration followed by a gloss from the translator (Cousin). Compare 51,16-17: *privatio et azoia (id est invitalitas).*

52,16 For *sui ipsius* (αὐτοῦ) understand *ipsius* (αὐτοῦ) (Boese).

52,19 *et hoc*, sc. καίτοι (Isaak Seb.).

53,4 *transortitur*, sc. μεταλαγχάνει.

53,9　　*latitante*, sc. οἰχομένης. Cf. *in Parm.* 171,24 (Steel): 'fugiens latito' = 833,29-30, φεύγων οἴχομαι.

53,17　　After *salvare* add, with Isaac and Boese, *le habens*. Cf. Isaak Seb. and *De prov.* 23,20.

54,4　　For *ipsius* (αὐτοῦ) understand *sui ipsius* (αὐτοῦ) (Boese).

54,22　　For *parypostasi aut veritate significante* understand παρυπόστασι<ν> τῇ ἀληθείᾳ σημαίνειν depending on δοκεῖ ὁ Σωκράτης (13). The final -ν- became η (*aut*).

55,11　　For *le* (τό) understand τῷ.

55,13　　The text is sound. It is not necessary to assume a lacuna.

56,10　　For *turpe* (αἶσχος) understand *adhuc* (πρός, as in Isaak Seb.) (Boese).

56,11-12　　Punctuate *impetibus – et enim appetitus non secundum rationem, et sensuum autem multi et fantasie precipites – quibus* etc.

57,6　　*le ornantium unumquodque*: probably understand τὸ κοσμητικὸν ἑκάστων. *ornantium* may be an error for *ornativum*; *unumquodque* stands for ἕκαστον, which may be a corruption for ἑκάστων.

57,8　　The text is sound. It is not necessary to assume a lacuna.

58,5　　There is a lacuna after *malum*, for which Cousin suggests *huic autem quod malum.*

58,6　　*inquietat*, sc. σαίνει (marginal gloss in MS Vat. lat. 4568).

58,7　　For *adversabitur* read *adversantur* (with *OSV*). For the formula compare Plot.1,1 [53] 12,6: τάχα δ' ἄν τις ἐξεύροι καὶ ὅπῃ μὴ μαχοῦνται.

58,8　　For *et* (καί) understand *si* (εἰ) (Boese).

59,6　　*conceptum*, sc. ὠδῖνα. For the expression see *in Tim.* 3,255,1: τὰς ἑαυτῶν ὠδῖνας ἀποπιμπλάντες.

59,14　　For *admittentis* understand or conjecture *animas admittentis*. Cf. Isaak Seb.

59,25　　For *ipsam* (αὐτήν) understand *seipsam* (αὐτήν, as in Isaak Seb.).

59,26　　Delete *esse* (with OSV and Isaak Seb.).

59,27　　*iniuriantibus*, sc. ἐξυβριζούσαις (ἐξυβρίζου according to the marginal gloss in MS Vat. lat. 4568).

59,27　　*competeret*, sc. ἐπέβαλλε, 'fall to the lot of' (hence indicating that which ought to be).

60,9　　After *est* a counterpart to the first member is missing: *preter naturam autem particularem* (Boese). Cf. Isaak Seb. and 60,23-4.

60,14　　For second *multa* (indefinite neuter) understand *mult(a)e* (sc. *figur(a)e*, Gr. σχήματα, neuter plural).

60,14   For *et idem* (καὶ ταὐτόν) understand *secundam ipsam*, sc. *ratio-nem* (κατ' αὐτόν, sc. τὸν λόγον) (Boese).

60,21   For *alii* (ἄλλῳ) understand *alio modo* (ἄλλως).

60,31   For *sic* (οὕτω) understand *huic* (τούτῳ, sc. *toti*) (Boese).

Select Bibliography

1. Editions and translations of the *Tria opuscula* and related texts

1.1. Proclus

Procli philosophi Platonici opera inedita quae primus olim e codd. mss. Parisinis Italicisque vulgaverat nunc secundis curis emendavit et auxit Victor Cousin, Parisiis, 1864 [= Frankfurt am Main, 1962].

Procli Diadochi Tria Opuscula (De providentia, libertate, malo). Latine Guilelmo de Moerbeka vertente et Graece ex Isaacii Sebastocratoris aliorumque scriptis collecta, ed. H. Boese (Quellen und Studien zur Geschichte der Philosophie, 1), Berolini, 1960.

Proclus. Trois Études sur la Providence, III, *De l'existence du mal.* Texte établi et traduit par Daniel Isaac, avec une note additionnelle par Carlos Steel (Collection des Universités de France), Paris, 1982.

Proklos Diadochos. Über die Existenz des Bösen. Übersetzt und erläutert von Michael Erler (Beiträge zur klassischen Philologie, 102), Meisenheim am Glan, 1978.

Two Treatises of Proclus, the Platonic Successor; The Former Consisting of Ten Doubts Concerning Providence, and a Solution of those Doubts; And the Latter Containing a Development of the Nature of Evil. Translated from the Edition of these Works by Victor Cousin by Thomas Taylor, London, 1833 [Reprinted as: *Proclus the Neoplatonic Philosopher: Ten Doubts Concerning Providence and a Solution of those Doubts and On the Subsistence of Evil.* Translated into English from their Latin Version by William of Moerbeke, Chicago, 1980].

Proclus. Trois études sur la Providence, I, *Dix problèmes concernant la Providence.* Texte établi et traduit par Daniel Isaac (Collection des Universités de France), Paris, 1977.

Proclus. Trois études sur la Providence, II, *Providence, Fatalité, Liberté.* Texte établi et traduit par Daniel Isaac (Collection des Universités de France), Paris, 1979.

Proklos Diadochos. Zehn Aporien über die Vorsehung. Frage 6-10 (§§ 32-66), übersetzt und erklärt von Ingeborg Böhme, Inaugural-Dissertation Köln, 1975.

Proklos Diadochos über die Vorsehung, das Schicksal und den freien Willen an Theodoros, den Ingenieur (Mechaniker) (§§ 1-32)), übersetzt und erklärt von Theo Borger, Inaugural-Dissertation Köln, 1971.

Procli Diadochi in primum Euclidis Elementorum librum commentarii, ex recognitione Godofredi Friedlein (Bibliotheca scriptorum Graecorum et Romanorum Teubneriana), Lipsiae, 1873.

Procli Diadochi in Platonis Rem Publicam commentarii. Edidit Guilelmus Kroll,

(Bibliotheca scriptorum Graecorum et Romanorum Teubneriana), Lipsiae, vol. I, 1899; vol. II, 1901.

Procli Diadochi in Platonis Timaeum commentaria, edidit Ernestus Diehl (Bibliotheca scriptorum Graecorum et Romanorum Teubneriana), Lipsiae, I, 1903, II, 1904; III, 1906.

Procli Diadochi in Platonis Cratylum commentaria, edidit Georgius Pasquali (Bibliotheca scriptorum Graecorum et Romanorum Teubneriana), Lipsiae, 1908.

PROKLOU DIADOKHOU STOIKHEIÔSIS THEOLOGIKÊ. *Proclus. The Elements of Theology*. A Revised Text with Translation, Introduction and Commentary by E.R. Dodds, Second Edition, Oxford, 1963.

Proclus. Théologie platonicienne. Texte établi et traduit par H.D. Saffrey et L.G. Westerink (Collection des Universités de France), Paris, *Livre I*, 1968; *Livre II*, 1974; *Livre III*, 1978; *Livre IV*, 1981; *Livre V*, 1987; *Livre VI. Index général*, 1997.

Proclus. Sur le Premier Alcibiade de Platon. Texte établi et traduit par A.Ph. Segonds (Collection des Universités de France), Paris, tome I, 1985; tome II, 1986.

Proclus. *Commentaire sur le Parménide de Platon. Traduction de Guillaume de Moerbeke*. Édition critique par Carlos Steel (Ancient and Medieval Philosophy, De Wulf-Mansion Centre, Series 1, 3; 4), Leuven, tome I, *Livres I-IV*, 1982; tome II, *Livres V-VII*, 1985.

Proclus. *Commentaire sur le Timée*, traduction et notes par A.J. Festugière, tomes I-V, Paris, 1966-68.

Proclus. *Commentaire sur la République*, traduction et notes par A.J. Festugière, tomes I-III, Paris, 1970.

Proclus' Commentary on Plato's Parmenides. Translated by Glenn R. Morrow and John M. Dillon with Introduction and Notes by John M. Dillon, Princeton, 1987.

1.2. Aristotle

Barnes, J. (ed.) 1984. *The Complete Works of Aristotle. The Revised Oxford Translation*, 2 vols (Bollingen Series, 71,2), Princeton.

Ross, W.D. *Aristotle's Metaphysics*. A revised text with introduction and commentary by W.D. Ross, 2 vols, Oxford, 1924.

Aristotle's Physics. A revised text with introduction and commentary by W.D. Ross, Oxford, 1936.

Aristotelis categoriae et liber de interpretatione, recognoverunt brevique adnotatione critica instruxerunt L. Minio-Paluello (Scriptorum classicorum bibliotheca Oxoniensis), Oxonii, 1949.

1.3. Chaldean oracles

Oracles Chaldaïques, avec un choix de commentaires anciens. Texte établi et traduit par Édouard des Places (Collection des Universités de France), Paris, 1971.

The Chaldean Oracles. Text Translation, and Commentary by Ruth Majercik, Leiden-New York-København, 1989.

1.4. ps-Dionysius Areopagita

Corpus Dionysiacum. I, Pseudo-Dionysius Areopagita, *De divinis nominibus* herausgegeben von Beate Regina Suchla (Patristische Texte und Studien, 33), Berlin-New York, 1990.

1.5. Isaak Sebastokrator

Rizzo, J.J. (ed.) 1971. *Isaak Sebastokrator's 'Peri tês tôn Kakôn Hypostaseôs' (De malorum subsistentia)*, Meisenheim am Glan (Beiträge zur klassischen Philologie, 42).
Erler, M. (ed.) 1979. *I. Sebastokrator. PERI PRONOIAS KAI PHUSIKÊS ANANKÊS*, Meisenheim am Glan (Beiträge zur klassischen Philologie, 111).
Dornseiff, J., 1966. *Isaak Sebastokrator. Zehn Aporien über die Vorsehung*, Meisenheim am Glan (Beiträge zur klassischen Philologie, 19).

1.6. Philoponus

Philoponus. *On Aristotle on the Intellect (de Anima 3.4-8)*. Translated by William Charlton with the assistance of Fernand Bossier (Ancient Commentators on Aristotle), London-Ithaca NY, 1991.

1.7. Plato

Platonis opera recognovit brevique adnotatione critica instruxit Ioannes Burnet (*Scriptorum classicorum bibliotheca Oxoniensis*), Oxonii, 5 vols, 1900-7.
Hamilton, E. & Cairns, H. (eds), 1973 [=1963]. *The Collected Dialogues of Plato, including the Letters* (Bollingen Series, 71), Princeton.
Cooper, J.M. & Hutchinson, D.S. (eds), 1997. Plato. *Complete Works*. Indianapolis / Cambridge.

1.8. Plotinus

Plotins Schriften. Übersetzt von Richard Harder. Neubearbeitung mit griechischem Lesetext und Anmerkungen fortgeführt von Rudolf Beutler und Willy Theiler, Hamburg, 1956-71, 6 Bände (Band Vc, *Anhang*: Porphyrios, *Über Plotins Leben und die Ordnung seiner Schriften*, zum Druck besorgt von Walter Marg).
Plotini opera, ediderunt Paul Henry et Hans-Rudolf Schwyzer (Museum Lessianum, Series philosophica), tomus I, *Porphyrii Vita Plotini. Enneades I-III*; tomus II, *Enneades IV-V. Plotiniana arabica*, Paris-Bruxelles, 1951; 1959; tomus III, *Enneas VI*, Paris-Leiden, 1973 [= 'editio maior', H-S[1]].
Plotini opera ediderunt Paul Henry et Hans-Rudolf Schwyzer, tomus I, *Porphyrii Vita Plotini. Enneades I-III*; tomus II, *Enneades IV-V*; tomus III, *Enneas VI* (*Scriptorum classicorum bibliotheca Oxoniensis*), Oxonii, 1964; 1977; 1982 [= 'editio minor', H-S[2]].
Plotinus, with an English translation by A.H. Armstrong (Loeb Classical Library), in seven volumes, London-Cambridge, MA, 1966-1988.
O'Meara, D. 1999. *Plotin. Traité 51. I, 8* (Les Écrits de Plotin), Paris.

1.9. Porphyrius

Porphyre. *De l'abstinence*, tome I, Introduction par Jean Bouffartigue et Michel Patillon. Livre I. Texte établi et traduit par Jean Bouffartigue (Collection des Universités de France), Paris, 1977.

1.10. Michael Psellus

Michael Psellus, *De omnifaria doctrina. Critical Text and Introduction.* Proefschrift [...] door Leendert Gerrit Westerink, Nijmegen, 1948.

1.11. Simplicius

Hadot, I. (ed.) 1996. Simplicius. *Commentaire sur le Manuel d'Épictète*. Introduction et édition critique du texte grec par Ilsetraut Hadot (Philosophia antiqua, 66), Leiden-New York-Köln.
Simplicius. *On Aristotle Categories 5-6*. Translated by Frans A.J. de Haas & Barrie Fleet (Ancient Commentators on Aristotle), London-Ithaca NY, 2001.

2. Secondary literature

Abbate, Michele. 1998. 'Parypóstasis: il concetto di male nella quarta dissertazione del Commento all Repubblica di Proclo', in *Rivista di Storia della Filosofia* 53, 109-15.
Alt, K. 1993. *Weltflucht und Weltbejahung. Zur Frage des Dualismus bei Plutarch, Numenios, Plotin* (Akademie der Wissenschaften und der Literatur. Abhandlungen der geistes- und sozialwissenschaftlichen Klasse, 1993, 8), Mainz-Stuttgart.
Armstrong, A.H. 1967. 'Plotinus', in *The Cambridge History of Later Greek and Early Medieval Philosophy*, Cambridge, 191-268.
Balaudé, J.-F. 1999. 'Le traitement plotinien de la question du mal: éthique ou ontologique', in *Les Cahiers Philosophiques de Strasbourg* 8, 67-80.
Baltes, M. 1982. Review of Erler 1978 (see part I 'Editions and Translations, Proclus'), in *Anzeiger für die Altertumswissenschaft* 35, cols 169-72.
Bechtle, G. 1999. 'Das Böse im Platonismus: Überlegungen zur Position Jamblichs', in *Bochumer Philosophisches Jahrbuch für Antike und Mittelalter* 4, 64-82.
Beierwaltes, W. 1962. 'Philosophische Marginalien zu Proklos-Texten', in *Philosophische Rundschau* 10, 49-90.
——— 1973. 'Die Entfaltung der Einheit. Zur Differenz plotinischen und proklischen Denkens', in *Thêta-Pi* 2, 126-61.
Beutler, R. 1957. 'Proklos. 4. Neuplatoniker', in *RE* 45. Hb. (XXIII-1), col. 186,10-247,3.
Blumenthal, H.J. 1996. *Aristotle and Neoplatonism in Late Antiquity: Interpretations of the De Anima*, London.
Boese, H. 1960: see part I. 'Editions and Translations, Proclus'.
Brams, J. & Vanhamel, W. (eds), 1989. *Guillaume de Moerbeke. Recueil d'études à l'occasion du 700e anniversaire de sa mort*, Leuven.
Charlton & Bossier 1991: see part I 'Editions and Translations, Philoponus'.
Cherniss, H. 1954. Harold, 'The Sources of Evil According to Plato', in *Proceedings of the American Philosophical Society* 98, 23-30.

Chiaradonna, R. 1998. 'Essence et prédication chez Porphyre et Plotin', in *Revue des sciences philosophiques et théologiques* 577-606

Colonna, A. 1963. Review of Boese 1960, in *Rivista di Filologia e di Istruzione Clasica* 91, serie terza, 92-4.

Cornford, F.M. 1935. *Plato's Theory of Knowledge. The Theaetetus and the Sophist of Plato Translated with a Running Commentary* (International Library of Psychology, Philosophy and Scientific Method), London.

Corrigan, K. 1996. *Plotinus' Theory of Matter-Evil and the Question of Substance: Plato, Aristotle, and Alexander of Aphrodisias* (Recherches de Théologie ancienne et médiévale, Supplementa, vol. 3), Leuven.

Costello, E.B. 1967. 'Is Plotinus Inconsistent on the Nature of Evil?', in *International Philosophical Quarterly* 7, 483-97.

De Haas, F.A.J. 1997. *John Philoponus' New Definition of Prime Matter. Aspects of its Background in Neoplatonism and the Ancient Commentary Tradition* (Philosophia antiqua, 69), Leiden-New York-Köln.

De Libera, A. 1995. *La philosophie médiévale*, Paris, deuxième édition (Collection premier cycle).

Dodds, E.R. 1963: see part I 'Editions and Translations, Proclus'.

Elorduy, E. 1959. *Ammonio Sakkas*, I, *La doctrina de la creación y del mal en Proclo y el Ps. Areopagita*. Burgos.

Erler, M. 1978: see part I 'Editions and Translations, Proclus'.

Festugière, A.-J. 1953. *La révélation d'Hermès Trismégiste*, III, *Les doctrines de l'âme*, suivi de *Jamblique. Traité de l'âme*. Traduction et commentaire, *Porphyre. De l'animation de l'embryon* (Études bibliques), Paris.

———— 1966-8; 1970: see part I 'Editions and Translations, Proclus'.

Fuller, B.A.G. 1912. *The Problem of Evil in Plotinus*, Cambridge.

Greene, W.C. 1944. *Moira. Fate, Good, and Evil in Greek Thought*, Cambridge, MA.

Guthrie, W.K.C. 1978. *A History of Greek Philosophy*, vol. V, *The Later Plato and the Academy*, Cambridge-New York-New Rochelle.

Hadot 1996: see part I 'Editions and Translations, Simplicius'.

Hager, F. 1962. 'Die Materie und das Böse im antiken Platonismus', in *Museum Helveticum* 19, 73-103.

———— 1987. *Gott und das Böse im antiken Platonismus* (Elementa. Schriften zur Philosophie und ihrer Problemgeschichte, 43), Würzburg-Amsterdam.

Henry, 1961 [=1938]. *Études plotiniennes*, I, *Les États du texte de Plotin*, Paris-Bruges.

Ihm, S. 2001. 'Neue Griechische Proclus-Fragmente aus dem Florilegium des ps.-Maximus', in *Traditio* 56, 1-14.

Isaac, D. 1977; 1979; 1982: see part I 'Editions and Translations, Proclus'.

Koch, H., 1895. 'Proklus als Quelle des pseudo-Dionysius Areopagita in der Lehre vom Bösen', in *Philologus* 54, 438-54.

Lloyd, A.C. 1987. '*Parhypostasis* in Proclus', in G. Boss & G. Seel (eds), *Proclus et son influence. Actes du Colloque de Neuchâtel, juin 1985*, Zürich, 145-57.

Long, A.A. 1968. 'The Stoic Concept of Evil', in *Philosophical Quarterly* 18, 329-43.

Majercik 1989: see part I 'Editions and Translations, Chaldean Oracles'.

Menn, S. 1999. 'Commentary on Steel', in *Proceedings of the Boston Area Colloquium in Ancient Philosophy* 14, 1998 [1999], 103-9. Cf. Steel 1999.

Narbonne, J.-M. 1994. *La métaphysique de Plotin* (Bibliothèque de l'histoire de la philosophie), Paris.

O'Brien, D. 1971. 'Plotinus on Evil. A Study of Matter and the Soul in Plotinus' Conception of Human Evil', in *Le Néoplatonisme. Royaumont 9-13 juin 1969*

(Colloques Internationaux du Centre National de la Recherche Scientifique, Sciences humaines, Paris), 113-46.

—— 1993. *Théodicée plotinienne, théodicée gnostique* (Philosophia antiqua, 57), Leiden-New York-Köln.

—— 1999. 'La matière chez Plotin: son origine, sa nature', in *Phronesis* 44, 45-71.

O'Meara, D. 1997. 'Das Böse bei Plotin (Enn. I,8)', in Th. Kobusch & B. Mojsisch (eds), *Platon in der abendländischen Geistesgeschichte*, Darmstadt, 33-47.

—— 1999: see part I 'Editions and Translations, Plotinus'.

Opsomer, J. & Steel, C. 1999. 'Evil without a Cause. Proclus' Doctrine on the Origin of Evil, and its Antecedents in Hellenistic Philosophy', in T. Fuhrer, M. Erler & K. Schlapbach (eds) *Zur Rezeption der hellenistischen Philosophie in der Spätantike*, Stuttgart, 229-60.

Opsomer, J. 2000a. 'Deriving the Three Intelligible Triads from the *Timaeus*', in A.Ph. Segonds & C. Steel (eds), *Proclus et la Théologie Platonicienne. Actes du Colloque International de Louvain (13-16 mai 1998). En l'honneur de H.D. Saffrey et L.G. Westerink*. Leuven-Paris, 351-72.

—— (2000b). 'Proclus on Demiurgy and Procession: a Neoplatonic Reading of the *Timaeus*', in R. Wright (ed.), *Reason and Necessity. Essays on Plato's Timaeus*, London, 113-43.

—— (2001a). 'Neoplatonist Criticisms of Plutarch', in Aurelio Pérez Jiménez & Francesc Casadesús Bordoy (eds), *Estudios sobre Plutarco. Misticismo y religiones mistéricas en la obra de Plutarco. Actas del VII Simposio Español sobre Plutarco (Palma de Mallorca, 2-4 de Noviembre de 2000)*, Madrid-Málaga, 187-99.

—— 2001b. 'Proclus vs. Plotinus on Matter (*De mal. subs.* 30-7)', in *Phronesis* 46, 1-35.

—— (forthcoming) 'Les jeunes dieux selon Proclus', in *Collection d'Études Classiques*.

Pépin, J. 1964. *Théologie cosmique et théologie chrétienne* (Bibliothèque de Philosophie Contemporaine, Histoire de la Philosophie et Philosophie Générale), Paris.

—— 2000. 'Les modes de l'enseignement théologique dans la Théologie platonicienne', in A.Ph. Segonds & C. Steel (eds) *Proclus et la Théologie Platonicienne. Actes du Colloque International de Louvain (13-16 mai 1998). En l'honneur de H.D. Saffrey et L.G. Westerink*. Leuven-Paris, 1-14.

Rist, J.M. 1969. 'Plotinus on Matter and Evil', in *Phronesis* 6, 154-66.

Rordorf, W. 1983. 'Sind die Dämonen gut oder böse? Beobachtungen zur Proklos-Rezeption bei Isaak Sebastokrator', in H.-D. Blume & F. Mann (eds), *Platonismus und Christentum. Festschrift für Heinrich Dörrie*, Münster, 239-44.

Rorem, P. & Lamoreaux, J.C. 1998. *John of Scythopolis and the Dionysian Corpus*, Oxford.

Saffrey & Westerink: see part I 'Editions and Translations, Proclus'.

Schäfer, C. 1999. 'Proklos' Argument aus De malorum subsistentia 31,5-12 in der modernen Interpretation, Philosophiegeschichte und Logische Analyse / Logical Analysis and History of Philosophy', 2, *Antike Philosophie*, 172-85.

—— 2000. 'Das Dilemma der neuplatonischen Theodizee. Versuch einer Lösung', in *Archiv für Geschichte der Philosophie* 82, 1-35.

Schröder, E. 1916. *Plotins Abhandlung POTHEN TA KAKA (Enn. 1,8)*, Leipzig.

Segonds, A. 1985-6: see part I 'Editions and Translations, Proclus'.

Sharples, R.W. 1975. 'Responsibility, Chance and Not-Being (Alexander of Aphrodisias *Mantissa* 169-172)', in *BICS* 22, 37-64.

———— 1994. 'Plato, Plotinus, and Evil', in *BICS* 39, 171-81.

Siassos, L. 1995, 'Le champ ontologique de l'apparition du mal chez Proclus et Denys', in *Diotima* 23, 43-5.

Siorvanes, L. 1996. *Proclus. Neo-Platonic Philosophy and Science*, Edinburgh.

Sorabji, R. 1980. *Necessity, Cause, and Blame. Perspectives on Aristotle's Theory*, London.

Steel, C.G. 1978. *The Changing Self. A Study on the Soul in Later Neoplatonism: Iamblichus, Damascius and Priscianus* (Verhandelingen van de Koninklijke Academie voor Wetenschappen, Letteren en Schone Kunsten van België, Klasse der Letteren, jaargang 40, 85), Brussel.

———— 1982a. 'Quatre fragments de Proclus dans un florilège byzantin', in D. Isaac 1982 (see part I 'Editions and Translations, Proclus'), 201-7.

———— 1982b. 'Un admirateur de S. Maxime à la cour des Comnènes: Isaac le Sébastocrator', in F. Heinzer & C. Schönborn (eds), *Maximus Confessor. Actes du Symposium sur Maxime le Confesseur*, Fribourg, 365-73.

———— 1996. 'La théorie des Formes et la Providence. Proclus critique d'Aristote et des Stoïciens', in A. Motte and J. Denooz (eds), *Aristotelica Secunda. Mélanges offerts à Christian Rutten*, Liège, 241-5.

———— 1997. 'Proclus et Denys: de l'existence du mal', in Y. de Andia (ed.), *Denys l'Aréopagite et sa postérité en Orient et en Occident. Actes du Colloque International Paris, 21-24 septembre 1994* (Collection des études Augustiniennes, Série Antiquité, 151, Paris), 89-116.

———— 1999. 'Proclus on the Existence of Evil', in *Proceedings of the Boston Area Colloquium in Ancient Philosophy* 14, 1998 [1999], 83-102; 109. See also Menn 1999.

Stiglmayr, J. 1895. 'Der Neuplatoniker Proclus als Vorlage des sogen. Dionysius Areopagita in der Lehre vom Uebel', in *Historisches Jahrbuch* 16, 253-73; 721-48.

Van den Berg, R.M. 1997. 'Proclus, In Platonis Timaeum Commentarii 3.333.28ff.: The Myth of the Winged Charioteer according to Iamblichus and Proclus', in *Syllecta Classica* 8 (*Iamblichus: the Philosopher*), 149-62.

Van Riel, G. 2001. 'Horizontalism or Verticalism? Proclus vs Plotinus on the Procession of Matter', in *Phronesis* 46, 129-53.

Volkmann-Schluck, K.H. 1967. 'Plotins Lehre vom Wesen und von der Herkunft des Schlechten', in *Philosophisches Jahrbuch* 75, 1-21.

Westerink, L.G. 1959. 'Exzerpte aus Proklos' *Enneaden*-Kommentar bei Psellos', in *Byzantinische Zeitschrift* 52, 1-10.

Westerink, L.G. 1962. 'Notes on the *Tria opuscula* of Proclus', *Mnemosyne* S. IV-15, 159-68.

Ziegler, K. 1934. 'Theodorus. 41. Mechaniker und Philosoph', in *RE* 2. Reihe, 10. Halbband (=V A 2), col. 1860,47-1863,43.

Zintzen, C. 1976. 'Geister (Dämonen), B.III.c, Hellenistische und kaiserzeitliche Philosophie', in *RAC* 9, col. 640-68.

Index of Passages

Texts cited by Proclus. References are to chapter and line of the Boese edition.

Subject Index

Numbers in italic refer to the notes to the translation.

Index of Names

Numbers in italic refer to the notes to the translation.